Fred Crawford
– Carson's Gunrunner –

∞

Keith Haines

Ballyhay Books

Published by Ballyhay Books,
an imprint of Laurel Cottage Ltd.
Donaghadee, N. Ireland 2009.
Copyrights Reserved.
© Text by Keith Haines 2009.
All rights reserved.
No part of this book may be reproduced
or stored on any media without the express
written permission of the publishers.
ISBN 978 1 900935 80 7

This volume is dedicated to the memory of Wesley Semple (1946-2007) whom, unlike Fred Crawford, life cruelly robbed of long years of retirement. Both of them were Collegians (pupils of Methodist College, Belfast). They both had enduring links with Campbell College, Fred as a Governor and Wesley as a member of staff, and they both sent their sons to the school. They both showed an interest in and appreciation of the natural world, manifested in membership of the Belfast Naturalists' Field Club (of which Welsey and his wife, Joan, were recent Presidents). Both men were loyal and generous friends. Wesley was particularly fond of the work of Horace. One of the latter's most famous quotations from his book of *Odes* – *nil desperandum* – could be aptly applied to Fred's spirit of adventure in April 1914. I hope that, through this biography, the words of the Roman poet may also apply for Wesley: *non omnis moriar.*

Acknowledgements

∽

This volume could not have been completed without the assistance of Fred Crawford's grandchildren, whose encouragement and co-operation has been incalculable. That I was able to track them down was due entirely to the Internet's search-engines. At the Devon Record Office I located a *Lark Rise to Candleford*-style collection of North Devon village life, compiled by Fred's eldest child, Helen Naomi Richardson. In turn, I was put in contact with her daughter, Brigid, and subsequently many of her cousins. Malcolm Crawford, John Crawford, Angela Carter, Heather Herring and, of course, Brigid Richardson have all been most generous and patient, and most tolerant of my vision and interpretation of their grandfather's life.

Acknowledgement must be made to the Public Record Office of Northern Ireland (PRONI), which houses the voluminous Crawford Archive. Dr Ann Mcveigh and all its staff have, over three years, proved unfailingly responsive, prompt and courteous. I am indebted to the Crawford family and PRONI for their permission to quote from the Crawford papers (the source of all references in the footnotes, unless otherwise cited); and also to Brian Dingwall for permission to quote from the diaries of Lady Spender. My gratitude is also extended to the librarians and staff of the Linen Hall Library, Belfast Central and Newspaper Library, Queen's University Library, and the Headmaster and Governors of Campbell College, Belfast. Trine Bogenes in distant Fjaere on Norway's southern coast deserves credit for her prompt response to enquiries about Captain Marthin Falck.

Acknowledgement is made to John Crawford for permission to use the image on the front cover - a portrait of Fred Crawford in his early 80s, painted by his daughter-in-law, Nina Morie Crawford, eldest daughter of the Prime Minister of Northern Ireland, the Rt. Hon. John Miller Andrews.

Contents

	Foreword	7
1.	Actively Employed in Doing Good	9
2.	Treasure in Heaven	21
3.	I Wish to God I Had Never Touched Starch	45
4.	Bathing In Acapulco	63
5.	A Lot of Naughty Men	85
6.	Pièce de Résistance	111
7.	The Ark and the Covenant	139
8.	A Box of Cigars	169
9.	A Non-manifest Manifest	187
	Images	209
10.	A Pink Pearl	225
11.	The Silver Casket	245
12.	Ulster's Watchdog	261
13.	I Trust in God and my Automatic	277
14.	The Garden of Consolation	299
	Index	317

Foreword

Historically, as a political entity, Northern Ireland is less than ninety years old. As a 'blow-in' who has lived here for forty per cent of its existence, I have long been surprised that no-one has written a biography of the individual who many contemporaries believed was integral to its creation. Many felt that Northern Ireland would never have existed at all if it had not been for the actions of Fred Crawford.

Inevitably that makes him a contentious figure. In a polarised and geographically exiguous community, history is viewed primarily as Orange or Green. Yet, having spent a quarter of a century trying to persuade students that the answer to all historical questions is 'yes and no', I believe that the spectrum is rarely that narrow. Fred himself may well have missed the irony that Protestants celebrate the Twelfth despite the fact that the Battle of the Boyne occurred on 1st July 1690, and that it was a pope who adjusted the date. Circumstances, opinions and interpretations change. Fred himself made the transition from taking pride in being an Irishman to calling himself an Ulsterman. The latter is itself problematical; Fred always referred to his post-1920 homeland as Ulster, despite the fact that he himself had pragmatically abandoned one-third of the latter's provincial counties.

Fred Crawford is effectively remembered as a consequence of a singular event – the Larne gun-running of April 1914 – and such is the current indifference to that treasonable action that a recent volume from one of Ireland's most respected academic publishers places it in

November 1913. There is no pretence that this is a definitive biography, or that this interpretation of such a controversial figure will satisfy all readers, but I hope that it will reveal that the Ulsterman was a more complex character. Fred Crawford inherited many of the traits of illustrious ancestors who counted inventiveness and vision, piety and charity, and both loyalty and rebellion amongst their genes. There will be those who view Fred Crawford as myopic, bigoted, truculent and obsessively loyalist; this work aspires to demonstrate that he was well-travelled and courageous, devout and charitable, courteous and tolerant.

He lived in turbulent times facing an uncertain future. Fred could never make a success of the family business, whose declining fortunes were compounded by the collapse of the post-First World War world economy. The north of Ireland found its industrial pride shattered by such events as the *Titanic* disaster; the Great War threw the established world order into turmoil; and the British Empire found itself under threat from such traumas as the Boer War and the post-1920 challenges within Ireland. Fred was not the kind of man to accept meekly these threats to his way of life. As he wrote to his brother at the height of his personal problems in mid-1923: "I will fight against trouble till the end and never lie down to it. God helped me thro' before and he will again".

Fred Crawford's story has never been fully told, perhaps because his reticence kept him out of the limelight. This volume attempts to rectify a lacuna in the history of Northern Ireland. It will not assess the rectitude or otherwise of his sentiments and actions; it is merely an attempt to present Fred's story, as far as possible, in his own words and from his own perspective.

Actively Employed in Doing Good

Only God ever brought Fred Crawford to his knees.

Like so much in his character, pious gratitude for divine intervention was congenital; in his diary, his father continually resorted to thanks to God for the condition of his family, health and business. He took nothing for granted. At the start of each year James Wright Crawford, an enduring hypochondriac, noted his astonishment that he had survived another year. On 1st January 1867 he duly – and with formality – wrote: "I thank Thee, Oh Thou Most High, that I see the beginning of another year", and a year later – at the age of 34 – he confirmed his insecurities by recording: "And am I spared so long?"[1] In spite of his fears, James Wright Crawford was to enjoy another 40 years of life.

James's father, Alexander Crawford, had established his chemical company in Coleraine, but transferred his factory to the centre of Belfast in 1836, where they later concentrated mainly on the manufacture of starch products.[2] Alexander Crawford & Son was one atom in the considerable explosion of industrial and commercial enterprise in Belfast – particularly in East Belfast – during the 19th century. This was a manifestation of the flourishing self-assurance and self-belief, which was most notably articulated in the concept of *Self-Help*. A volume bearing this title was published by Dr. Samuel Smiles in 1859. One of his sons established the Belfast Ropework Company at Connswater in East Belfast in 1875, which became the largest such company in the world.

Such self-confidence was viewed by James Wright Crawford as fatal arrogance and, if he had lived another five years, he would have been one of those who regarded the *Titanic* tragedy as divine nemesis. As Professor John Wilson Foster – born and raised within sight of Harland & Wolff – expressed it: "The technical and social hubris that contemporary commentators identified in the case of *Titanic* accorded with the Christian idea of retribution: this was God in the guise of Nature putting Man in his place".[3]

James Wright Crawford feared such presumption: "Am I proud?" he enquired of himself. "I fear I am. I think I want, and would like, to be humble"; and he knew where to direct his appreciation of his good fortune: "Lord, I must record my thanks to Thee for the special goodness to us in our business".[4] His diary illuminates the misery he encountered on the streets of Belfast, and mentions several sudden deaths amongst those with whom he was acquainted in the Victorian city. For all his own family's relative prosperity in the second half of the 19th century, it did not escape its share of misfortune and tragedy: his second son, John Richard Wolfenden Crawford, had died on 25th July 1859, aged only 14 months; on 24th February 1866 his six-year-old son (and namesake) James Wright died from scarlatina; illness precluded his father from attending the interment. Finally, James's only daughter, Caroline Elisabeth Madge, died in January 1881 after a lengthy illness, aged only fifteen.[5]

Although a rift was to develop later between James W. Crawford and his eldest son, Alexander, when the latter left to seek his fortune in Australia, the father had been delighted when his first-born, at the age of only ten, had returned home from an open-air religious meeting and revealed that: "he felt that he loved Jesus and that Jesus loved him", and that he had asked "God to pardon his sins".[6] Whilst this may appear to be the consequence of impressionable youth, such occasions clearly retained their resonance for Alexander as, when he was to be re-introduced to Revival hymns nearly twenty years later in Australia, he revealed that: "It quite warmed my heart to hear them".[7]

Fred also adopted this biddable, acquiescent piety. For all the fame – or, more accurately, notoriety – which he was to acquire as a consequence of his gun-running exploits, he tended to spurn public acknowledgement. As did his father, Fred placed his trust, and his life, in the hands of God. During a visit to Jerusalem in 1890, Fred's diary recorded the aspiration that he would be a better man for having trodden on holy ground.[8]

Even in his twenties, suffering persistent and painful attacks of sciatica, Fred viewed the affliction as a personal sounding-board and an inspiration to more intense devotion: "If God in His merciful goodness gives me strength to recover without an attack of sciatica, I will strive to show my gratitude to Him by living a better life than I have been doing lately".[9]

Throughout his life, Fred emulated the social conscience exhibited by his father, who regularly visited the poor and endeavoured to improve their lot. Fred served on church committees, worked with charities, and promoted institutions (including the YMCA, the British Legion, and the Disabled Ex-Servicemen's Association) dedicated to assisting less fortunate groups in society. Generous himself, he was reluctant to accept charity and, when his personal and family fortunes were at a very low ebb in the early 1920s, he indicated that he did not wish to be a burden upon the public purse, rather he sought a post that was "straight and honourable".[10]

Despite the severe neglect and financial haemorrhage suffered by his business as a consequence of his gun-running venture, he refused to accept a single penny of compensation. Crawford's interpretation was that his actions had been undertaken in the service of his country and that any success was due not to himself but to the protective and guiding hand of God. In later reflections upon the episode of 1914, he observed: "I trusted in God, and when almost in despair … I realised that in the past He had never really let Ulster down, though she had come through some very dark days during the last 200 years". There were, in April 1914, to be many narrow escapes and occasions of good fortune, and he attributed them all to the intervention of the Lord, and acknowledged that: "I felt like sinking on my knees and thanking God from the bottom of my heart". At one difficult juncture he did so again: "I went into my cabin and threw myself on my knees and, in simple language, told God all it meant to Ulster, and pointed [out] what the unselfish and Christian aims were that Ulster had ... I rose from my knees somewhat comforted".[11]

THE CRAWFORD DYNASTY

Faith in the justice and righteousness of one's cause is a variable guarantee, as the United Irishmen had discovered in the summer of 1798. As several thousand of them gathered that June on Donegore Hill, they will have trampled through the graveyard which is the final resting place of some of Fred Crawford's ancestors.[12]

The future gun-runner was the sixth generation of Crawfords born in the north of Ireland after the arrival of his ancestor, Thomas Crawford (born 1625), from Ayrshire. Thomas married Janet, a daughter of Rev. Andrew Stewart, Presbyterian Minister of Donegore (1627-1634), whose family also hailed from the same area of Scotland. Thomas Crawford succeeded to the incumbency of Donegore in 1655, and was buried in the churchyard close to his father-in-law in 1670.

These were dedicated and devout forebears, described in the *Fasti of the Presbyterian Church in Ireland* as "an able and sincere Minister of Christ" and "a man very straight in the cause of God". Fred Crawford set great store by personal dignity and respectability, and would probably have been unamused that Rev. Thomas Crawford's brother-in-law, also named Rev. Andrew Stewart – minister at Donaghadee – described many of the immigrant Scots of the early 17th century on the littoral of Antrim and Down as "generally the scum ... who, for debt, or breaking and fleeing from justice, or seeking shelter, came hither, hoping to be without fear of man's justice in a land where there was nothing, or but little, as yet, of the fear of God".

"Yet", he continued, "God followed them when they fled from him". The tombstone of the younger Stewart bore the legend: "A Pious and Faithful servant of Jesus Christ"[13] – an epitaph with which Fred himself would have been satisfied.

These men were courageously loyal to their native Presbyterianism in difficult and dangerous times. Rev. Thomas Crawford and the younger Rev. Andrew Stewart suffered arrest and exile, as did many others, in the early 1660s as a consequence of the reassertion of the Episcopal Church, and the alleged complicity of Presbyterian ministers in the plot of Thomas Blood.[14] Thomas's son, Rev. Andrew Crawford (died 1726), minister at Carnmoney, married a daughter of Rev. David Brown, minister at Urney (Co Tyrone), who himself had died in 1689 as a defender in the siege of Derry. In spite of the fact that such personal sacrifice ensured the survival of the Episcopal Church, Presbyterianism was shown little gratitude, and continued to suffer disenfranchisement and disadvantage. Fred would identify similar injustice in Great Britain's ungrateful treatment of Ulster following the latter's sacrifice during the First World War.

Fred Crawford could boast many illustrious professional ancestors – medical and scientific, as well as ecclesiastical. Rev. Andrew Crawford's son, another Thomas (died 1782), was minister at Crumlin for 58 years. The latter was Fred's great-great-grandfather, and the signs are that his distant descendant perused the eulogy presented at Thomas's funeral, which declared that he was "sprung from a flock of respectable and pious ancestors …". It recalled a character which was echoed in that of his descendant: "His gentle disposition had always secured him from feeling that rancour and virulence, which too many have been seen to indulge against those who held a different faith … He entertained a warm and universal benevolence for mankind …". Whilst it is undeniable that, as a consequence of their actions and methods, Fred proved vitriolic, even unforgiving, towards Irish nationalist rebels in the early 20th century, he never decried anyone simply for their faith or religion.[15] Alexander Crawford & Son was located in a district that was to become predominantly nationalist and the company was quite prepared to engage Roman Catholic labour; even during the dangerous days of 1920, Fred indicated that he was well acquainted with "several of the local RCs, whom I have obliged at different times".[16]

Rev. Thomas Crawford of Crumlin, who married Anne Mackay, also of Scottish descent, sired four illustrious sons, all of whom entered the medical profession.[17] In 1776, in a letter to one of these (John), he stated with some pride that the family was "generally not most distinguished by their blood than they were by their virtue". They were to retain the latter, but Thomas would probably have been delighted to know that they each also achieved distinction.[18]

John (died 1813) became a surgeon in the East India Company, and later lived in Baltimore where he "had been successful in practice especially by the use of mercury, almost considered a panacea in liver complaints in America". William Drennan, regarded by many as one of the chief inspirations of the United Irishmen movement, studied at Edinburgh University with a second Crawford brother, Adair (died 1795), whom he described as "an awkward-looking lout".[19] Adair, nevertheless, fulfilled the promise recorded by Drennan that he was "the most ingenious student of medicine at present in this University", by becoming a respected physician and chemist. He was recognised for his investigations into the property of heat and recommended a cure for scrofula; later he was Professor of Chemistry at Woolwich and was elected to the Royal Society in 1786. Adair Crawford was to acquire an international reputation in the years before his death with research into the mineral strontianite and its related element, strontium.

One of Adair's sons, also named Adair (died 1879, aged 88), enjoyed an even more celebrated European reputation. Only five years old when his father died, an uncle took him to France where he lived until the downfall of Napoleon. He "received a very superior education, especially in the medical schools, where he obtained a prize for comparative anatomy, which occasioned his being recommended to the Emperor and appointed a lecturer on that subject and consulting adviser as to the management of the Imperial stud". One of the family heirlooms which passed into Fred's possession was a silver medal (which he, in turn, bequeathed to a grandson) presented to "Dr. Adair Crawford by order of Napoleon for services rendered to the Emperor by vetting one of his horses before a battle". Adair Crawford continued his studies, both on the continent and in Scotland, and suffered spinal trouble as a consequence of "prolonged stooping over a microscope".

He became an itinerant physician on the continent, spending three months in Vienna "both very agreeably and profitably". His principal role was as physician to the Ambassador, Henry Wellesley, younger brother of the Duke of Wellington, who introduced him to such notables as Metternich. He then travelled to many major cities, including

Prague, Dresden, Strasbourg and Berlin, "stopping a few days to see the medical schools".[20] In July 1827 he was appointed chief of the Dublin Fever Hospital. The testimonials he obtained for this position echo the high regard in which he was held, and reflect the calibre of Fred Crawford's ancestors. One of these was penned by one of the leading surgeons of the day, Sir Astley Cooper: "I have the greatest pleasure in certifying that Dr. [Adair] Crawford is the most skilful physician and a most amiable man. With him and his connection I have been long acquainted, and the more I have known of them the greater have been my esteem and regard. Dr. Crawford may be recommended in the most unbounded confidence both medically and morally".

In 1830 he returned to London, where his patients included the Irish nationalist leader, Daniel O'Connell. Subsequent to the break-down of his health he travelled extensively, gaining the acquaintance of another future Emperor, Louis Napoleon. He became, for an unspecified period, family physician to the Grand Duke of Oldenburg, who was related to the Russian Imperial family. In April 1910 Fred was to write to the Grand Duke's grandson in St. Petersburg: "When an outbreak of cholera occurred in 1849 or 1850, Dr. Crawford left your father's household to go into a hospital in St. Petersburg to make a study of this disease. Before he left, your honoured father was kind enough to present him with a handsome gold watch as a souvenir of his regard and esteem. This watch has descended to me ... I understand that Dr. Crawford was very fond of Your Grace when you were a little boy and frequently used to go out riding with you then".[21]

The quintessential congenital piety of the Crawford dynasty was encapsulated in an obituary to Dr. Adair Crawford (junior); his "chief happiness was drawn from his sincere and simple faith in that Almighty Saviour ... It was his chief object to ... uphold the Scriptures".

The eldest son of Rev. Thomas Crawford was William (died 1800),[22] who was ordained Presbyterian minister at Strabane in 1766. His interests, however, were more literary and political rather than theological. He established an Academy at Strabane in 1785, which almost acquired university status, but was to suffer as a consequence of the emergence of the United Irishmen movement in 1791. William Crawford had been a leading, respected figure within the Volunteers and the first publication of the Strabane printing press was one of his sermons to the Strabane Rangers. He was a delegate at the 1782 Dungannon Volunteer Convention, and his *History of Ireland* (1783) gave prominence to the role of that organisation. William appears to have died in straitened circumstances soon after his acceptance of the incumbency in Holywood in 1798 but, nevertheless, he attracted retrospective admiration of which Fred would have been proud: "… his life was not only blameless, but actively employed in doing good".

Although he appreciated the reasons, William had disagreed with the transformation of the Volunteers into the United Irishmen. His youngest brother, Alexander (died 1823)[23] – Fred's great-grandfather – however became a prominent member of the latter body, and was arrested in March 1797 on a charge of high treason and, for a period, joined Henry Joy McCracken in Kilmainham gaol.[24] Over the next century or more the political scene was transformed radically in the north of Ireland and the prospect of a more representative Dublin-based government – so vehemently sought by the United Irishmen – was to become anathema to Fred Crawford, but the latter inherited his great-grandfather's dedication to political principle and a willingness to go out on a limb and take risks.

For all his political diversion and enthusiasm, Dr. Alexander Crawford retained his professional commitment. He was a respected physician in Lisburn, where he was one of the early occupants of Roseville,[25] and where he created employment at his extensive chemical works. A grateful community was to express its appreciation and respect by presenting him with his portrait and one patient made a gift of damask linen bearing the Crawford family crest and coat of arms as "a small expression of gratitude on his life saved … by the doctor's skill and kind assiduity during fever 1817".[26]

Alexander developed a formula for producing chlorine bleach – beginning his account prosaically: "You must have a stone still with a metal bottom lined on the bottom with fire brick …".[27] By 1785 it had been shown that bleaching with chlorine speeded up the process of linen production and he established the Vitriol Bleachworks at the Lisburn Island, in addition to running the chemical works which he inherited from his father-in-law. Although there is some evidence that the Bleachworks went bankrupt, Alexander's son, named after his father, continued the chemical manufacturing. Alexander junior married Elizabeth Wright, daughter of James Wright of Lisburn, and they moved to Laurel Hill near Coleraine, whence he transferred his chemical production. In 1836 he moved to Belfast but, whilst the products of Alexander Crawford & Son may have changed, the family retained a pride in its contribution to the development of chlorine. Alexander later built two adjacent homes on the Malone Road and, spurning more glamorous names, christened them Chlorine House (where he died on 22nd May 1873, aged 76)[28] and Chlorine Villa.

The Crawfords were a dynasty with a pronounced, even profound, social conscience. Alexander junior's son, James Wright Crawford, who succeeded to the family business, could be reduced to melancholy at the condition of Belfast's poor, and Fred was to inherit this sensitivity. Although the latter expressed his concern at the lack of moral fibre amongst the rank-and-file soldiers during his service in the Boer War, he was always sympathetic to their desperate plight and circumstances, and was to hint at this during his fleeting visit to the front lines during the First World War. In February 1916 at Auchonvillers, acknowledging that he was there only temporarily, he recorded that: "My British warm jacket and waterproof were frozen like boards today when I returned from the trenches". This sentence was prefaced by the observation that: "I would much rather be shot than gassed".[29] It was perhaps a symptom of Fred's ignorance of the scientific history of the family business, which he reluctantly inherited, that he made no reference to the contribution made by his great-grandfather to the development of the brutal and fatal chlorine gas which had first made its appearance on the Ypres front in April 1915.

Notes

1. D/1700/3/1, 1 January 1867 and 1 January 1868.

2. The company provided a brief portrait of its own history in *Industries of Ireland* (part 1) in 1891, reproduced in *Industries of the North one hundred years ago*, introduction by W. H. Crawford (Friar's Bush Press, Belfast, 1986), p.105.

3. John Wilson Foster (Professor Emeritus at the University of British Columbia), *The Titanic Complex*, (Belcouver Press, Belfast/Vancouver, 1997), p.58.

4. D/1700/3/1, 24 May 1867 and 5 August 1867.

5. D/1700/3/1, June 1866, 5 February 1869. There are also some genealogical details entered in a family Bible in D/1700/4/7. A letter to Fred on 12 April 1880, from his friend John Horner, indicates that Caroline was ill at that time. When his father died in 1907, Fred Crawford inherited portraits of his sister and brother (James), in addition to those of his paternal grandparents and his own father and mother. They were quite probably still in Fred's possession at the time of his death in November 1952, but they are not itemised in his will.

6. D/1700/3/1, 18 June 1867.

7. D/1700/5/2/22, 30 April 1884 to his brother, Fred Crawford, from Linton in Victoria.

8. D/1700/3/8, 3 May 1890.

9. D/1700/3/9, 25 May 1892. Fred eventually found more mundane relief from sciatica in the brine baths at Droitwich: D/1700/10/1/804, 6 June 1910.

10. D/640/11/2, p.108.

11. D/1415/B/34, pp. 45, 51, 55, 59, 60, 86 and 121.

12. The sources for the Crawford ancestry are too copious to itemise them in detail. The material in the following paragraphs is taken principally from the following sources: D/1700/4/4, D/1700/4/7, D/1700/5/1/8 and –/15, D/1700/6/1/-, D/1700/8, D/1700/10/-, D/2456/2; Revs James & S G McConnell, *Fasti of the Presbyterian Church in Ireland 1613-1840*, (Presbyterian Historical Society, Belfast, 1951); entries for William and Adair Crawford in the *Oxford Dictionary of National Biography [ODNB]*; Thomas Witherow, *Historical and Literary Memorials of Presbyterianism in Ireland 1623-1731*, (William Mullan & Son, Belfast, 1879), pp.26-32, and *Historical and Literary Memorials ... 1731-1800*, (1880), pp.203-207.

13. Rev. Andrew Stewart, minister at Donaghadee was the son of his namesake at Donegore. John Stevenson, *Two Centuries of Life in Down 1600-1800*, (White Row Press, Dundonald, 1990), p.45. Rev. George Hill (ed), *The Montgomery Manuscripts*, (Belfast, 1869), pp.61n.48, 240n.77.

14. Following the dissatisfaction of some Cromwellians with the Restoration Settlement, Blood (later involved in the theft of the Crown Jewels) plotted to seize Dublin Castle and the Lord Lieutenant. An attempt to engage Ulster Scots in the affair brought (unwarranted) suspicion upon Presbyterian clergymen.

15. One of the grand-daughters of Rev. Thomas Crawford (died 1782), Sarah Anne Radcliff, daughter of Adair Crawford (died 1795), wrote to a brother from Adelaide in Canada on 7 December 1837, outlining circumstances similar to those which Fred Crawford and Ulster were to experience: "This is now a most important period to us settled in Canada, as the Lower Province is in a state of open rebellion against the British Government and, if they succeed in establishing their independence, it will not only injure us in a communal way, but it may set

all the Radicals in this Province going, and they are willing to do anything bad":
D/1700/5/1/15.

16. D/640/11/2, pp.19-20.

17. For much of what follows, see D/1700/8; Thomas Witherow; *ODNB* for William and Adair Crawford; J Dooher & M Kennedy (eds), *The Fair River Valley: Strabane through the Ages,* (Ulster Historical Foundation, Belfast, 2000), pp.113-117, 252-253, 355-356; Rev. Edward Cupples, *Glenavy Statistical Survey,* (1814); *Record,* 18 June 1879.

18. D/1700/4/4, 20 June 1776.

19. Jean Agnew (ed), *The Drennan-McTier Letters (1776-1793),* (Irish Manuscripts Commission, Dublin, 1998), I, 41.

20. D/1700/5/1/8, 12 March 1826.

21. This information is found primarily in *Record,* 18 June 1879; D/1700/8; D/1700/10/1/776. In a declaration on his family history in D/1700/10 Fred confuses some details of this Adair Crawford with the latter's father. The Grand Duke of Oldenburg in 1910 was a grandson, not the son, of the Grand Duke served by Adair Crawford in the 1840s.

22. The sources disagree over the year of William's death: Witherow (1880) places it in 1801; The *Fasti* and *ODNB* give the date as 4 January 1800.

23. Fred Crawford states that Alexander died in Sligo in 1823 – D/1700/10 – although Agnew states, in all three volumes, that he died in 1820.

24. Agnew, II, 312-314. A T Q Stewart, *The Summer Soldiers,* (Blackstaff Press, Belfast, 1995), p.56.

25. For Roseville, see D/1700/10; *Belfast News Letter,* 20 May 1960; and Kathleen Rankin, *The Linen Houses of the Lagan Valley,* (Ulster Historical Foundation, Belfast, 2002), pp.66, 70. By coincidence, between the two World Wars, Roseville, long associated with the Island Spinning Co, was sold to Messrs Henry Campbell of Mossley, whose founder had bequeathed his inheritance to the establishment of Campbell College, where Fred Crawford was to be the longest-serving Governor from 1898 to 1951.

26. Fred Crawford inherited these heirlooms in late 1922, following the death of Rev. James Hamilton of Donaghmore, who was also a great-grandson of Alexander Crawford senior: D/640/11/2, p.99.

27. See Alexander Crawford's personal manuscript of 27 April 1822 in D/2456/2.

28. Alexander Crawford was buried in the family plot in Belfast City Cemetery, where Fred Crawford was also laid to rest: Tom Hartley, *Written in Stone: history of Belfast City Cemetery,* (Brehon Press, Belfast, 2006), pp.66-67.

29. D/1700/5/17/1/127, 23 February 1916. At least one pupil at Campbell College – Francis Leonard – was to die at the end of April 1916 from the effects of chlorine gas during the First World War.

Treasure in Heaven

~∞~

Alexander Crawford junior moved to Belfast around 1836 and had established himself as a manufacturing chemist at 26 Mill Street almost immediately.[1] He lived for some years at Mount Prospect on the Lisburn Road, but towards the end of 1860 his son indicates that they had moved closer to Belfast.[2] Alexander probably began the construction of Chlorine House (which he occupied) and Chlorine Villa (which was occupied by his son) on the Malone Road about this time, as they were in occupancy by 1864.[3] To distinguish more readily between them, these homes were re-christened Chlorine and Cloreen.[4] The will of James Wright Crawford (which he made on 17th July 1907, three months before he died), also suggests that his father had been acquiring property in Belfast at least as early as 1844. These leases were in Millfield and Wilson Street, where the starch factory was established, and adjacently at Letitia Street, Campbell Street and Johnston Street.

Alexander Crawford & Son appears to have become established quite quickly, as James W Crawford recorded on 1st November 1861, in his account of the Great Revival of 1859-1863, that: "I also determined to thank God before the men [of the Works] for His goodness in prospering my father in business".[5] The earliest direct reference to starch manufacturing at the two-acre Wilson Street site is 1864.[6]

By the late 19th century, a large percentage of the population was so reliant upon the linen trade for employment that Belfast became known as Linenopolis. Alexander Crawford & Son was one of the innumerable subsidiary, supply companies which lubricated and sustained the industry. Another of these was the Clonard Foundry, founded by George Horner, which constructed hackling machines for the linen factories. The latter's son, John, was one of the original intake of pupils at Methodist College in Belfast in 1868, along with Alexander Crawford's two grandsons, Alexander and Fred, and the three boys retained their friendship into later life.[7] Twenty years later, the former wrote to Fred from Victoria state in Australia about his nostalgia for home: "Mother, Father and you and John Horner are about the lot at home" for whom he cared.[8]

Whilst starch may have lacked the glamour and profitability of engineering, it remained an integral cog of the trade and Alexander Crawford & Son developed and diversified its product range. In various sources the company is described as starch, cornflour and chemical manufacturers, and also drysalters and black soap and candle manufacturers. They produced starches adapted for various types of manufacturers, including calico printers, bleachers, finishers, lace dressers and laundries – their best known product being 'Snow-white Starch'. Additionally they manufactured 'Amylaceous Food' (starch-based), advertised as "a pure wheaten food, easily digested, very nutritious, and a pleasant article of diet ... highly commended by eminent physicians as a food for children and invalids". Much of the creativity and success was primarily due to Alexander's son, James W. Crawford, who appears to have been engaged by his father at about the age of eighteen, about the time when the company was established.

Alexander, the antipodean, had written to his parents in mid-1884: "I had a letter from Chlorine last week saying you were sending starch and cornflour to two exhibitions. I hope you will be awarded first prize at them". Indeed, they seem to have done so, as the company was to boast Gold and First Prize Medals at Exhibitions in Belfast (1870), Dublin (1872), Cork (1883), London (1884), Edinburgh (1886) and Glasgow (1888). They also exhibited starch "and cornflour of their own preparation" at other events, such as the Dublin Exhibition of 1882.[9]

The decade that stretched between the success at Dublin and Cork possibly reflects the change of hand on the company's helm. Alexander

Crawford had provided a solid foundation for his company but, after the best part of three decades in Belfast, his powers and his health were on the wane and he became increasingly reliant upon the contribution of his son. The latter always saw the positive side of ill-health; he welcomed it as an exhortation to, as he expressed it, "prepare us all for the nobler mansions above".

James W. regarded sickness as a credit balance for gaining access to the Pearly Gates. In January 1868 he had noted that: "My little Fred and baby [Caroline] are not in good health. Oh, how great a boon is the thought to have them all, my little dears, in Heaven – where, if it be God's will, we shall meet". Just over a year later his eldest son, Alexander, had just recovered from measles. "Baby is very ill", he continued, "but we don't know what it is. Fred does not appear strong". Additionally, his mother-in-law had slipped and hurt her side and wrist. At this time – February 1869 – his father had also been "seriously ill with bronchitis for several days". In June the latter had visited Portstewart for a week, but fell ill with recurring symptoms. James W. added: "These sudden attacks [are] coming now so often; the cause is not to be without serious apprehensions. He is 73 years [he was actually 72], and he enjoys such good health that any change from this alarms us".[10] Alexander Crawford eventually contracted painful and debilitating catarrh of the bladder and passed away (aged 76) at his home at Chlorine on 22nd May 1873.

James Wright Crawford

As he became more engaged in the family business, James W. Crawford discovered that trade bore a remarkable resemblance to the spirit – it was subject to pressure and fluctuations. In the final months of the 1860s his diary indicates that "the Lord has blessed us so much in business this past half year, without one seeking orders", and that they required additional space as they could "scarcely keep our customers going with starch". However, they had had to survive a downward trend in the market place, and others had been struggling even more. Early in 1867 they had been fortunate to rein in £1000 of assets, which came at a time when his father's bank had warned him that the company was "over-checked". The son expressed relief that it was "a great blessing that we were not in the position of many of our poor fellow beings, who are obliged to stop and meet their creditors". Later in the same year (1867) he admitted that profitability was low, "but we have a number of first-class customers who pay promptly".

One of the most encompassing and revealing entries in the diary of James W. is that of 13th January 1868:

> We have settled our books, and find the balance on the right side to a considerable amount. To God be all praise. It was Thou who put it into my heart to make the starch ... as it is found specially suited for those purposes required. To this we owe the profits of the past half year specially. May we not waste one penny of what Thou in mercy givest, but may all be used for Thy glory. The fact that trade has been so dull with others in the same business makes it all the more marked that it is from God.

This best reflects his philosophy. He believed that hard work would reap its own rewards, that it was necessary to be charitable to others and that the hand of God can be discerned in all things. It combines the belief that one should earn God's pleasure, with the faith that God will dispense and dispose as one needs. These were eternal truths to James W, who felt it incumbent upon each generation to instil them in the next, as his private notes acknowledge: "I thank Thee, oh my Lord, for such teaching as I had from father and mother. May I train up my little ones in Thy love and fear".[11]

The young Fred inherited this willingness – even enthusiasm – to give thanks to God for all the blessings he enjoyed and, as his father had appreciated his own prosperity in business, so Fred ultimately was to express his gratitude for what he was to regard as the salvation of Ulster. Of course, as Fred's mother so rightly advised, one must avoid presumption; there were no guarantees. As Fred set out in mid-1885 to Hong Kong as an engineer on board the White Star Line's vessel, *Gaelic*, she warned:[12]

> We will be disappointed where we expected most. It is wisely ordered so that our minds may reach something higher and often. When lowest down, the Most High makes use of these things to bring us into closer communion with Himself. You will often be perplexed and distressed in

many ways, but Fred, dear, always raise your heart to Him and He will enable you to be calm and will help you in every time of need.

For all his reliance upon divine disposition, James W. Crawford proved a practical, industrious and creative businessman. Perhaps because of the uncertainty in the starch trade, in October 1883 he began to lease – at an annual rent of £250 – the Belfast Nursery, adjacent to Chlorine, from Alexander Threlkeld, an active fellow-worshipper at University Road Methodist Church. The nursery covered seven acres, and at one time enjoyed a frontage of 350 feet along the Malone Road; it was asserted that it was the largest nursery in the north of Ireland, and "most famous for horticultural excellence". Its size was eventually reduced as a consequence of the growing demand for land, as exemplified by the construction of Fisherwick Presbyterian Church at the very end of the 19th century.[13] Crawford employed a large staff on the site, which was intensively cultivated, and it boasted fourteen glass houses, in addition to "a lofty rose house" and an orchid house. The same source which described this addition to the Crawford commercial portfolio stated that: "Mr James W. Crawford … is well-known and highly respected in Belfast circles. He devotes all his attention and energy to the development of the business with an enthusiasm and persistence which are so essential to complete and permanent success".[14]

He also manifested such positive qualities in the family's traditional commercial base – the Wilson Street Works – and once, rather surprisingly, eschewed his usual reticence to emphasise his personal contribution, if privately, in his diary. Having sublimated any personal ambitions, as a young man he made a commitment to his father's company. During the 1850s and 1860s he worked diligently and developed new products – particularly starches – and sought new customers and markets in England and Scotland.

He spent lengthy periods of time experimenting and researching to create products specifically suited to individual customers. Occasionally, he was disposed to admit that this was not always as successful as he would have hoped and in September 1869 he noted that: "Nearly all my spare moments have been filled up with plans and experiments for our new starch". This occasion caused him to record an unaccustomed note of pique, brought on by professional and personal strain.

In addition to the inadequacies of the new starch, the company was having difficulties with a new well that had been installed on the premises at Wilson Street. In late June 1869 they had just completed the construction of the bore (which was 17 feet wide at the base), which was to supply between 5000 and 6000 gallons of water per day. This was a major investment, but within a month leaks had appeared and James W. recorded that: "This, with other things, has caused us a great deal of worry, so that, along with trying to keep the starch right, they bother me a great deal". This coincided with the period when his father was subject to increasing "sudden attacks" and, consequently, an increasing workload was falling on his shoulders.

James W. confided in himself that: "I feel that this drain of so long a time on my powers of body and mind is telling on me. I am still in the position as regards my interest in the business as what I was ten years ago – £200 salary and one-eighth of the profits. I consider this unfair when I do the work". He admitted that this was the same as his father paid himself, but his uncharacteristic complaint continued: "I would speak to father, only for accusing him in his old age. On the other hand, when I look at Madge and the children I am not sure that I should be thus kept back from speaking as all my energies are devoted to the business, as if every penny came to myself. Many other things of a like nature prey on my mind …"

The success of the company, at least partly represented by competitive prizes, after Alexander's death in 1873 was clearly the result of his son's efforts. James W. brought his own son, Fred, into the company's employment by 1886 – with the same financial arrangement which his father had bestowed upon him! Within a couple of years Fred was informing his older brother, Alexander in Australia, that the company was beginning to struggle.[15]

After leaving Methodist College, Alexander had been sent to Queen's College in Belfast and then to study at Albert Agricultural College at Glasnevin, near Dublin – training which was to stand him in good stead in Australia. However, by the time of the death of his own father in 1873, James W. probably determined that he needed his elder son's assistance at Wilson Street. Alexander can have worked only briefly for his father before he left the company, ostensibly on grounds of ill-health.[16] There are indications that Alexander's father regarded him as both a sickly and a wilful child; when his son was only 12 years old he wrote that he was "a soft child, yet has several traits in his character [that] may lead him into trouble".[17]

Alexander had departed from the family business by 1875, when he spent most of the year travelling through North America. He then sought a healthier climate in South Africa before arriving on the east coast of Australia. He then travelled to Linton in Victoria to visit the farm of one of his mother's brothers. The rift between father and son was not simply to be caused by a clash of personalities, but by affairs of the heart. In Linton, Alexander Crawford fell in love with his cousin – Eliza Jane Mathews (whom he referred to as Lillie) – and he returned to marry her on 3rd March 1885. A year earlier he had written to Fred:[18]

> 'Tis true [Father] never mentions Lillie or anything about her in his letters, but at the same time he takes other ways of showing his dislike to her and to my marriage, and in a mean way. Thus if Mother or you put in your letters something kindly about Lillie, Father has at different times scored it out and written something else over it in no way connected … He has no reason to think me unfeeling or ungrateful, for he said most distinctly before I left home that I had to choose between Lillie and him. I took my choice and I have not repented … it is Father's own fault that I am not at home now. I was willing to wait a year or two and stay at home in the business, if he would promise to give his consent at the end of that time, but he would not.

Subsequently, Alexander visited Belfast only briefly in 1886 and 1906, the year before his father's death.[19] James W. was never enamoured of the departure of his son, and almost thirty years later he still bore a grudge, expressed in a caveat in his will: "… it is my will that if my son Alexander shall not come to reside in this country …". There is an irony in Alexander's deprecatory observations about his father's financial incompetence, as he himself was to struggle financially all his life. The latter's own son (also named Alexander) wrote to Fred, his uncle, in late 1936: "Father himself was a very bad businessman, and I really think he had but little idea of what his own financial position really was … I know latterly his bank worried him quite a bit endeavouring to try and make him reduce his overdraft, which apparently he found great difficulty in doing".[20] It was this penury which ultimately prevented Alexander from returning home as he would have wished.

Alexander admitted that his attitude towards his father reeked of ingratitude, but was firm in his analysis: "I know I ought not to be the one that would say anything, for I have cost him a great deal, and even now I am indebted a considerable sum that I would gladly pay off if I could, and which I hope to do by degrees – but that does not make me blind to what to me seems to be wrong".

Fred had evidently at this time (1889) complained to his brother about the cost of a new well on the company premises. These were a major capital expenditure – another was installed in 1893 [21] – and Alexander replied: "The well has cost a lot of money; I hope you will not have to lay out any more on the work for some time to come. It seems as if money were forever being spent on the Works". Profitability was rapidly vanishing and the emigrant rather sardonically wrote to Fred: "If you want my microscope to be able to find your dividend, just cable, and I will send it [by] first steamer"!

Three months later his concern had intensified:

> I am very sorry to hear that business is so bad. Could you not persuade Father to try and sell the business and have done with it? I do not think he will ever make anything out of it, and he ought to be able to get something for it and that, together with what he should make out of the Nursery, ought to keep Mother and him very comfortably, and at the same time give him congenial employment. Then you [Fred] would be free to return, if you wished, to your old business, or anything else you wished.

In 1923, as he poked through the ashes of the family business, Fred was to acknowledge his father's improvidence: "I never could understand dear old dad; he never made any effort to pay off the depositors"; and he specified that: "These were the people father, at their own request, had taken money from, [who] were depending for a livelihood on the interest". He prefaced this by revealing to his brother that, at the time of their father's death (1907), the company had owed depositors and the Bank over £10,000, that it was making an annual loss, and that there was "the usual loss of £50 on the Nursery, which had lost money for years previously".[22]

Back in 1889, Alexander had identified the underlying problem: "If prayer could help you", he continued to Fred, "you would be in a good way now … I would greatly like to know that you were all in comfortable circumstances, although I do not think Father would ever save anything if he had £10,000 a year. I believe he would spend it, and what he calls have faith for the future, but I do not see it at all in that light. It seems to me like reckless improvidence and, had he been careful, he might have been beyond all care in the way of money matters".

Treasure in Heaven

Alexander Crawford inherited much of his father's piety, devotional zeal and moral rectitude. In December 1884 he wrote from Queensland to his parents that he was surrounded by quite a lot of ladies: "I join in, although several of the younger ladies have done their best to make me dance, but I would not give in to them. They are an extremely worldly lot, and I often feel I am out of place among them".[23] Despite this similarity to his father, Alexander was a perspicacious judge of the older man's character and temperament.

His father's priority was not worldly prosperity; as early as December 1859 James W. Crawford had written: "God help me to lay up treasure in Heaven … I pray God help me to live for Himself alone". This goal acquired added urgency in his own mind as, despite the fact that he lived to the age of 75, he always believed that his life teetered on the edge of the abyss. In his thirties he suffered recurrent epistaxis, with nose-bleeds often lasting several days. He felt that the additional work required in his Works "has been injurious to my health". All his ailments amplified his fears; in late 1868 he attributed swollen ankles and hands to "kidney disease or fatty degeneracy of the heart, or both". He envied those with a robust constitution, as he aspired to labour "for the salvation of sinners".

As he sought his own spiritual salvation, he seemed afflicted by hypochondria of the soul! "I feel as if I need the whip of affliction hanging over me", he wrote, "to keep me from becoming too worldly". He struggled to master self-denial, but bewailed his failure: "Oh Lord how often I yield to what I should not. I loathe myself. I am a poor wretched sinner".

He claimed that he suffered from "fearful temptations" and recorded that, at times, "I am almost consumed by them". This is an unexpected confession from an individual whose inflexible moral perspective appeared to be infused by the very starch which he manufactured. These temptations are never specifically identified, but the indications are that they arose from his attempt to divert girls from prostitution. As will be seen, William Gladstone was to become one of Fred Crawford's *bêtes noires*, but James W's efforts to rescue young women from the thrall of prostitution very much echoed those of the Liberal Prime Minister.

In late 1852 Gladstone recorded, discreetly in Italian, in his diary: "Tonight I saw a most beautiful unnamed girl of 18. I accompanied her to her house, where we lingered over a talk; she hates her way of life, yet lacks the courage for the expense and sacrifices of detaching herself from it. God have pity on her".[24] Seven years later the Ulsterman noted in his diary that he had been approached by a girl in the street, who had been "only five weeks at this life. She admitted that she was doing wrong, and said what could she do, as she could not starve". Crawford added that he took her home and gave her a little money; later he found her a post and added that she was doing well. He recorded other personal approaches, as on 29th December 1868 when he tried to keep a girl on the corner of Marquis Street "from going astray", and one night in April 1863, after visiting the Night Refuge, he revealed that: "last night … the temptation was probably pressed on me". He stated on another occasion that: "I have like a great hankering after the fleshpots of Egypt, that nothing but God's grace keeps me from falling into outward sin, yea of deepest dye".

In February 1890 his younger son found himself en route to this country of fleshpots. Fred's own diaries reveal that he suffered more temptation at the sight of a pretty woman than did his brother and, like his father, felt compelled to record these distractions. Within a week of leaving England on board the *SS Britannia* his eyes had wandered and the 29-year-old confided to his private pages: "There is a very attractive widow on board; had a chat with her today, and felt bad after it as she has beautiful eyes. It is well for me I shall be getting off in 48 hours [at Malta]. If I had gone to Australia I don't know what might have happened". Sent to guard prisoners at St Helena during the Boer War, he paid a visit to Longwood, Napoleon's former prison. He noted an encounter with a "well-favoured" lady with several daughters and expressed concern at the need for propriety and rectitude: "I felt happy for once at least I was a married man, and that I had not in consequence been guilty of a flirtation with a young lady, though if I had not been married I think I should have been very tempted, as she was very pretty".[25]

It would be impossible to differentiate between what personal qualities were genetically inherited by Fred and which may have been nurtured, but there are many echoes of his father's self-directed jeremiads in Fred's own devotional reflections. At the close of 1892 he recorded one Sunday: "Poor day for the Kingdom – failed litterly [sic] in resisting temptation. God help me withstand the Evil One. I am so weak". The New Year began on an equally despondent note: "I have had a very bad week to start the New Year. I have given way shamefully to temptation ... I seem to fall deeper than ever".[26] Later in the year he was to note that: "Temptation [is] raging like a prairie fire", and by the end of the year he concluded that he was "the chief of sinners ... never has there been such a sinner as I".

Like his father, Fred was inclined to regard physical pain and illness as the consequence of personal transgression. As he travelled to the Holy Land in 1890, he noted that he had been enduring unimaginable distress from sciatica: "What a life I have had of pain and suffering these last two years, no person will ever know". He suspected that he had to bear this because of his unworthiness, and asked that God "will remove the fire when the dross of lust or passion has been burnt up ... Sanctify, Oh Christ, the affliction", he urged, "but do not make it permanent".

In His Works and in His Works

Even if both men were to feel that they did not measure up to divine expectations, both father and son aspired to a life of service. Fred pleaded between the pages of his diary: "Oh God, let me live so that I can be of some use". His father expressed it more positively and dynamically: "I always feel as if the principal object of my life was unattained unless I do some good each day of my life". This he endeavoured to achieve both in his charitable works and in his Wilson Street Works.

Fred's rueful observation in the 1920s that his father had shown no inclination to prioritise the claims of the investors in Alexander Crawford & Son was a symptom of the company's quixotic paternalism. When, however, long-serving William McKee felt that he had to give up his post in 1916, Fred demonstrated that he had inherited this casual indulgence; he responded to his employee: "Don't say you have given up your position ... It is still open for you to come and go when you like; but look upon it as a pastime and not a duty".[27]

One of James W. Crawford's most valued employees, David Marmion, died on 27th October 1868, at a time when the company was particularly busy. Consequently, he had to rise at 5 o'clock each morning at Chlorine to compensate for the loss of an essential worker. Crawford's principal concern, however, was for Marmion's family and salvation: "Davy died this morning. I hope and believe in the hope of everlasting life. Thus ends a loving, faithful and good servant. Oh that he may receive such a welcome above… To his wife and little orphans [sic], this will be an irreparable loss. May God take care of them all".

At the very start of 1867, when reflecting upon "drink, the curse of our land", Crawford mentions that "McLorinan we have taken back". Clearly the latter was a troublesome and ill-disciplined clerk, for exactly one year later the diary reveals that "Poor unfortunate McLorinan we have at last been obliged to part with. What will become of him, such a debasing horrible life he is leading". Even though a replacement clerk was engaged within a week, more work devolved upon the owner, who complained that "the close confinement of the office at night has been injurious to my health". Crawford's diary entreaty that the arrival of William McKee may prove a blessing was answered.

William McKee, who was 31-years-old at the time, stayed until his 80th year (1916). So trusted and valued was his service that he was appointed one of the trustees and executors of his employer's will – for which he was rewarded with a payment of £200, a year's salary. By March 1916 McKee found the return journey to Bangor physically too demanding and he could no longer get to work, but discovered that Fred – the third generation of the family he had served – continued to pay his full salary. Mindful of the company's precarious financial circumstances, McKee found this to be an embarrassment, but by

December he was still on full pay. He wrote to his employer expressing gratitude, but insisting that he would only take half. Fred demonstrated that he had learned all he knew about commercial financial management from his father by replying that he would not accept this sacrifice although, as he wanted to increase the salary of his principal employee (Ernest Knowles), he would agree to a £50 per annum reduction.[28]

James W's philanthropy also extended to those in the vicinity of the Works, whether employees or not, and it is arguable that this ultimately paid dividends. Ulstermen, and women, boast long memories, as one legend bears witness. In the aftermath of the Battle of the Boyne, King Billy was riding through the woods when he heard someone sobbing profusely. He encountered his father-in-law, King James II, crying his heart out. King Billy asked what was the matter and James explained that his life was no longer worth living: he had lost a battle; he would never regain his throne; he had let down his supporters and loyal subjects; his daughter (Billy's wife) would no longer talk to him; and he would become a laughing-stock. A little embarrassed, King Billy tried to cheer him up, and said: "Sure, don't worry, everyone will have forgotten about it in a week"!

Of course, they did not, and just over two and a quarter centuries later Orangemen were adding new heroes to their banners – as with LOL 100 of Comber, which embellished its banner with portraits of Edmund de Wind, winner of the Victoria Cross in 1918, who was a pupil at Campbell College when Fred became one of its first Governors, and of Colonel R. H. Wallace, one of Fred's closest Unionist associates. By the 1920s, social and political dichotomies had widened and intensified, but – although it failed to deal with the economic challenges of the age – Alexander Crawford & Son survived the violence and sectarianism that destroyed so much property around it.

The company had always been spared during sporadic periods of violence in the 19th century. It can be argued that this was a consequence of the personal standing and reputation of James W. Crawford and his younger son. Rioting had occurred not too distantly from the Crawford Works around the Twelfth in 1857. It returned with a vengeance in August 1864, and Fred's father described them as "situated in the midst of the Seat of War". The severity of the outbreak was such that many mills and factories were forced to close – and the starch manufacturer proved to be no exception.[29] The rioting was to cause considerable economic distress to the working classes, and for a while shortages of certain essential goods were experienced. Damage was extensive, and one of those whose property suffered was the baker, Bernard 'Barney' Hughes. Even Lady Donegall found this surprising and she sympathised with singular use of the language: "It is wonderful that they should destroy your property, for you are so liberal to all classes".

James W. believed that the Lord was protecting him: "When it was a risk for anyone to go to the Works in Wilson Street", he wrote, "I went, as my duty is daily to go up about 10 o'clock as usual, but chose what I thought was the quietest route". The streets were unaccustomedly deserted, with "Houses closed up, windows barricaded, if not smashed, streets covered with stones and brickbats". He said that one Friday, following a fearful fight in the adjacent streets, he felt it unwise to venture down to the factory and at one stage: "We only got one load out of the Starch Works for four days – the Friday when our cart was coming by Millfield". The concerned owner adds that, despite a readiness to destroy, "the mob looked at the name on the cart but said nothing".

This was arguably the consequence of the fact that James W's missions' work of the previous five years was well-known and appreciated in the locality. His diary records that, during this distressing summer:

> Protestants living in Catholic districts received notice to quit instantly, or within a few hours. Catholics received the same. Both parties requested shelter for their furniture from us. Of course, we gave it, and for four or five nights some families slept in our store. One poor woman called Doherty married to a Catholic was obliged to leave. We gave her furniture, family and pigs shelter. Her husband, a poor old man, although a Catholic, received from his own party a blow with a large stone on the knee.

Over half a century later his son was to receive a similar approach. In September 1920, in the midst of the rioting, Fred recorded that:[30]

> *Two RC women who keep a marine store, came to me and asked me could I save some valuable furniture in a Public House that was broken into, and the rest taken out and burnt in the street ... They appealed to me to try to help them. I spoke to the Commissioner of Police and the women informed me that their furniture had been protected and thanked me for what I had done.*

A few years earlier Fred was to mention to a correspondent in passing that they were trying to alleviate the local distress during the difficult times of 1908: "... and every shilling I send you will be one short of what I can spend to assist the starving children and women we have about our doors".[31] Such encompassing compassion would remain in the local public memory and may well account for the fact that, despite threats, attacks and some incursions, the Works were to remain intact during the vicious events of the early 1920s, whilst Fred witnessed many of his neighbours being burned to the ground. As we shall see, he was to take necessary protective precautions – he was very much a realist, revealing that: "I trust in God, but I also keep my powder dry"[32] – but by then he had become notorious for his partisan gun-running escapades. It was, however, recognised that he was fair to all men; on one occasion two Nationalist men, who had seriously assaulted him, later came by to apologise. If Fred's political outlook was cloistered, he lacked bigotry and would have concurred with his father's aspiration: "Oh Lord, turn all people, Catholic and Protestant, to Thyself".

One action which demonstrated the family's lack of political or religious discrimination was its distribution of one vital commodity – water. Although wells were sunk on the company's property for manufacturing purposes, in 1865 James W. recorded: "now, when there is such a dearth of water in town, we are thankful to be able to give free water to thousands from our wells". He clearly viewed this as part of his charitable works and concluded the entry: "God is very good to put us in circumstances to keep our fellows for both worlds. Praise His name".

According to one source,[33] the company had housed a Mission Room at the Works since 1859, a product of James W's commitment to the Great Revival of that year.[34] As one source points out: "The 1859 Ulster Revival ... was not the work of professional revivalists. Rather the initial impetus seems to have come from pious laymen operating in communities, with at least a smattering of biblical knowledge and familiarity with the basic Christian concepts of salvation and damnation". The working classes were particularly affected, even entire factories, mills and bleach works,[35] such as those of Alexander Crawford and Son.

James W. revealed that, in 1859, he had begun to find worldly possessions and pursuits unsatisfying and that during a Revival meeting he had been affected by comments made by his brother-in-law, Lawson Brown,[36] about the power of prayer and had left the occasion with an intense and over-powering sensation. This sense of redemption encouraged him to begin visiting the pariahs, poor and underprivileged of society, either in their homes or by regular forays into the back streets and lanes around the Wilson Street Works. He claimed that he regarded it to be an unalloyed privilege that "I am able and willing to visit the poor". He was also prepared to give money to, or to help find work for, the disadvantaged of society.

Even before the close of 1859 the Wilson Street Works was hosting weekly Bible classes, and sermon and prayer meetings, which accommodated both the employees and the local community. Within a year the attendance had risen from about fifty to double that number, which often included many prostitutes. These meetings continued throughout the 1860s and at some stages the company was holding five meetings a week. James W. Crawford's diary contains the exhortation: "May many souls be saved in Wilson Street" – and clearly he believed that this proved to be the case. In August 1865 he records: "Last Thursday evening, I was told, was the first evening for the last four weeks that there was not someone converted at the Starch Works. Lord, how great the privilege to be in a position to open a place where the poor can get their souls blessed without money and without price".

The pages of the starch manufacturer's diaries preserve the names of some of the most wretched and unfortunate members of mid-19th century Belfast society, whose existence would ironically have been erased from the memory of history, but for their misery and adversity. Crawford exhibited personal sadness, even grief, when he records their deaths – although he rejoices at their success and salvation.

It is to their credit that men such as James W. Crawford persisted with their community work, as the lack of hygiene could be particularly testing. It was said with regard to Rev. Robert Workman of Newtownbreda, who worked in the Belfast Mission in the 1860s, that: "The greatest physical trial in connection with Mission work arose from the filthy habits of the people and the vermin with which they were infested". Workman wore a separate suit during his visits as he was very susceptible to fleas. Fred was to find the latter troublesome during his travels and one night at Ramleh in the Holy Land in 1890 he recorded: "I never in my life suffered from fleas as I did last night. I destroyed a host and it did not seem to make the least impression on them".

Social conditions do not appear to have changed in half a century. On 4th May 1914, (the future) Lady Spender, the wife of one of those most closely associated with Fred in the development of the Ulster Volunteer Force, noted in her diary that she had been obliged to go to the Shankill Road Picture House to view a film of Carson's recent visit. She admitted that the film was excellent, but recalled that: "The atmosphere in the house was the very worst I ever encountered anywhere, for the audience was drawn exclusively from the slums and the smell was <u>appalling</u>! Tobacco smoke has the most delicate perfume to it, and I would have welcomed it as a disinfectant, but they were too poor to smoke". The following month she described an Orange Hall, selected for use as a dressing station, as "the most unspeakably dirty place I ever was in".[37]

As a consequence of his walks around the streets off Wilson Street and Mill Street James W. gauged that nineteen out of twenty homes "are in poverty ... owing to drink ... the poor children in rags, filth and hunger. Thank God", he continued, "many who come to our meetings, once drunkards, are led to give up the bad habit, and I hope and pray they may be converted". He was distressed by the misery imposed upon families – particularly upon the children – by the excesses of drink. He mentions William Scott, a wood turner, whose death left six or seven children as orphans and the death of James Kerr, "son of drunken John ... poor little fellow deprived of the necessaries, much less comforts, of life by the abominable drunken excesses of his father".

He despaired of the Gilmores: "a heathen family – such drinking, such destitution, nakedness, poverty and sin".

In February 1861 he witnessed "two drunken women staggering along Brown Street (at about midnight) with a little child of about three years old walking between them". Crawford believed that "the great sufferers are the poor children" and, like many with a social conscience, aspired to do something practical to deal with the problem. Although he made no further progress on the idea, at the end of the 1860s he suggested the opening of an institution "for the poor helpless boys and girls who work in Mills, and who make not sufficient to keep them without asking assistance. Many of these are orphans, depending on the uncertain help of neighbours or the benevolent".

In common with most social reformers, he posed the rhetorical question: "When will drink, the curse of our land, be done away with?" As elsewhere, it was an endemic problem in 19th century Belfast. As early as 1834 it was estimated that there were over 750 outlets for alcohol in Belfast alone. Half of the disciplinary action taken against Belfast police constables in the 19th century was the consequence of inebriation, and applying the full sanction of dismissal "would have meant having no experienced policemen in the force". Drinking was equally ignored or condoned on the railways, which could result in accidents such as that at Ballymacarrett (East Belfast) on 13th May 1871, in which two young people were killed. Neither was inebriation uncommon amongst professional people, such as bank employees.[38]

Most businessmen recognised the problem that alcohol presented to their prosperity. In 1871 the Andrews flax-spinning mill in Comber engaged a new spinning master and advised him that "Unless you are <u>strictly sober</u> you need not think of coming to us".[39] The Andrews family set an unimpeachable example and Thomas Andrews senior raised his four celebrated sons – one of whose daughters was in 1933 to marry one of Fred Crawford's sons – to be life-long teetotallers.

James W. recorded that his company "had our first public Temperance meeting in common with our Works" on 10th January 1862. He would rejoice when men – such as a pair of shoemakers, "for 14 years, companions in sin, drunkenness, fighting, and all the consequences they suffered" – abjured alcohol. He would despair at its prevalence and baleful influence, as with the Gilmores. One of the final entries in his personal diary (27th September 1869) expressed his concern on the issue: "When I see the fearful ravages caused by drink, I never feel free in my heart to allow any kind of it into my house". It was a disposition, *aux* Andrews, which he transmitted to his sons. On 22nd June 1921 Fred was invited to meet Their Majesties at City Hall; he recalled that: "The lunch was a good one; the champagne wine was 1911 brand and must have cost about £2 a bottle. I, of course, did not benefit by this luxury as I don't take any stimulant except when ill or ordered by the doctor".[40] One entry in his diary of the riots and disturbances of the early 1920s reveals that Fred did keep a bottle of whisky in the house;[41] his spelling suggests either that it was Scotch, or that he simply did not understand the difference between that and whiskey!

Methodists

The Crawford family commitment to the temperance movement derived from its links with the Wesleyan Church. Earlier generations of the Crawfords, as we have seen, were Presbyterians – and, indeed, at least until the 1930s Fred was also paying pew rent at Fisherwick Presbyterian Church [42] which was constructed on the edge of the Chlorine estate at the close of the 19th century. The family, however, became dedicated Methodists, occupying pews at University Road Methodist Church [43], which opened on 23rd April 1865. The change of allegiance probably stemmed from James W. Crawford's marriage on 29th April 1856 to Margery – always known as Madge – Mathews, the daughter of Hugh Mathews of Annagh House, near Portadown.[44]

Fred would never have known his grandfather,[45] who attended Thomas Street Wesleyan Chapel in Portadown. A tribute was to say of the Methodist Leader: "It is the force of moral character, evinced in the consistency of Christian deportment, that even the profane commend the person that they fail to imitate, and pronounce the goodness of the character whose practice condemns themselves. Such was the testimony borne by the most worthless, as well as the most worthy, that Hugh Mathews was a good man". He had once tolerated drink, but became "sickened and revolted" by what he saw and was teetotal for the last four years of his life.

James W. also instilled in his two surviving sons the value of church attendance and worship and Methodism was the principal vehicle. His elder son was to become a Trustee of Perth Central Methodist Church in Western Australia, with which he was linked intermittently for 55 years. On 25th June 1934 he regaled a gathering in Perth about the pioneer days as they celebrated the building of the first Methodist Church in the territory.[46] As his father had done,[47] whenever Fred went on his travels he sought out a Wesleyan service – or preferably two – on Sundays, although, for practical reasons, he was not always denominationally fastidious.

He did, however, expect to be uplifted spiritually on the Lord's Day. En route to the Holy Land in 1890 he noted, upon reaching Brindisi (2nd March) that: "We had a Presbyterian service. It seemed rather strange in this hotbed of Roman Catholicism to have a real good sermon just like home, without even the Church service". Perhaps it was only right that he should get the hump on Quasimodo Sunday (24th April) 1892 on board *SS Cuzco* when there was "no parson on board of any denomination, at least among 2nd class …" to provide a service. They did unearth one later in the day from 1st class "and he held a service there this morning, but did not give us the pleasure of a sermon".

Methodism was no easy option for its adherents; the Church expected its members' character to be disciplined and its mettle to be tested. One commentator was to observe, with a touch of irony, that:[48]

> During the Boer War, a leading religious [Methodist] newspaper severely criticised the British Commander-in-Chief because he fought two important engagements on Sunday! It was plainly hinted that this in itself was sufficient to account for his defeats. Apparently it was considered permissible to trifle with the eighth Commandment providing the letter of the fourth was unbroken.

The minister at University Road Methodist Church at the turn of the 19th century, Rev Charles Inwood, was a fearsome figure. He had alienated his previous congregation at Knock (East Belfast), asserting that they were "not possessed of much out-and-out religion". References in his diary to 'back-sliding' and admissions that he had also failed to make an impact upon his new charges, reveal that he lacked personal charisma, but his letters are peppered with terms such as 'revival', 'conversions', 'special mission' and 'open-air work', which must have resonated with individuals such as his parishioner, James W. Crawford.[49]

In the early years of the 20th century, and particularly in the 1920s fractured by the aftermath of the First World War and the tribulations of Partition, Methodism was in the vanguard of social welfare and pastoral work. In the late 1860s, Fred's father had railed against "the dreadful sins caused by this hellishly selfish system" of spirit licences and he believed that "the time will come when the temptations of such a sort will be removed from the people". He was mistaken, but it was the Wesleyans who proved most vigorous in promoting pro-temperance legislation in the new Parliament of Northern Ireland, to diminish the corrosive impact of alcohol upon Ulster society.

A large number of prominent individuals – such as Sir William Whitla and John Cleaver – took an active part in the Methodist Laymen's Missionary Movement.[50] Fred Crawford was also actively engaged in the charitable social work pioneered by his father (as with the YMCA, the British Legion and the Royal Victoria Hospital). James W. would have viewed this as a satisfying outcome to his prayerful aspiration, at the very start of 1866: "Be it my duty to bring our offspring up for glorious duty in this world. May they all be employed in Christ's Kingdom".

Notes

1. He is listed at this address in the 1839 *Belfast & Ulster Street Directory*. It may have been on small scale at that time, as he is listed in 1842 between a publican and chandler.

2. D/1700/8, 13 December 1860. After the departure of the Crawfords, Mount Prospect was for some time occupied by James Wright Crawford's brother-in-law, Lawson Brown; by 1878 the latter lived at 5 Chlorine Place close to Chlorine House.

3. The dates and details of occupancy are uncertain, but James Wright Crawford allowed his sister, Abby (probably Abigail) Agnes Luther to occupy Chlorine Villa from 1878. She was married to Dr H Waldemar Luther, who died around 1896. The couple had at one stage lived a couple of doors along the Malone Road at Fernleigh House, but are listed as living in Chlorine House from 1890. Abby died in September 1908.

4. The Register of Methodist College, Belfast, states that in 1868 the family of James Wright Crawford was living at Cloreen.

5. This account is found in D/1700/8.

6. The Wilson Street Works are mentioned in James Wright Crawford's diary on 21 August 1864. The first reference in the *Belfast & Ulster Street Directory* is 1865-1866. The obituary of James Wright Crawford in *The Northern Whig*, 28 October 1907, is probably incorrect when it states that the starch factory had been in Wilson Street for sixty years.

7. In a lengthy letter of 12 April 1880 John Horner indicated their friendship, and expressed his sympathy over the illness of Fred's sister, Caroline: D/1700/5/2/12.

8. D/1700/6/1/4, 14 May 1888 from Warragul, Victoria, to Fred Crawford at Chlorine. John Horner was a multi-talented individual, known as a skilled engineer, polished linguist, noted scientist and botanist: J W Henderson, *Methodist College Belfast 1868-1938*, (Methodist College, Belfast, 1939), p.34.

9. *Industries of the North one hundred years ago*, introduction by W H Crawford (Friar's Bush Press, Belfast, 1986), p.105. *The Freeman's Journal*, 14 August 1882.

10. D/1700/3/1, 21 January 1868, 8 February 1869, 5 July 1869.

11. D/1700/3/1, 12 March 1868.

12. D/1700/5/2/35, 4 July 1885 from Hotel Imperial in Glasgow. There seems to have been an expectation that he was visiting his brother, Alexander. If this is the case, the latter must have travelled to Hong Kong from Australia to meet Fred.

13. The area was being developed as early as 1895, and it was necessary to widen the road (now the Malone Road). The Belfast Town Clerk notified Fred that they were willing to erect "a neat wooden fence" along the new frontage, but Fred retorted that it "must be a wall": D/1700/5/2/49: 22 February 1895.

14. W H Crawford, p.105. Obituary in *The Northern Whig*, 28 October 1907.

15. This information is derived from two letters from Alexander to Fred dated 7 January & 24 April 1889: D/1700/5/2/42 and D/1700/6/1/5.

16. See Alexander Crawford's entries in the *Australian Dictionary of Biography*; in W T Pike, *Ulster Contemporary Biographies*, (Brighton, 1910), p.78; and in H M Coffrey & M J Morgan, *Irish Families in Australia and New Zealand 1788-1983*, I, 169-170.

17. D/1700/3/1, 27 September 1869.

18. D/1700/5/2/21, 4 April 1884.

19. In correspondence with Alexander on 31 December 1906, Fred notified his brother that "Father [is] much as he was when you were home": D/1700/10/1/25.

20. D/1700/6/2/5, 14 December 1936, from Alexander's home in Victoria (also

named Cloreen) to his uncle, Fred Crawford, at Cloreen.

21. In Fred's devotional diary: D/1700/3/10, 15 September 1893.
22. D/1700/6/1/18 July 1923 (Fred at Cloreen to Alexander in Perth).
23. D/1700/8, 20 December 1884 from Coorabelle, Springsure, Queensland.
24. M R D Foot & H C G Matthew (eds), *The Gladstone Diaries, IV 1848-1854*, (Clarendon Press, Oxford, 1974), p.465; D/1700/8 (1859).
25. D/1700/3/7, 27 February 1890; D/1700/3/2, 6 May 1900.
26. Much of this is taken from Fred Crawford's Devotional Diary: D/1700/3/10.
27. D/1700/5/17/129A, 28 March 1916.
28. For this, see D/1700/5/17/129-130, –/134-135.
29. Crawford's diary, D/1700/8, 21 August 1864. Jack Magee, *Barney: Bernard Hughes of Belfast 1808-1878*, (Ulster Historical Foundation, Belfast, 2001), pp.144-165. Jonathan Bardon, *A History of Ulster*, (Blackstaff Press, Belfast, 1992), pp.349-352.
30. D/640/11/2, p.20.
31. D/1700/10/1/517, 30 November 1908 to Rev Charles Duncan.
32. D/640/11/2, p.98.
33. Pike, p.79.
34. Much of this material is taken from James Wright Crawford's account of the Great Revival: D/1700/8; and also from other sources such as Rev W L Northridge, 'Irish Methodism and Evangelism' in *Irish Methodism in the 20th Century: a Symposium*, (Irish Methodist Publishing Company, Belfast, 1931); D L Cooney, *The Methodists in Ireland: a short history*, (Columba Press, Dublin, 2001); and David Hempton & Myrtle Hill, *Evangelical Protestantism in Ireland 1740-1890*, (Routledge, London, 1992). Fred continued to give a £5 donation each Christmas to the Wilson Street Mission until at least the late 1930s: D/1700/7/1.
35. Hempton & Hill, pp.150, 156-157.
36. Lawson Brown married James Wright Crawford's sister, Jane. He was a timber and slate merchant based in Chichester Street. When Crawford moved in the 1860s from his home at Mount Prospect on the Lisburn Road, Lawson Brown occupied the latter.
37. Margaret A K Garner, *Robert Workman of Newtownbreda 1835-1921*, (William Mullan & Son, Belfast, 1969), p.71. D/1700/3/7, 29 April 1890. D/1633/2/19.
38. For all of this, see B Griffin, *The Bulkies: Police and Crime in Belfast 1800-1865*, (Irish Academic Press, Dublin, 1997), p.55; K Haines, *Human Frailty and the 1871 Ballymacarrett Rail Accident*, (Ballymaconaghy Publishing, Belfast, 2002), pp.99-111; Lyn Gallagher, *The Ulster Bank Story*, (Ulster Bank Ltd, Belfast,

1998), p.196; Fred Allen, 'Ardent Spirits, Pawnbroking and the Belfast House of Industry', *East Belfast Historical Society Journal*, Vol.2 no.4 (1989-90), pp.16-24.

39. D/4189/A/2/2, 12 January 1871.

40. D/640/16/2. In June 1922 Fred collapsed with pain when Dr William Killen was treating a damaged ear, and "he gave me some whisky, which pulled me thro' ": D/640/11/2, p.93. Fred does not appear to have indulged in that other social pastime: smoking. In 1910 he advised his brother to smoke less because of his health, adding: "I have tried smoking and I have had to give it up tho' I like it very much; still, I found it does not suit me": D/1700/10/1/805-806, 8 June 1910.

41. D/640/11/2, p.96.

42. D/1700/7/1.

43. Fred was to leave the church £100 in his will, "for such purposes as the Committee ... may decide".

44. This information is taken from 'A Brief Memorial of Hugh Mathews of Annah' (sic), *Irish Evangelist*, April 1863. In an appended personal note, Fred Crawford, whose middle name was Hugh, reveals that he was named after his maternal grandfather. Madge's sister, Lizzie, married Rev John Oliver of Omagh and Fred was to keep in regular contact with the latter's son (i.e. his own cousin), Rev Turner Barrett Oliver.

45. Hugh Mathews died, aged 77, on 2 April 1862, when Fred was only seven months old. In a letter of 14 September 1909 to Methodist College he states that his great-grandfather had been a Methodist: D/1700/10/1/688-689.

46. D/1700/6/1/13, –/26.

47. D/1700/3/1, 7 November 1866, 30 May 1869.

48. R H Foster, 'Irish Methodism and War', in *Irish Methodism in the Twentieth Century: a Symposium*, (Irish Methodist Publishing Company, Belfast, 1931), p.68. During his service in the Boer War, Fred declined to be photographed with his fellow Officers because: "I don't like breaking Sunday and turning it into an ordinary day": D/1700/3/2, 3 June 1900.

49. Archibald M Hay, *Charles Inwood: his Ministry and its Secret*, (Marshall, Morgan & Scott, London/Edinburgh, no date), pp.84-90.

50. Hay, p.90. Northridge, pp.56-58. R Lee Cole, 'One Methodist Church', Vol. IV of *The History of Methodism in Ireland*, (Irish Methodist Publishing, Belfast, 1960), p.119.

I wish to God I had never touched Starch

∞

Despite James Wright Crawford's innate pessimism, at the time of Frederick Hugh Crawford's birth – 21st August 1861 – the prospects looked good both for the family and the company. It may possibly have been the arrival of a new grandson, as well as the development of the Wilson Street site, which encouraged Alexander Crawford to build two new homes on the Malone Road.

The death of two young children by 1866 caused Fred's father to be overly cautious about his children's health and he was inclined to believe that Fred "does not appear strong". Occasionally Fred and his younger sister, Caroline (who died aged fifteen in 1881), were taken by their mother to Omagh to aid recovery from various ailments and, often for several weeks at a time during the late 1860s, the entire family would decamp to Mr Lamont's establishment on Sandy Row (now Queen's Parade) in Bangor for the beneficial air of the Co Down coast.[1]

Such concern on his father's part was transmitted to Fred, who became very attentive to the ailments of his own five children: "None of my youngsters is really strong", he noted in 1908.[2] The simple reality was, however, that – in an age when commonplace remedies and antibiotics had yet to be discovered – all of them were susceptible to prevalent illnesses and diseases, such as measles, whooping cough, diphtheria, tuberculosis, scarlet fever and influenza. Fred's elder son, Stuart, contracted the latter in January 1907, at a Sunday School party, and at one stage his mother "thought he was dead". Occasionally Fred would send a child to his own mother for isolation, as the impact of some illnesses could be enduring; the family was in quarantine for five months in the summer of 1908 as a consequence of mumps and they endured whooping cough for the whole of the summer of 1910.[3]

Compared to many, such as those who lived in the penumbra of the Crawford Works, the family resided in very pleasant and salubrious circumstances. James W. admitted as much: "How blessed a thing", he acknowledged, "to have the comforts of life, especially when many are in sickness". The final entry of his diary in autumn 1869 was penned at Cloreen: "I am now sitting looking through my open window on the grounds outside which are made so beautiful by the clear atmosphere and deep blue sky, with shades of clouds of various hues. Lord, why am I thus, and not shut up like so many others in close, dirty, dark and miserable streets?"

Fred was raised in this congenial ambience, away from the grime and cacophony of the industrial heartland of central Belfast, and defied his father's belief that he was a delicate child. From a young age, he rose as early as 5am.[4] He pursued a full-term apprenticeship in shipbuilding, a physically demanding career, and between 1885 and 1892 several journeys across the globe, as well as participation in the Boer War between 1900 and 1901, testified to his fitness and energy. As had his mother, Fred survived to celebrate his 91st birthday.

Methodist College

His early home was on the fringes of the seven-acres of Threlkeld's nursery that his father was to acquire. The lower end of what is now the Malone Road was primarily open ground. William Corry, a mineral water manufacturer, built his home, named Chatsworth, across the road from Methodist College in 1879. Lennoxvale, later owned by family friend and physician, Sir William Whitla, was designed only three years earlier.

As a very young child, Fred played on the open ground on which Methodist College was constructed from the mid-1860s.[5] At this time Methodism boasted an impact upon the social and political scene in Ireland that belied its attenuated numbers – 40,000 adherents out of a population of five million. Methodist College – now almost universally known as Methody – was originally rather inelegantly named the Wesleyan Methodist Collegiate Institution. It was established for two primary reasons: as a college for students of the Methodist ministry and as a grammar school for the sons of ministers and others.

The links between the College and its neighbour, University Road Methodist Church (opened in April 1865), were close. The latter asserted that it was "enriched by the close association" and its highly-regarded minister in 1879, Rev. Dr. Joseph W. McKay, became the President of Methody from 1880. He was a powerful and dignified man, and "such a record of work and honour can scarcely be found associated with any other name in the annals of Irish Methodism".[6] It is rather surprising then that, by the time of the latter's death in 1891, the most recent Headmaster and his deputy (both poached by Campbell College as joint-Headmasters in 1890) were, respectively, an Episcopalian and a Presbyterian.

In the middle of 1868, James W. had prayed: "May I, with Madge … train up our remaining three children, Alexander, Freddie and Baby [Caroline], to be burning and shining lights". Two months later he evidently felt that he had found the means to pursue this aspiration when he noted in his diary, on the day before Fred's seventh birthday, that: "this day Alex and Fred have gone to the Methodist College … May the College in all its departments be a blessing to all concerned. May it not be ever used for the glory of man".

In retrospect, therefore, he must have been truly disappointed by the appointment of the new Headmaster in 1890, Henry Spillar McIntosh, for the latter was an irascible man who placed worldly glory above academic achievement. He was obsessed with rugby, particularly with winning the prestigious Schools Cup, to the extent that it was recorded early in 1893 that "McIntosh made a speech to [the rugby team] at the beginning of term, in which he told them to mind Football first, work afterwards". As one source suggests, he probably regarded it as blasphemy when he was advised by the President of the College in 1906 that "a little less football would be rather for the advantage of the College".[7]

During the first decade of the 20th century, numbers began to decline at the school. By this stage, Fred was himself a parent of pupils at the College, and was perhaps mindful of the inadequacies of his own education, and the emphasis placed upon the precept of manliness or 'muscular Christianity'. Despite – or, more accurately, because of – the fact that he described himself as "a very pronounced Wesleyan Methodist",[8] like so many others, he became less enamoured with the institution.

By mid-1908 Fred reported to his brother that he felt that his eldest child, Naomi, was not making good progress at Methody, so he had sent her to another Methodist foundation, Queenswood College in London, "where I trust she will be able to lay the foundation of a university education". He had expressed reservations, directly to McIntosh in late 1907, complaining that the homework of Naomi and Stuart was not being properly marked. At this time he had flirted with The Leys School in Cambridge – described as the first Methodist Public School – indicating that he would like his son to be "brought under the influence and teachings of this denomination". By September 1909, Fred was berating McIntosh that Stuart "is learning, as far as I can judge, absolutely nothing", and he threatened to find another school for his son.

Probably symptomatic of the financial problems facing his company at this time, he became embroiled in a rather trivial wrangle with the Head of Science at Methody, J. Stewart Kerr. In 1907 Fred's brother, Alexander, sent his own son – also named Alexander – to reside briefly in Belfast (at Cloreen). Fred continued his nephew's education at the school, but received a letter of complaint in February 1909 that the boy had not acquired correct equipment. Fred responded that: "Alex informed me that he was required to get some instruments, and among other things a pencil at 4d [four old pence]. I objected to pay this price for a pencil to be given to a boy 13 years of age who would likely lose it, so I got a pencil at 2d that I can stand over and which I used for the finest work when I was a Marine Architect at Harland & Wolff".

For all his pride in and attachment to Methodism, Fred Crawford articulated an ambivalent opinion of the school. Having been a pupil there himself, and having a family home only a stone's throw distant, he cannot have been oblivious to the nature of the College. He notified McIntosh, however, that if his elder son, Stuart "goes into the Army [which he was to do] or some other profession, I do not want him branded educationally as Methodist or any other sect. I object to denominational education, and the name of Methodist College is a great mistake from a business standpoint". He felt that the Governors should face the fact that this deterred others from applying.

Nearly a year later, before the start of the 1910 academic year, he informed McIntosh that he also disagreed with co-education beyond the age of eight or nine, and that he had removed his son to Campbell College – where Fred had been a Governor since 1898 – as "I think a boy educated at any school called by a sectarian name is very much handicapped in after life".

The starch manufacturer was to prove equally critical about the lack of academic application made by his son at Campbell College and wrote a complaint to its Headmaster, R. A. H. MacFarland, who was a more fervent exponent of 'muscular Christianity' than was McIntosh. Always solicitous of his children's health, during Stuart's first term he told the school – which permitted local walks at weekends within rigidly specified bounds – that he did not want his son out of school on Sundays "until his cough is better". Others appear to have been even more concerned about the ailments which afflicted their sons on the Belmont campus and, exactly one week after Fred had contacted the Housemaster (William Allison), the father of another pupil, who had joined only in September 1910 with Stuart Crawford, withdrew his son permanently because of his concern for the boy's health. Thus ended Stuart's acquaintance with the young C. S. Lewis. Nevertheless, Fred persisted with Stuart's education at Campbell College and he remained sufficiently convinced to send his younger son, Adair, a decade later.

There are indications that, as they grew older, Fred's five children found the domestic environment to be difficult and their father to be a hard-taskmaster. He admitted [9] that: "I try to impress upon all the children that they will have to make their own way in life". He did, however, always demonstrate considerable paternal anxiety for, and attentiveness to, their health and education.

Within a year of their father's death, Fred confided to his brother that he might soon be seeking other employment, admitting that: "when there is a wife and five children to provide for, it leaves a sickly sinking at the pit of the stomach".[10] When he had to beg Sir James Craig for a position in 1923, after his business had collapsed, he admitted that, as a result, "my three younger children's education can be completed, thereby giving them a decent start in life".[11] Surviving personal cash books reveal that even well into the 1930s Fred was paying substantial medical bills for operations and treatment for his children, as well as for himself, in addition to educational fees and costs for his daughters.[12]

In passing it should perhaps be pointed out that, as he grew older, Fred lost track of the depreciating value of money. His cash books reveal that from at least 1927 he was giving his wife, Helen,[13] a monthly housekeeping allowance of £29 3s 4d, or £350 per annum. This sum was also specified in his will made in 1941 which, in turn, appears to indicate that this particular amount had been set since 1918! Helen Crawford struggled to cope with this situation until her husband's death in 1952 and, following the grant of probate of the will, their son Adair wrote to his siblings suggesting that "the £350 named will not be a very robust income for anyone, and I think we should hesitate to draw our full share of the surplus income".[14]

Shooting Star

Fred's own education at Methodist College to 1875 appears to have been unspectacular. He was then sent to complete his education at University College School in an insalubrious part of London, at which his younger son later claimed that: "his academic ability was assessed by his ability to throw a cricket ball further than others". Whilst disdainful, this observation does no more than reflect the growing emphasis upon 'muscular Christianity' in schools, and it seems that at this time academic subjects remained optional at Gower Street, whilst games were encouraged.

Fred distinguished himself as an athlete and at rifle shooting, for which he won a silver-plated ink-stand in 1877,[15] and it may well have been here that he first developed his abiding interest in guns – in Jerusalem in 1890 he could recognise such weapons at a glance: "... the Martini Henry rifle with sword bayonet". He established several rifle clubs in Ulster, revived old ranges and created a new range on Lord Ranfurly's estate in Dungannon. Much later he recalled: "I started a secret society called 'Young Ulster'. A condition of membership was the possession of one of three weapons: a Martini rifle, a USA Cavalry Winchester rifle, or a .455 revolver ... and one hundred rounds of ammunition". He was appointed Vice-President of the Ulster Rifle Association in 1908, and described himself, even in later life, as "a dead shot"; in June 1936, at the age of (almost) 75, he demonstrated his talent at Ligoniel Rifle Range by scoring an 'inner' from 1000 yards.[16]

Apprentice

The partnership of Edward Harland and Gustav Wolff, which eventually flourished into the largest shipyard in the world, was signed only four months before the birth of Fred Crawford. Shortly after the latter's seventeenth birthday, James W. purchased for him, at a cost of £200, a premium apprenticeship in the yard "to learn the art and trade of an Ironshipbuilder". Fred's service was computed from 23rd September 1878 for five years, with his pay set at 4 shillings per week in the first year, rising incrementally and annually to 10 shillings per week.[17] Seventy years or so later, Fred's grandson, Malcolm, was to follow a similar apprenticeship and his grandfather's original tools – bearing the legend 'FHC' – returned to the yard.

His first three and a half years involved practical labour on the ships, followed by a year and a half in the drawing office. He appears to have found the latter more congenial as he then worked "as a journeyman draughtsman for about a year and nine months" and later, in his irritated communication to Stewart Kerr at Methodist College about the quality of a pencil, described himself as "a marine architect at Harland & Wolff".[18]

Edward Harland and Gustav Wolff created thousands of jobs, but they were hard taskmasters and disciplinarians. Thomas Andrews, future designer of the *RMS Titanic* – and posthumous uncle-in-law to Fred's younger son, Adair – obtained a premium apprenticeship under his uncle, William Pirrie. The latter insisted that his nephew be shown no favours, and "by his own efforts and abilities he must make his way". The yards opened at 6am and punctuality was an obligation upon the employee – Fred's indenture punished him with two days' service for each day he was absent.

The shipyards, like the mills and factories, were treacherous workplaces at this time; injuries were commonplace – with little or no chance of any financial compensation. A private letter from an acquaintance, James Panton Ham junior, in November 1878 indicates that Fred had injured himself in the work-place quite early in his apprenticeship.[19]

Fred became well-acquainted with the Carlisle and Pirrie families, who played a dominant role in the shipyards. William (later Viscount) Pirrie, who later became Chairman of Harland & Wolff, was in his final year as an apprentice when Fred started at Queen's Island, and Fred became friendly with one of Pirrie's cousins and future brother-in-law, James Carlisle.

In retrospect, it seems unlikely that a Headmaster of English at Royal Belfast Academical Institution, John Carlisle, would sire a brood that would dominate the world's premier shipyard. One of his sons – Alexander – became a Managing Director, and a daughter – Margaret – married (in 1879) her cousin, William Pirrie. Even the rich and powerful, however, could not alter fate, and another of John Carlisle's sons – James – died in an accident sustained at the shipyard.[20]

He was injured towards the end of April 1880, and died a month later. Agnes Carlisle, the elder sister, wrote to Fred on the death of her brother, forwarding as a memento a pencil case that had belonged to him, as he had been "very fond" of Fred.[21] They had clearly been very close friends – James Carlisle had kept a photo of Fred – and this was confirmed in a later letter from Agnes Carlisle recording her condolences, in early January 1881, on the death of Fred's teenage sister,

Caroline. Along with her sympathy, she adds: "We will always think of you as 'Jimmie's friend', and you are often spoken of by us when we talk of our darling Jimmie".[22]

The occasion of the future Lady Pirrie's letter to Fred in July 1880 was to express regret at an eye injury he had suffered at the shipyard: "I do hope it is nothing serious, and that you will soon be all right. If you feel well enough to let me know how you are, I should very much like to hear from you".

The amiable relationship with the Carlisle and Pirrie families did not prove enduring. Early in 1908 Fred was approached by an acquaintance in Buncrana to use his influence with Alexander Carlisle to assist a friend in obtaining a position in Harland & Wolff. Fred replied that if Carlisle knew he were involved "this alone would be sufficient to damn him ... since Carlisle stood for West Belfast [in the General Election of 1906] and split the Unionist vote, and made us lose the seat, he and I are not very friendly". Later that year, in correspondence with the Earl of Ranfurly, Fred expressed growing disquiet amongst his Unionist acquaintances at Pirrie's political views as a Home Ruler: "I have been asked by quite a number of people: How did Pirrie get to be a peer – I could not answer the conundrum. I pass it on to you ... if you know the answer. A lot of my friends would like to know it".[23]

Following his early mishaps, Fred avoided further self-inflicted wounds, but the dangers of the shipyard were underlined by an incident in which he became involved in December 1881. On the first day of the month a gang-plank gave way at lunch-time at the Abercorn basin as a large number of workmen left the steamer *Shannon* being built for P&O. Thirty to forty men fell into the freezing water and became trapped beneath a raft of logs. Fred initially helped rescue three or four of his colleagues, but the water was littered with tanks, broken timber and foul sewage. Hearing that one man was still missing, he swam to a raft, took a boathook and used it to bring painter Thomas Moore to the surface. The first impressions were that Moore was dead but, after being taken to the steam boiler, he later recovered in hospital. In February 1882 his fellow workmen presented Fred with an illuminated address and an inscribed silver Presentation Cup for his "noble conduct and perseverance". He was also awarded the Bronze Medal of the Royal Humane Society.[24]

Earlier in 1881 he had been sent on a journey from Hull to the Norwegian fjords, and it was perhaps his acquaintance with Pirrie which resulted in his being sent to visit the latter in Liverpool. However, he did confide in an acquaintance early in his apprenticeship that he felt "bound" to the company, although he was repelled and challenged by the coarse, often offensive, language of his fellow workers.[25] He found the drawing office more congenial, deliberately extending his training as a draughtsman. During this period (primarily in 1883) he worked, sometimes at Liverpool, on several vessels – often joint cargo and passenger ships, such as the *British Princess, Irishman, Ionic* and *Doric* – and he filled several notebooks with detailed personal instructions and memoranda, which reveal an attention to detail.[26] The final reference he received recorded that: "He leaves of his own accord to get some experience at sea. He has a good practical knowledge of his business and is perfectly trustworthy and obliging". Fred was to retain some interest in the glamour of shipbuilding, as he accepted tickets from (the future Sir) George Clark, of Workman Clark Ltd, to view the launch of the *Olympic* (sister ship of the *Titanic*) on 20th October 1910.[27]

His departure from Harland & Wolff may have been partly occasioned by his disappointment early in 1884 at not being appointed a sub-manager at Queen's Island.[28] He joined the White Star Line, paying some heed to advice given by his former school-friend, John Horner, who had suggested that he should get "a year or so in the Engine Shop. I think you would like the work … and I am sure it would be most useful to you, even if you never required it, for you will always find that a good mechanic can service almost anything; it opens the mind and expands the ideas". It was demanding work and when he departed from Larne harbour on a visit to America in June 1886 the engines of his vessel were stopped; he noted, *qua* mechanic, in his diary: "I remember the work I had to do when anything went wrong, and felt sympathy for them".[29]

The skills, however, did – as John Horner predicted – prove invaluable. During his service in South Africa he noted that there was "plenty of room for my experience as an engineer to come into play", particularly with regard to laying mines.[30] His expertise also allowed him to improvise on the *Fanny* during the gun-running of April 1914, and enabled him to manufacture home-made hand grenades during the disturbances in 1920.[31]

WHITE STAR LINE

Fred honed these skills as Fifth or Sixth Engineer on various vessels of the White Star Line between July 1885 and March 1886 and, when he gave up this employment, Ismay, Imrie & Co. certified that he "gave every satisfaction, being strictly sober and attentive to his duties". His duties would have been onerous and physically demanding and he evidently appreciated breaks from the confines of the Engine Room. His first journey was to China (Hong Kong), where he possibly took the opportunity to meet his brother,[32] and a year later, as he watched the sunset off the coast of Mexico, he noted that it "was the most beautiful colouring I have seen since I was in the China seas".[33]

Such episodes attest that Fred regarded Nature as a form of communion with God. When he had been disappointed over the sub-managership at the Yard, his cousin, Rev Turner Oliver, advised: "Don't trouble yourself about affairs at the Island; just leave them and all your concerns in a higher hand, and it will all turn out well. I often think of what you told me about going up the mountain in Switzerland covered over with trees. The spots that seem the darkest will appear the brightest when we get over yonder".[34]

Whilst in Hong Kong – where, he later revealed, he "was always followed by an inquisitive crowd" [35] – Fred was offered the position of Manager of the small shipyard. It is impossible to say whether or not he was seriously tempted, but he declined the offer. If he had not done so, the history of Ulster might have proved dramatically different.

THE FAMILY CONCERN

Fred was later to indicate that he started at Alexander Crawford & Son in 1886, probably during the last few months of the year after he had returned from his trip to Central and North America.[36] He never makes it clear as to why he joined the firm started by his grandfather, but it may have been out of a sense of obligation to his father, who would wish to ensure dynastic continuity. As he was the owner who ultimately presided over the company's demise, some commentators have concluded that he was a reluctant, neglectful and inadequate businessman. There is a grain of truth in this assessment, confirmed by the statement which he made to his brother in 1923 when the company was on the verge of collapse: "I wish to God I had never touched starch; it has been a nightmare ever since I went into it".[37]

There is the insinuation that his "boyish spirit of adventure" resulted in absenteeism and indifference to the plight of the company.[38] Certainly he was absent for several months in 1890 when he visited the Holy Land and Near East, where he was to return for a number of months in 1896 on his honeymoon. He spent most of 1892 on a visit to his brother in Australia. He joined the Donegal Artillery, with whom he spent about fifteen months serving in South Africa during the Boer War, and he continued to enjoy participating in the military training attendant upon his Artillery membership during the first decade of the 20th century. During the late 1890s and early 1900s he also spent some time on the political campaign trail.

It would, however, be unjust to label all this absence as negligence on his part towards his business responsibilities. Fred was perhaps not the easiest of employers; he admitted to William McKee in 1916 that: "Many times I am afraid I have showed impatience and perhaps spoken sharply to you without thinking. When I did so, I always had a bad time after".[39] His irascibility was, however, probably induced by the stress of trying to maintain the viability of the company. Much of the absence listed above was taken during the time when his father (who died in October 1907) was effectively still managing the company and, from the outset, he had given his son little incentive to dedicate himself to the trade. Bearing in mind that twenty years earlier James Wright Crawford had bemoaned his relative penury, as a consequence of the remuneration which his father gave him, twenty or thirty years later Fred cannot have been inspired by the fact that his father gave him an identical stake in the business,[40] and there is no evidence that he was given a controlling hand.

In spite of this, Fred struggled for forty years to keep the business afloat and, as a sexagenarian, was to spend many a lonely and dangerous night trying to protect the company's premises against the very real threat of destruction during the Troubles of the early 1920s – despite the fact that, as he admitted, he could claim compensation if the Works were burned down and that, in light of the depressed contemporary trading circumstances, he might have preferred such an opportunity.[41] The *paterfamilias* maintained his sense of duty and responsibility towards those in his care, saying to his brother that the loss of the Works (or his death) "would be awkward for the family".[42]

Fred may not have demonstrated any enthusiasm for the family business, but neither was it a trade for which he had been trained. There is, however, no evidence that he did not apply to the company the same meticulous planning and attention to detail which characterised all his other work and activities – whether it be as apprentice at Harland & Wolff, preparing for war in South Africa – he was proud of the fact that "we are the only Company who had the foresight to bring any spare stores" [43] – or organising the gun-running operation.

As the starch manufacturer revealed to his brother, neither was the company in a particularly sound condition, financially, when he started in 1886.[44] When he inherited the business in 1908, he had to survive a general trade depression and, at the end of that year, he wrote to Rev. Charles Duncan in Desertegney (Buncrana) that: "Business is very bad. I never remember a worse year since I joined my father's company twenty-two years ago".[45] He had sent the latter a gift of 10 shillings towards a parochial hall fund, whilst reminding him that the company was still heavily committed to the work of the Mission around Wilson Street. After the First World War the company's trade was decimated – like that of so many – by the global economic contraction and cheap competition.

Certainly in 1914 he absented himself from the company premises whilst undertaking his secret gun-running activities, and subsequently travelling to the continent to evade arrest. However, by that stage, whatever trade Alexander Crawford & Son was doing could be handled by able lieutenants such as William McKee and Ernest Knowles. If he can be criticised as a businessman for travelling to South Africa at the start of the 20th century, so could very many others such as James Craig, who did likewise.

His travels in 1890 had been the culmination of two years of painful and debilitating sciatica that made it almost impossible for him to work: "What a life I have had of pain and suffering these last two years no person will ever know … I cannot be doing anything scarcely. I am no use for business, and a burden and a bother wherever I go". Whilst staying in Cairo in March the affliction proved recurrent, and it even prevented him from getting to church. On another day he had to crawl to the local gardens. Inevitably he viewed this as a test of faith and spirit from God; asking to be spared the pain, as we have seen, he added: "but if it is still His will to send it, may He send me grace to bear it in the right spirit … Sanctify, Oh Christ, the affliction, but do not make it permanent".

During the journey to his brother two years later there are hints of a recurrence and, between the pages of his diary, he promised that if he recovered: "I will strive to show my gratitude to Him by living a better life than I have been doing lately".[46] Ultimately, his plea that God have mercy on him, "and give me back, while I am still young, the complete use of my limbs", appears to have been answered by visits to the brine baths at Droitwich, where he was – physically, at least – completely cured.[47]

These years of travel may have helped to broaden Fred Crawford's perspective of the world, but they could not liberate him from his self-imposed spiritual shackles. During one tedious Sunday (16th October 1892) – "Sunday is always with me a very dull day on board ship" – as he skirted the Falkland Islands, he reflected: "I am not living a Christian life … My life is a complete failure; I do wish I were an out and out follower of my blessed Jesus. Oh God help me to live for Christ and not for the world".[48]

Notes

1. Much of this is taken from James Wright Crawford's diary: D/1700/3/1.

2. D/1700/10/1/476-477.

3. For examples, see D/1700/10/1/29, –/50, –/546, –/847.

4. His father acknowledged this: D/1700/3/1, 13 December 1868.

5. Ronald Marshall, *Methodist College: the first hundred years 1868-1968,* (Methodist College, Belfast, 1968), pp.82-83.

6. *A Brief History of University Road Methodist Church*: CR/6/5N/1. Information on McKay supplied by Edgehill College Archives.

7. Marshall, pp.67-69. D/3642/B/2/4.

8. The following is taken from a miscellany of letters written between 1907 and 1911: D/1700/10/1/171-172, –/176-177, –/239, –/476-477, –/522, –/571, –/686, –/688-689, –/817, –/827, –/852 and –/986.

9. D/1700/10/1/476-477 in a letter to his brother, Alexander, 29 September 1908.

10. D/1700/10/1/515-516, 26 November 1908.

11. D/1700/8, letter to Sir James Craig, 19 July 1923.

12. D/1700/7/1 (1927-1941). Throughout this period he was also paying for subscriptions to *The Northern Whig* for Naomi and Bea (Bethia), and providing them with a monthly allowance for most of the period of £2 10s.

13. Although most of the family knew her as Helen (her correct name), Fred always referred to her as Nellie.

14. Clause 24 of Fred Crawford's will, 1941. D/1700/8, letter of 1 December 1953. Probate was granted on 5 November 1953.

15. This was bequeathed to his daughter Bethia in his will.

16. H J K Usher et al, *An Angel without Wings: a history of University College School 1830-1980,* (University College School, London, 1981), pp.19, 40, 44-46. Fred H Crawford, *Guns for Ulster,* (Belfast, 1947), pp.10-11. *Belfast News Letter,* 27 March 1934. Obituary in *Irish Times,* 6 November 1952. D/640/11/2, pp.82, 83, 90. D/1700/10/1/344, 29 February 1908. A T Q Stewart, *The Ulster Crisis: Resistance to Home Rule 1912-1914,* (Faber & Faber, London, 1979), p.90. His will shows that he won a silver bowl for the best Battery shooting in the Donegal Artillery. D/1700/3/8, 3 May 1890.

17. Fred's indenture to Harland & Wolff, D/1700/10, 20 March 1879, plus a memorandum of 18 July 1885.

18. D/1700/10/1/571 in 1909. Marshall, p.70.

19. Ham, the son of an author on spiritual and doctrinal matters, wrote on 21 November 1878: "I trust you have not hurt yourself seriously": D/1700/5/2/8.

20. On 22 July 1880, the new Mrs Pirrie had written from her home in Comber to Fred; in the letter she mentions: "We all miss our dear Jamie dreadfully; everything seems so lonely and changed. Twelve weeks today since the darling boy was hurt …": D/1700/5/2/15.

21. D/1700/5/2/13, 25 May 1880.

22. D/1700/5/2/16, 7 January 1881. M Moss & J R Hume, *Shipbuilders to the World: 125 Years of Harland & Wolff, Belfast*, 1861-1986, (Blackstaff Press, Belfast, 1986), pp.93, 307.

23. The Nationalist Joe Devlin took West Belfast by 16 votes, when Carlisle polled a mere 154 votes in the Election. D/1700/10/1/318, 3 February 1908 and D/1700/10/1/500, 10 November 1908.

24. D/1700/10. *The Northern Whig* and *Belfast News Letter*, 2 December 1881. D/1700/5/8/19B, 22 February 1949: case no.21533 of the Royal Humane Society. Thomas Moore lived at 34 Fox Street, Ballymacarrett, East Belfast.

25. D/1700/3/3 (Fred's personal notebooks). D/1700/5/2/10, 4 April 1879.

26. D/1700/3-5. D/1700/5/2/20.

27. D/1700/10/1/845. Clark was later to chair the secret committee formed in 1913 to import guns for the Ulster Volunteer Force.

28. D/1700/5/2/22, 30 April 1884, from his brother in Linton, Australia.

29. D/1700/5/2/13. D/1700/3/6, 5 June 1886.

30. D/1700/3/2, 27 October 1900, 12 February 1901.

31. D/640/11/2, p.25: "I also got twenty hand grenades of a very simple pattern. I gave a sketch to a plumber to be made in a hurry … they were simple and safe if not lighted".

32. D/1700/5/2/35, 4 July 1885. Alex had sent a postcard saying that he hoped to hear from Fred when he (Fred) reached the Cape. It seems that their mother believed Fred was going as far as Australia.

33. D/1700/3/6, 24 July 1886.

34. D/1700/5/2/24, 28 May 1884.

35. D/1415/B/34, p.66.

36. The date of his return is unrecorded; his last diary entry was for 31 July 1886 in San Francisco.

37. D/1700/6/1/18, 8 July 1923 from Cloreen to his brother, Alexander, in Perth.

38. Dr A P W Malcomson, Chief Executive of the Public Record Office of Northern Ireland, in the Statutory Report 1997-98, p.70. Dr Malcomson is a former pupil of Campbell College, at which Fred Crawford was the longest-serving Governor.

39. D/1700/5/17/1/129A, 28 March 1916.

40. D/1700/6/1/5, 7 January 1889. James Wright Crawford was given £200 salary and one-eighth of the profits: D/1700/3/1, 28 July 1869.

41. D/640/11/2, p.15. On 17 July 1922, Alexander Crawford wrote from Perth,

commiserating with Fred "for you having to keep your midnight vigil at the Works": D/1700/6/1/14. D/640/11/3, 11 July 1921 in a letter to his daughter, Marjorie (Doreen): "I am alone in the Works as they are supposed to be closed this week". It is likely that she was named after her grand-mother, although the latter's name was spelled as Margery. Fred appears to have referred to his daughter as Marjorie, although everyone else called her Doreen: D/1700/6/1/18, 8 July 1923. When he was evading the authorities on board the *Fanny* in April 1914, Fred kept changing the name of the vessel; he used the names of each of his three daughters, opting (in the case of his middle daughter) for *Doreen*: D/1415/B/34, p.63.

42. D/1700/6/1/11, 31 July 1920.

43. D/1700/3/2, 11 April 1900

44. In 1889 Alexander suggested selling the business: D/1700/5/2/42, 24 April 1889.

45. D/1700/5/2/42. D/1700/10/1/476-477, –/517.

46. D/1700/3/7, 15-19 March 1890. D/1700/3/9, 24-25 May 1892. See also comments in correspondence with Alexander: D/1700/5/2/42 and D/1700/6/1/5.

47. D/1700/10/1/464-465, 9 September 1908, and –/804, 6 June 1910. This visit may have been some time during the 1890s; in his Boer War diary, he records that he had been away one Christmas at Bath "with sciatica": D/1700/3/2, 24 December 1900.

48. D/1700/3/9.

Bathing In Acapulco

∞

Long before he visited Germany, under various aliases, to purchase guns and ammunition for the Ulster Volunteer Force, Fred Crawford had circled the globe under his own name. For an individual who resided his entire life on the Malone Road (either at Chlorine, Cloreen or Marlborough Park), and who has been perceived as parochial and politically myopic, he was exceptionally well-travelled.

It was not a trait that was manifestly inherited from his father. The latter travelled to Scotland and England, as well as to southern cities in Ireland, both to seek business and to promote his products at major Exhibitions. After visiting his sister, Abby, in Blarney in late 1867, James Wright Crawford professed a disinclination to travel, as it "interferes with my regular times of devotion. This is bad for me". A year previously, accompanied by his wife, he had travelled to the Channel Islands and northern France, including Paris, but the homeward journey from Le Havre to Southampton he recalled as dangerous and fearful. He invested this with the characteristics of biblical, Pauline shipwreck and tragedy; he wrote, in thankful vein: "I am so peaceful when in my Father's hands … May I ever recount Thy mercies and deliverances".[1]

With what is probably a degree of exaggeration, one source asserts that by 1910 Fred Crawford "had visited nearly all the countries of Europe".[2] Some of this may be accounted for as a consequence of ports of call, such as Gibraltar and Brindisi, during his travels to the Holy Land (1890) and Australia (1892), and during his honeymoon in 1896. Incidental comments in correspondence, however, indicate that he had made journeys to Europe by the mid-1880s. His cousin, Rev. Turner Oliver hints that he had visited Switzerland [3], and in July 1886, as he arrived at San Salvador, Fred himself noted that the coastline was reminiscent of "a sail down the Rhine from Mainz to Cologne".[4]

Globe-trotting

Between 1886 and the end of 1892, Fred travelled the best part of 50,000 miles around the world.[5] The first of these journeys was to North and Central America. He departed from Larne Harbour, where a dozen large whales had gathered to bid *SS Baltic* 'bon voyage' on Sunday 5th June 1886. He noted "a boundless expanse of troubled water" before reaching the sanctuary of New York harbour nine days later.

Whilst it is likely that much of this trip was sight-seeing (as around the Panama Canal and Mexico), the full nature of the venture is unclear. A quarter of a century later (October 1910 to July 1911) James Samuel Davidson, General Manager of, and heir to, the Sirocco Works in East Belfast, was to travel around the globe on a journey that was principally designed to promote and develop sales of the company's tea-drying machinery.[6] If Fred joined his father's firm early in 1886, it is not impossible that Fred travelled to America with a view to seeking new markets for the products of Alexander Crawford & Son; he recorded that on 27th June (1886) he went to Downtown New York and "left some samples, with Mr Copeland, of starch". The balance of probability is, however, against such an interpretation. Whereas James Davidson had fulfilled a full apprenticeship at Sirocco Works long before departing on his business trip, Fred can only just have started at Wilson Street, and had no experience of, or expertise in, his company's products.

It would seem unlikely that James W. would have permitted his son to go to America for so long, so soon after joining the business, and it is more likely that Fred finally started at Alexander Crawford & Son after his return from America. The length of Fred's visit is, however, uncertain. His diary ends with his arrival in San Francisco on 31st July 1886; the precise details of his travels after that date are conjectural. There remains an intriguing comment by his sister-in-law, Lillie (the wife of Alexander), in a letter to Fred from Australia in late December 1887, when she notes that he had "been flying about all over America", adding that she hopes that he had had a good trip.[7] A passing reference in Fred's Boer War diary makes it clear that he was not absent from home at Christmas 1886,[8] but there is no clear evidence that he returned to America during 1887. If Fred did cross the Atlantic again with business in mind, he never specifically mentions the project and clearly the financial difficulties of Alexander Crawford & Son in the late 19th century would suggest that the American market did not respond to Belfast starch.

After touring the sights of New York, he departed on the 196th anniversary of the Battle of the Boyne, on a steamer bound for the Caribbean end of the Panama Canal. It had proved a costly construction; Fred later observed of the adjacent railway: "for every sleeper laid down, a life was sacrificed to the climate or disease".[9] It was not to be a stage of the journey which he recorded or recalled with affection: "We are slung in canvas bags [three deep] along the deck for sleeping … The way we feed is every man for himself – the food is put down on one common table and every one helps himself with his own knife and fork". The resident rats were numerous but were not troubled by the ship's dozen cats, as the traditional enemies "lay down together".

He was not enamoured of some of his travelling companions, and may have felt that the purchase in New York of an 1851 Colt Navy black powder revolver – favoured by Wild Bill Hickok and General Robert E. Lee – for his personal protection had been a wise decision. He noted that: "The two fellows above me [in the canvas berths] are just what you would expect to see in the Spanish or Italian mountains, with pistols and knives in their belts".

Such imagery is reminiscent of characters encountered by another Ulsterman, Arthur Moore – a traveller, adventurer and journalist – who was completing his career as a scholar at Campbell College as Fred was beginning his role as the school's longest-serving Governor. Whilst trapped in the siege of Tabriz in northern Persia (Iran) in the early months of 1909, Moore depicted such characters, who sang during their revels "with a contagious rolling swing that might have lit the fires of revolution in the soul of a usurer. Swarthy, deep-chested merry fellows, with the inevitable bandoliers and Mauser pistols on them even at their feasts". A year earlier, when reporting from Salonica (now Thessaloniki) on the Young Turk Revolution, the journalist witnessed "Men who had held the hills for years, sleeping by day and waking by night, [come] down to the town ... Wild, fierce figures with whom no brigand that has ever trod the stage of a theatre could compare in dressing for the part, shaggy men with Mannlichers, knives and revolvers and a double-burdened belt of cartridges marched in proudly ...".[10]

These were, of course, revolutionaries – men who could change the course of history – and Moore generally accepted them for what they were, without "even the smallest feeling of superiority in their company, or the slightest objection to shaking their hands". Fred, on the other hand, sought more conservative company and viewed those who challenged the divinely-disposed, imperial equilibrium with undiluted suspicion. He could not conceive why anyone would deliberately disturb the established order of what he perceived as good governance. Moore was to spend twenty years as Assistant, and later Managing, Editor of *The Statesman* newspaper in Calcutta and was ultimately (in 1942) to suffer dismissal at the hands of the Viceroy, as a consequence of his endeavours to encourage a greater role for Indians in their own affairs, which the India Office was reluctant to countenance. Such a vision would have been anathema to Fred, who fought in South Africa in 1900-1901 against a threat to the Empire and who played a more enduring and significant role in Ireland against those he considered to be murderous rebels.

Patriotism

It has to be admitted that, although he enjoyed the experience of foreign cultures, Fred did not readily adapt to the company of indigenous populations. En route to the Holy Land in February 1890, on board P&O's *SS Britannia*, he appeared pleased that: "as far as I can judge, we are entirely free from foreigners, which is a great blessing, not being of a cosmopolitan disposition. I always like to mix with my fellow countrymen".

In the late 19th century his patriotism contained a certain ambivalence. His nationality was British, which he wore with gravitas: "With all the Briton's little failings, insularisms, I am proud I am a Briton. There is no country", he noted in March 1890, with casual syntax, "in the world – a people, I should say – that know the true meaning of fair play like the British or how to treat people of other countries with due respect and mutual fairness".

Nevertheless, Fred did manifest a patina of pride in being Irish. Over Easter 1890 in Cairo he met Surgeon Thomas Parke. The latter was both companion and physician to the explorer and journalist, Henry Morton Stanley, whose book, *Through the Dark Continent,* the Ulsterman had read whilst crossing the Atlantic in 1886. Fred enthused that Parke – whom he was to meet again in London at the end of his Near Eastern visit (2nd June 1890) – "struck a note of joy in my soul when he informed me that he was an Irishman. It makes one proud of his country when such heroes belong to the same side". This admission did not survive the corrosive post-First World War years; in July 1920 he informed his brother, Alexander, that: "The world is in a strange condition … I am ashamed to call myself an Irishman. Thank God I am not one. I am an Ulsterman, a very different breed".[11]

That Easter in Cairo, however, Fred had attended a multi-national function with a German, a Russian, two Swiss, an Armenian, a Syrian, a Maltese, two Italians, a Frenchman, and an American. In this assemblage he readily described himself as an Irishman. He displays no shame when he reveals that, apart from three of them, the group conversed in French: "Three, besides myself, could talk English", adding with a tinge of sarcasm, "the American included". American travellers appear to have attracted adverse comment for at least a century or more. Crossing the Pacific to San Francisco in 1911, Sirocco's James Davidson observed that: "A great many of the passengers are Americans of the pushing objectionable type who think everything belongs to them".[12] Fred hinted at similar irritation when he had visited the America Mission in Cairo; he had received a cool reception as he had believed it to be Methodist instead of Presbyterian. He paid them the courtesy of a return visit, but had suffered during the address as the speaker had "an abominably American accent ... If I go back there, I trust they will have a better preacher, or one more intelligible to the English people".

INCONVENIENCES

After travelling down the eastern littoral of the United States and past the Cuban coast, Fred reached the point of transfer across Central America to Panama, by train. The Canal was, at that stage, under its earliest construction and he recalled the scenery as "beautiful in the extreme", although punctuated by the growing number of graves of "many a stranger far from home". On 10th July he embarked on *SS San Blas* for a three-week voyage to San Francisco, which provided far more charm and enchantment than the journey down the eastern coast. With much irony and vexation, however, as an Irishman he found the potatoes served on board on the Twelfth "simply vile".

This proved a minor prelude to a four-page diary rant as he reached the Californian coast, convincing himself that this was the worst-disciplined ship on which he had ever travelled. No doubt accustomed to the stricter discipline of the White Star Line, he complained that the captain showed no interest in, or sense of responsibility towards, his charge. This was compounded by the fact that the rest of the crew paid no attention to their duties and were rude and insulting to the passengers. The consequence of this indifference was appalling food and a total lack of hygiene. Fred noted on 25th July that, when he disembarked at Mazattan in Mexico, he had his first decent meal – "soup, fish, entrées, omelette, steak, fried potatoes, dates and tea" – since he had left New York on the first day of the month.

The crew was merely one of the hazards and privations experienced during 19th century travel. Fellow-travellers could prove an annoyance and inconvenience. The principal exception to this, noted by Fred on a number of occasions, was a pretty woman, but even the latter could elicit disappointment. He revealed that : "All Mexican women of the lower classes smoke cigars like the men" and, as he passed the coast of Greece in May 1890, he praised the beauty and carriage of some fine-looking Italian women, who proceeded to disenchant him by smoking in a masculine manner.

His most awkward encounter with a woman during his world travels came when he crossed the bed of a dry river, a branch of the Nile, just outside Cairo. His prudish western Victorian sensibilities were offended by a local woman who removed her clothes "and stood in all her natural beauty … displaying her charms". He had no choice but to pass close to her, and he felt that: "This was the most indecent piece of audacity I have seen since I came here … The women here shame themselves". This moral outrage was matched by a note of xenophobia. One Saturday (in March 1890) he had spent the entire day sight-seeing at the Pyramids – where he was given a lesson in the laws of probability, losing 2 shillings to an Arab who bet him that he would climb the Great Pyramid and return in under ten minutes – and at the main buildings in and around the capital. On the following day he visited the Turkish baths, "but when I looked in it was enough for me for the place was full of Arabs, and I have a natural horror since yesterday of having Arabs too near me".

His pejorative outbursts could, however, also be directed at fellow Europeans. As he neared the Australian coast at the end of May 1892, after five weeks at sea, he described some of the passengers as "a shoddy lot of colonials". He was particularly vitriolic towards those who, unlike himself, could not resist the distraction of alcohol. A number of those who, near the start of the voyage, had ventured into Naples "came aboard in a state of beastly intoxication". Two years earlier he had noted that some of those who avoided the more cultural diversion of the Opera in Valletta "went in for what they called having a night of it and, judging from the noise they made, they had a night and no mistake". It was perhaps appropriate that the journey to the Holy Land had commenced by demanding of him the patience of a saint; his first night had been interrupted by the drunken return of his cabin mate, which occasioned the sound advice entered in his diary: "It is always desirable to choose a table at which your room companion does not sit, because frequently there are slight differences of opinion below in the state room that had better not be brought to the table in the saloon".

Further discomforts of travel included second-class accommodation, which Fred adopted – either as a result of thrift or principle. Whilst the coast of Greece by moonlight could add romance to an evening, he confessed that aboard the *Hydaspes* – the vessel he had joined at Brindisi in March 1890 – "the second class saloon is scarcely worthy of the name". With a few notable exceptions, such as the Holy Land, which had been receiving travellers and pilgrims since before the Crusades, many locations were simply not geared for the embryonic tourism of the age. He despaired that there were few concessions to his status as an importer of foreign currency. Egypt was a nightmare: "The impudence of the porters is astounding", he moaned in Alexandria, but he was even more blunt in Cairo: "the beggars here make me inclined to punch their heads".

Vermin was probably the biggest affliction to beset the traveller. With no apparent logic, he was prepared to tolerate cockroaches, explaining in Colombo in May 1892 that: "I don't mind them as they are little brown fellows". During his visit to the Near East two years previously, however, he rebelled against the unpleasant attentions of mosquitoes, fleas and lice, all of which he felt provided confirmation of the episodes of Biblical plagues. The lice, he argued, "are ugly-looking customers", and he found them even harder to bear than the fleas which "are everywhere in Egypt". He suffered augmented attacks at Ramleh: "I destroyed a host and it did not seem to make the least impression on them", and a few days later in Alexandria he conceded that: "I thought I had got used to them but I am sorry to have to alter my opinion". It has to be admitted, however, that such conditions attended the working-class and industrial neighbourhoods of Belfast in the final decade of the 19th century.

Diversions

Nelson Russell, who would have been known and respected by Fred, left Campbell College in 1914. He was awarded the Military Cross two years later for leading the first daylight raid of the First World War, and in 1951 was to become Sergeant-at-Arms at Stormont. Between these dates he led the 38th Brigade in Sicily in 1943 to what his superior officer described as "a feat which will live in the annals of British arms". During this campaign Russell recalled that: "I had one of life's outstanding baths in the river Simeto with my behind on a fairly smooth stone and the cool mountain water rushing over a very sweaty, smelly, dusty body …".[13] Fred himself expressed similar sentiments of gratification over fifty years earlier. Facilities for the late Victorian traveller were at a premium and, as the starch manufacturer sailed up the Pacific seaboard of Central America, enduring the privations of *SS San Blas*, he may well have equated the state of rigidity of his body and clothing with that of his products. Disembarking at Acapulco – appropriately, in Mexico, on the Feast of Margarita (20th July) – Fred went for a long walk along the shore, "and had a splendid bathe. I never enjoyed a bathe so much in my life as I had not changed my clothes for twenty days".

Whatever misery and discomfort Fred may have endured during his travels, it was probably balanced by the pleasure which he derived from his encounter with the natural world. Even during the short, tense train ride from Oslo (then known as Christiania) to Bergen in March 1914 to purchase the *Fanny* for the purpose of gun-running, he was alert to "the lovely scenery, of the grandest description in some parts".[14] On a number of occasions he commented upon the beauty of sunsets; as he passed San Salvador he was entranced by the sight of an erupting volcano. In Australia (August 1892) he wrote of a waterfall that: "It is quite impossible to convey the grandeur of this gully" and he waxed lyrical for three pages in his diary about the majesty of the Imperial Cave at Magretta.

His reverence for nature is best encapsulated in his memory of his visit to the Egyptian capital, where he yearned "for a painter's brush and a poet's pain to paint on canvas or in words, and keep forever, the scene I now drink in … It is the nearness of the beautiful green fields to the bleak tho' beautiful desert that forms such a contrast … never shall I forget the beauty of a sunset as seen from the Citadel of Cairo".

Fred Crawford's name tends to be remembered purely in a political context, but he established a broad spectrum of friends and acquaintances – most of whom he outlived. His range of interests embraced natural history and he was a member of the Belfast Naturalists' Field Club (which was only two years his junior), whose objective was 'the practical study of the Natural Science and Archaeology of Ireland'. His fellow members included the leading botanists and natural historians and scientists of the age, such as R. J. Welch, Francis Joseph Bigger and Robert Lloyd Praeger.[15]

During his travels, and even amongst the martial detritus of the Boer War, Fred displayed a keen interest in the natural world and his diaries are punctuated with observations on the local wild life. At sea, he relished seeing whales, dolphins, porpoises, swordfish and turtles. In Botany Bay he took time out to witness the swooping kingfishers "who would never miss a fish". Lurking in Fred's psyche, however, was an ambivalence towards the world's fauna, which was nevertheless totally contemporary.

In April 1890 he visited Heliopolis near Cairo, the site of the oldest obelisk (3800 years) in Egypt. This caused him to reflect upon the fragility of human life: "how true does that [Biblical] passage come home to us as we stand gazing at this milestone of history: Man's days are but a span". There were some who seemed determined to prove it, when Heliopolis became a training ground for young pilots during the First World War. Fred himself was interested in the incipient pastime of flying and took his wife to Blackpool in November 1909 "to see the flying, but [we] saw nothing but the machines as the weather was so bad after we arrived".[16] Others such as Campbell College's adventurous pupil, Arthur Moore, were totally fascinated by flight. Despite his advanced age (37), Moore endeavoured to master it at the training ground at Heliopolis in late 1917 – crashing five planes in the process! One other fellow pupil – Richard Patrick Hemphill (from Birr in Co Offaly) – was not so fortunate; he had died of injuries sustained in a crash at Heliopolis in March 1917.

Twenty-seven years earlier, Fred's interest in the locality had proved a little more down-to-earth. He paid a visit to an ostrich farm, which so impressed him that he returned six years later whilst on honeymoon.[17] Appended to his description of the birds, their egg-laying and rearing, was an expression of sadness that the birds suffered for the sake of ladies' fashions. Such farms were certainly commercially active. In the 1930s Fred was to inherit a large painting (*The Irish House of Commons 1790* by Henry Barraud and John Hayter); the first private owner of the canvas was Dr Thomas Corry of Belfast, one of whose close friends and executors was William Ireland, who was described as an ostrich feather merchant (of Upper Arthur Street, Belfast).

The contemporary world was, however, less well-disposed to the welfare and conservation of wildlife. Another of the earliest pupils at Campbell College, (the future Sir) Edward Bennet, later a High Court Judge at Allahabad, participated in a six-month safari (early 1913) and, in his aptly-named *Shots and Snapshots in British East Africa*, recorded "having spent the happiest six months of my life" shooting buffalo, guinea fowl, partridge, oryx, gazelle, antelope, impala, zebra, colobus monkeys, a lioness, hyena, kudu, hippopotamus, dik dik, oribi, hartebeest and egrets. As a Governor of, and regular visitor to, Campbell College, Fred would have been witness to Bennet's beneficence to the school in the form of an African rhinoceros head to his *alma mater*.[18]

On occasions, Fred displayed a willingness to engage in the hunt and, during his visit to his brother in Australia in June 1892, he records shooting a coot, a grebe and wedge-tailed eagle, in addition to spending a few days hunting wallabies, kangaroos and possums. One suspects that these were easy prey for a crack-shot, but he does hint at the scorn of the wildlife during one shooting match: "There were a lot of jackasses in the trees about that seemed to think shooting a splendid joke; every time the rifles were fired they would set up a shout of laughter, whether at the bad shooting (it was not good, and lots of misses) or at the novelty of the noise I can't say, but they did laugh as tho' they enjoyed the whole scene". During the Boer War he allowed a young baboon to sleep under his bed, although this may have stemmed from a sense of guilt that, a few months' earlier, he had spotted several baboons occupying a kopje (hill) about one mile distant: "I must see if I can shoot one", he revealed in his diary.[19]

Over a century later, such pastimes sit uncomfortably with the aspiration of conservation, but they were typical of their age. As we have seen, however, Fred generally embraced the enchantment of the natural world, symbolised by his comment about porpoises that: "every time I see these playful creatures, I think better of the world".

Pilgrimage

One of those whom the Ulsterman befriended in the Belfast Naturalists' Field Club was a respected amateur botanist, Corrie Denew (always known as 'Chevy') Chase. The two men became very well-acquainted, as the latter was associated for sixty years with Campbell College, where he acquired the demeanour, appearance and reputation of the fictional character 'Mr Chips'. He was Head of Modern Languages, and founder of the Officer Training Corps in 1909. There were a number of coincidences in the relationship between the schoolmaster and the Governor, although there is no unequivocal evidence that either man was aware of them!

One of the most marginal and delicately-balanced political constituencies at Westminster was that of West Belfast, and between 1895 and 1897 Fred acted as Honorary Secretary of its Registration Association.[20] The sitting Member, since 1892, had been Hugh Oakley Arnold-Forster – and it was the loss of this seat, following the MP's departure in 1906, that was to cause Fred so much bitterness in his relationship with Alexander Carlisle of Harland & Wolff. Arnold-Forster was the grandson of Thomas Arnold, celebrated Headmaster of Rugby School, and his own father (Thomas's son) died young, and Arnold-Forster was adopted by his uncle – by marriage – W. E. Forster, who had been Chief Secretary for Ireland from 1880 to 1882. The latter gave his name to the Educational Act of 1870, in which he was supported by another brother-in-law, the poet Matthew Arnold, whose career was that of a schools' inspector.

Both the Arnold and Forster families resided in the English Lake District, and were close acquaintances of the Vicar of Ambleside, Rev. Charles Henry Chase (1882-1891), the father of 'Chevy' Chase who arrived at Campbell in 1905. What Fred may never have realised, with regard to his association with the Arnold-Forster connection, and with 'Chevy' Chase, is that the clergyman from Ambleside was one of his companions on the visit to the Holy Land in 1890! Both Fred and Chase senior were pictured together in a group photograph on the Mount of Olives.[21]

Shortly before both men had set out on their visit to the Holy Land, the vicar had published a slim volume entitled *Alpine Climbers*, in which he equates travel with the ultimate pilgrimage – the journey through life. Along the way, he asserts, there are many, often unseen, dangers. In his diary, Fred refers to the dangers and pitfalls which one encounters that entice the individual into sinful ways. Both men emphasised the necessity of submitting to God to ensure salvation; suffering intense and persistent pain from sciatica, Fred writes: "At least may He send me patience and resignation to His Holy Will and give me strength to say from my heart: Thy Will be done … I confess, Oh Christ, I have been a very wayward servant, sometimes in open rebellion to Thy Holy Will, sometimes led captive by the Devil … Oh Jesus have mercy upon me and purify me".[22]

There is little doubt that Fred viewed his journey as a pilgrimage and religious experience. At the hub of his journey – Jerusalem – he wrote: "The sight to one who considers the city and what events have happened here is sublime – sacred. I thank God he has permitted me to see this city, and I trust I shall be a better man for having seen the actual ground our Saviour trod when on earth".

To some extent his readiness to absorb the fullness of the experience appears to have left Fred open to a degree of credulity. For someone who was a supreme political realist (ultimately acknowledging that force of arms was a *sine qua non*), and who sneered at the pilgrim relics as worthless fakes,[23] he accepted many Biblical 'locations' without adverse comment. Some of these have acceptable historical reliability, such as the Mount of Olives, the Garden of Gethsemane and even the Via Dolorosa. Others were more debatable, such as the house where the Last Supper occurred, but – although he does once hint at doubts about the precise location of such sites – he notes without suspicion that he has seen the spot where the Magi first caught sight of the star after leaving Herod, the home of Elijah, a cave where Jeremiah had composed Lamentations, and the place where the angel sat when appearing to the shepherds! It could be argued that such uncritical acceptance differed little from that placed in the Holy House at Loreto in Italy (declared to be the Nazareth home of Jesus, Mary and Joseph, transported there from the Holy Land by angels in the 13th century) by the 350 Irish pilgrims who visited it only three years later en route to Rome.[24]

Fred Crawford's personal account of his journey in 1890 must be a revelation to those who are familiar only with the gun-runner of a quarter of a century later, who vigorously resisted Home Rule and Irish nationalism, which became equated with Irish Catholicism. The Ulster Methodist demonstrated an inquisitiveness about, and tolerance of, other religions.[25] His eventual prejudices were to be centred on politics and not focused on a religion. During his visit to the Holy Land he happily accepted Franciscan hospitality, and noted that: "I am as well-treated as anyone".

He struck up a brief correspondence with an Irishman named Patrick Ryan, who worked at the Commissariat at the Kasr-el-Nil Barracks in Cairo (perhaps as a civilian employee), and who probably assisted Fred with travel arrangements and other facilities. Fred forwarded a gift of rosary beads and expressed sentiments about the impact of Holy Places upon the pilgrim. Ryan concurred: "I do not see how any ordinary Christian could visit the places where our Lord was born, toiled, taught, suffered and died for us, without being impressed with a sense of awe and reverence". Ryan added that he had guessed that Crawford was a Protestant, noting that: "I see very little distinction in matters of faith", which was an accident of birth. Fred responded, evidently expressing his views on religious denominations, which Ryan rehearsed: "You are quite right about Roman Catholics and Protestants. Christ came to save sinners. He did not come for Jews alone, nor for Catholics, nor for Protestants, nor Calvinists. He came for all, and all who believe in Him …". During his lengthy journey to Australia in 1892, to help pass the hours as they crossed the Indian Ocean, Fred borrowed a copy of a Thomas à Kempis work (probably *The Imitation of Christ*) from a fellow passenger, and concluded that: "if all Catholics lived up to the doctrines there expounded, no-one could find fault with their religion".[26]

Alexander Crawford

Although Fred maintained a fraternally amicable correspondence with his brother, Alexander, for over half a century, his visit to Australia in 1892 was one of only three occasions on which he met his brother following the latter's departure from Belfast around 1875.

The younger brother departed from Gravesend on 22nd April 1892 and, via the Suez Canal and Indian Ocean, reached Australia at the end of May. At the very end of August he crossed the Bass Strait to Tasmania, then toured New Zealand. In the final days of September he caught a boat home and, sailing via Tierra del Fuego, the Falkland Islands, Rio de Janeiro and Tenerife, arrived back in Plymouth on 13th November. He punctiliously recorded that he had travelled 31,351 miles.

Outliving two wives, and marrying a third who was almost forty years his junior, and despite the fact that he was a persistent smoker, Alexander was 78 years old when he died in Perth (Western Australia) on 8th November 1935.[27] He had arrived in the antipodes on the steamer *SS Otway* at Fremantle around 1877. "Western Australia was very easy to enter", he later recalled, "but hard to leave" – you had to obtain a certificate from a Police Magistrate testifying that you were a free man. He claimed that these were years of great hardship, but that the young pearlers and squatters he met manifested friendship. He was asked to share a drink, but "unfortunately for them, my education in that direction had been sadly neglected; there was never an alcoholic liquor in my home, and I had not then, nor have I since, tasted alcohol".

Fred met his brother on 13th June 1892 at Reid's Coffee Palace in Ballarat – which is still extant. This style of hotel had been built in the 1880s as part of the Australian Temperance movement and did not serve alcohol. Despite Alexander's integrity as a teetotaller, and the pursuit of a vigorous, often outdoor, life, his health conspired to fulfil his father's prophecy that he was "a soft child",[28] and, in spite of a posthumous entry in the *Australian Dictionary of Biography*, his career never really approached his personal aspirations.

In his early years in the antipodes Alexander endeavoured to put his educational training in agriculture to some use by undertaking sheep-farming in Victoria and New South Wales; in 1879 he managed a sheep station in northern Queensland. During his first twenty years on the continent he was prepared to traverse it several times in search of work. At the close of the 1870s he was engaged in gold prospecting and surveying potential routes through Western Australia for the transcontinental railway. In November 1881 he became part-owner of a sheep-run at Moorarrie, near Murchison, in the western state. In May 1883, however, he wrote to his parents to reveal that he had recently had 700 sheep killed, several horses stolen and had incurred an expense of £350. Additionally, he had had "a serious encounter" with thirteen natives which had resulted in an injured knee and rendered his left arm useless for several days: "… so altogether things are not looking very promising just now. It is not all prosperity, a squatter's life in Australia, any more than in business elsewhere". He sold his share in the enterprise, and by early 1884 had moved to Victoria.

This was to prove equally unrewarding. He penned a couple of letters to Fred in April 1884 from Linton, rehearsing his sadness about his father's attitude towards him. In passing he mentioned that he had recently shot a large platypus: "I am getting it stuffed and will send it to father when finished". Whether this was intended as a gift, a peace offering, or a coded comment is unclear. It is also uncertain whether it arrived, as it does not appear to be mentioned again; indeed, the only Australian legacy which featured at the Crawford home on the Malone Road was a collection of fourteen boomerangs listed in the inventory of the contents of Cloreen after Fred's death!

Alexander revealed that he had found no work and, two months later, notified his parents that he could not "find any openings here that will suit me. I started work last week felling trees but it was such hard work that I knocked my hands up, and I find I could scarcely make my tucker out of it, so I gave up".

To Fred he admitted that he was weary of the peripatetic lifestyle, and wanted to find something that would enable him to settle down and marry his cousin, Lillie (Eliza Jane Mathews), and his courage or pride asserted that: "I do not think I will go home. I am going to try and make a home here, or at least in the Colonies somewhere". Later that year he moved to Sydney and then on to Queensland, although – almost inevitably – suffering his share of further misfortune. He informed his parents in late December 1884, from Springsure in Queensland, that he had "had to walk seventeen miles barefoot one day; my boots gave out and the ground was burning hot".

Alexander married Lillie Mathews at Linton, Victoria, on 3rd March

1885. He then appears to have returned home briefly to Ireland, before visiting other parts of Europe and North America to study dairying at various agricultural colleges. On his return to Australia in 1886 he was offered the leadership of a group exploring the district around Eucla (Western Australia) at the head of the Great Australian Bight. Alexander's wife labelled him "very untakecareable" and, as well as suffering attacks of sciatica and diphtheria, he was nearly killed as a consequence of being rolled upon by a camel, which left him insensible for two months, and he took a further year to recuperate.

In May 1888 Fred received a letter that Alexander had become quite thin since the accident, but that he was feeling well, and "am on the lookout for something else to do". He had bought some land at Warragul in Victoria, and had placed some of it under grass and clover. He had also invested £300 in silver mines but, with unerring Crawford timing, found the market depressed. He was managing to sell some timber but, perforce, was living "cheaply and plainly". He admitted that he and Lillie were nostalgic, but that their financial plight precluded any possibility of them returning home.

In 1888 Alexander entered Government employment, although on 24th April the following year he confided to Fred, in a very lengthy letter, that "how long that is likely to last I have no idea ... They are very sure pay days but they are very slow"; he claimed that he was owed salary and needed it to pay off a land purchase. He had been appointed manager of a travelling dairy by the Victoria State Government, and in April 1891 became manager of the Victoria Creamery & Butter Company. He and his wife moved into a new home that she had planned, but the gloss was corroded from his new-found security and stability by Lillie's death in November 1891. On 5th April 1893 he married his sister-in-law, Martha (Mattie) Linton Mathews.

A letter of April 1896 notified Fred that his brother was returning to Western Australia to start his own business, but he was actually employed by the Bureau of Agriculture in Perth. Within a decade he was appointed acting Director (1903-1905) and acting Under-Secretary (1905-1908), but in 1905 his career was adversely affected by the investigations of a Royal Commission into the butter industry in Victoria, which alleged irregularities in the accounts of the Victoria

Creamery & Butter Company. Crawford argued that he had never been employed in the accounting department, but his career appears, somewhat unjustly, to have suffered a backward step.

In light of the failing health of his parents, Alexander paid a dutiful visit to Belfast in 1906. James Wright Crawford had been in poor health for a year and eventually died in October 1907. Although Madge Crawford was also unwell during this period, she survived until 1915. This visit gave the elder son the encouragement to consider returning to his roots. As a preliminary step he sent his oldest son (by Mattie), also named Alexander, to stay with Fred from the end of 1907.[29] He wanted to send his wife and two other children (a son and a daughter) to follow, but his mother set herself against the idea – and Fred concurred – as Alexander (senior) had had two or three serious illnesses, and she feared that he would have no-one to care for him if he took a turn for the worse. Ultimately the decision was determined by a downturn in his financial fortunes.

In late 1906 he declined another bureaucratic position, but continued to work for the Western Australian Government. In late 1908, however, his salary was reduced (for an unspecified reason) and, in view of the fact that, at that time, there were no pensions paid in Australia, Alexander admitted that this scuppered any hope that he may have harboured of returning to home soil. In the following year he lost savings as a result of over-ambitious investments, and had to raise money (£400) by selling the farm on Islandmagee that he had recently inherited from his father.[30]

He served the Western Australia Bureau of Agriculture for a decade from 1909 as Chief Inspector under the Rabbit & Vermin Act, and enjoyed trips by camel to inspect the world's longest rabbit-proof fence! Mattie died of consumption on 22nd April 1921, but he indicated to Fred that he continued to work and was kept occupied in charge of 200 men scattered over a range of 2000 miles, as well as in managing a horse-trading and camel-breeding station.

A year later, at the age of 65, he had retired, buying eight acres of land near Perth, growing fruit and vegetables and raising poultry – but still unsure of his Government pension. His financial circumstances, like those of his brother, had always been parlous. Writing to his uncle in December 1936, Alexander junior had encapsulated his father's cavalier approach to financial management.[31]

Alexander senior continued to be active in the Methodist Church and, at the age of 66, on 4th July 1923 he married a 28-year-old widow, by whom he had another daughter. Such virility aside, he had been dogged by ill-health for many years, probably compounded by heavy smoking. In January 1906 he had nearly been poisoned (by some unspecified means), and in July 1909 Fred remarked in a letter to his brother that the latter had been "chronically ill with your old complaint". A year later Alexander had most of his right ear removed, probably as a consequence of cancer, as well as enduring an operation for the removal of haemorrhoids. Fred sympathised: "You, poor old fellow, have had a terrible time of suffering, even when I was out with you seventeen years ago".

He suffered additionally from rheumatism and endured further surgery in 1934 (at the age of 77), observing to Fred that "neuritis has me well in its grip. For the past two months or more I have had continual pain", which was "sometimes very acute". He died on 8th November 1935 and was buried in the expansive Karrakatta Cemetery on the outskirts of Perth.

The company of eight First World War Victoria Cross winners in the same cemetery is an undeniable indication that, despite the distance, Australia was not shielded from, or indifferent to, world events. It did, however, mean that expatriates such as Alexander Crawford did not have to experience the local political turbulence in Ulster in the post-War world. He did nevertheless keep a weather eye on political developments in his native island. He admitted that "in my very young days I thought Home Rule would be a fine thing", but continued that he had "got more sense" and, in the days following the assassination of Field Marshal Sir Henry Wilson in June 1922, he commented, in pre-emptive sentiments not too far removed from those of his brother, that: "For the atrocities that have been committed, not only now but all along, I think Lloyd George should be tried and hung".

Alexander's chief concern, however, was for his brother. On 17th July 1922 he wrote from Perth to Fred at the Wilson Street Works:

I am awfully sorry that things are in such an awful condition in Belfast, and I do feel deeply for you having to keep your midnight vigil at the Works … The strain of ever being on watch must be awful, and I do not wonder at the Commissioner of Police wondering how you have escaped for so long. I have been continually dreading to hear that you have been assassinated.

This was not simply idle or arrogated speculation on the part of the Crawford family. The City Commissioner of Police had said that he could not account for the fact that the gun-runner who had attracted such notoriety had never been shot and Fred admitted that he was indeed fortunate. On 7th January 1922 as Fred and his younger son, Adair, pushed their bicycles along Berry Street (a tributary of Royal Avenue), the thirteen-year-old reported to his father that he had turned round and had overheard two men, one of whom said (looking at Fred): "There is a man that ought to be out of the way, dead".[32]

By that time the charitable, God-fearing traveller had been transmogrified into one of the most notorious figures in Ireland.

Notes

1. D/1700/3/1, 7 November 1866, 29 October 1867, 19 November 1867.

2. W T Pike, *Ulster Contemporary Biographies*, (Brighton, 1910), p.79.

3. In later years Fred was to make regular visits, on business, to Blattmann AG – who were (and still are) in the starch trade – in Wädenswil, near Zurich. On these earlier occasions he will probably have travelled with his father.

4 D/1700/5/2/24, 28 May 1884; D/1700/3/6, 16 July 1886.

5. The following information on Fred's travels is derived primarily from his diaries to Central and North America, D/1700/3/6; to the Holy Land and Near East, D/1700/3/7-8; and to Australia, D/1700/3/9.

6. D/3642/B/3/1-52. See also Keith Haines, 'James Davidson, heir to Sirocco, *Ulster Local Studies*, Vol.19 no.2 (1998), pp.45-59.

7. D/1700/6/1/3, 20 December 1887.

8. D/1700/3/2, 24 December 1900.

9. D/1415/B/34, p.112.

10. W A Moore, *The Orient Express*, (Constable, London, 1914), pp.64, 190.

11. D/1700/6/1/11, 31 July 1920.

12. D/3642/B/3/44.

13. Nelson Russell, *The Irish Brigade in Sicily, July and August 1943*, pp.7-9: D/3574/E/7/7.

14. D/1415/B/34, p.38.

15. As an example, Fred Crawford is listed amongst the membership in 1928: *Proceedings of the Belfast Naturalists' Field Club*, Series II, Vol.IX, Part 1.

16. D/1700/10/1/709, 1 November 1909.

17. D/1700/3/11, 23 March 1896.

18. Edward Bennet, *Shots and Snapshots in British East Africa*, (London, 1914), pp.87-171.

19. D/1700/3/2, 2 October 1900, 8 May 1901.

20. Fred H Crawford, *Guns for Ulster*, (Belfast, 1947), p.12.

21. Keith Haines, *'Chevy' Chase … a real Mr Chips*, (Ballymaconaghy Publishing, Belfast, 2005), especially pp.27-32, 46-50.

22. Rev. Charles Henry Chase, *Alpine Climbers*, (SPCK, London, 1889). D/1700/3/7, 16 March 1890.

23. He stated that some items that were claimed to be found in Egyptian graves were made in Cairo and Italy, and added that: "The Arabs drive a trade here in these curios, the same way that the guides on Waterloo do with bullets that are made in Birmingham and sent over": D/1700/3/7, 8 March 1890.

24. Rev. J Nolan (parish priest of All Saints, Ballymena), *History of the Irish National Pilgrimage to Rome*, (1893), pp.60-74.

25. This included the Moslem faith; for instance, he was impressed with the Dome of the Rock in Jerusalem: D/1700/3/9, 3 May 1890.

26. D/1700/5/2/43-44, 11 and 15 May 1890; D/1700/3/9, 15 May 1892.

27. The sources for Alexander Crawford are copious. Much of the material taken from Pike, p.78; H M Coffrey & M J Morgan, *Irish Families in Australia and New Zealand 1788-1983*, Vol.I, 169-170; and *Australian Dictionary of Biography*. There are numerous letters between the brothers in D/1700/5/2/- D/1700/6/1/- and D/1700/10/1/- which cover the full span of Alexander's years in Australia. Fred's diary of his 1892 visit is found in D/1700/3/9.

28. D/1700/3/1, 27 September 1869.

29. Fred sent him to Methodist College for much of his time in Belfast and finally placed him on a boat home at Tilbury on 18 February 1910, after 27 months: D/1700/10/1/742, –/748, 19 and 26 January 1910.

30. Milliken's Farm (9 acres) at Mullaghdoe, Islandmagee, which James Wright Crawford had purchased from Samuel Milliken on 26 January 1903.

31. See Chapter 2. D/1700/6/2/5, 14 December 1936, from Alexander junior at Cloreen, Pine Avenue, Camberwell, Victoria to uncle Fred, at Cloreen in Belfast.

32. D/1700/6/1/14. D/640/11/2, pp.81-82.

A Lot of
Naughty Men

∞

The significance and value of the volume of the diaries, correspondence and memoirs of Fred Crawford is that they provide a distinctively personal insight into many of the central themes (such as poverty and commercial enterprise) and local events (such as the political turmoil) of the late 19th and early 20th century Belfast; they add depth and individual comment to nebulous and generic subject material. Fred was never reticent about proffering his opinions upon the events and people, central and tangential to his life – and the war in South Africa (or Boer War) was one of these.

Two years to the day after he embarked at Queenstown (now Cobh) for his journey to Cape Town he was addressing the Literary & Debating Society at Campbell College on his recent experiences and it was recorded that: "It was to this personal aspect of the war – the scene-shifting, the side-lights of personal reminiscence, the character of the actors, the tragedy and the comedy of the drama that was being acted in that vast theatre of operations – that we were introduced by Captain Crawford". Much of this is still preserved in his personal diary of that distant conflict.[1]

Receptive to, and absorbed by, all that he witnessed during his itinerant years, his travels cemented his credo that the British Empire was the most rewarding, reassuring and civilising confederation on the globe –

a sentiment that could inspire hyperbole: "Oh England, England, you have been the home of thousands who will never look upon your white cliffs and rural villages again. What proud mother you should be; the best, the truest and the pluckiest men that the modern and medieval world ever saw – you have given birth to, and reared to be a blessing to, Mankind at large".[2]

Ten years before he volunteered to venture to the southern tip of Africa, he had written less elegantly and extravagantly: "There is no country in the world – a people, I should say – that know the true meaning of fair play like the British, or how to treat peoples of other countries with due respect and mutual fairness".[3] The war on the veldt was, however, to give a severe jolt to his equanimity.

His absence from Belfast in 1885 as a White Star Line engineer, and in 1886 en route to the Americas, meant that Fred did not become actively engaged in the anti-Home Rule furore at that stage, but as he returned from Australia at the close of 1892 he "found Ulster in a fever of political agitation over the proposed [Second] Home Rule Bill",[4] which went before the House of Commons on 13th February 1893.

Despite the fact that the two came from a different socio-economic background, Fred's outlook and approach – and even character – in the 1890s very much reflected that of one of the most influential Irish Unionist voices, and most prominent critics of the Second Home Rule Bill – Edward Saunderson of Co. Cavan.[5] Like Fred, the politician displayed "a profound, if occasionally histrionic, religiosity, deep devotion to mother and wife, and an element of doubt and insecurity … He was a flirt, though sufficiently earnest and responsible … [and] he was a sincere Christian gentleman". Although they ministered to different social groups, both men were active religious evangelists.

On his return from Australia Fred quickly became engaged in political campaigning – particularly in the volatile and insecure constituency of West Belfast, which had only recently been won at the 1892 General Election from the nationalists by Hugh Oakley Arnold-Forster. Although he never became a politician, Fred was to be one of the Ulstermen most involved, over the next score years, in the fight to preserve the geo-political integrity of the United Kingdom.

Empire

During the last decade of the 19th century this sense of political identity and unity was to acquire an imperialist patina. Ulster became the standard-bearer of the preservation of the Union; if Ireland were allowed to secede from the Empire, then other component members would wish to follow suit. A threat to this integrity was also detected at the very end of the 19th century in South Africa. Visiting that country in the winter of 1897-1898 "Saunderson increasingly perceived and articulated a parallel between the plight of the Irish minority apparently threatened by majority aggression and the plight of an English minority in the Boer republics, apparently threatened by an Afrikaner majority".

The Boer War was to consolidate the devotion to Empire of others who, within a decade, became more closely associated with Fred Crawford. In his rather rambling and fulsome biography of Lord Craigavon, St John Ervine observed of Captain James Craig, in words that could equally have applied to the starch manufacturer:[6]

> *South Africa taught him more than he yet realised ... the British Empire had become a reality to him ... At the bottom of all his actions and beliefs was his faith in the British way of life. The Empire was ... as good an organisation as the mind of Man had yet imagined and developed ... the union called the Empire in 1900 ... was a fact, and on this fact he founded his faith. All else in his life was subsidiary to that.*

Fred expressed an equally inflated perspective on the worth of Empire and was to experience considerable pride in his personal membership; as he approached Cape Town on board his overcrowded troopship in April 1900 he recorded that:

> *It seems scarcely possible that I am within measurable distance of taking part in one of the great Empire-making upheavals of the greatest nation God ever permitted to rise in the world, and that I shall form a unit in the great military power by which England means to assert her rights, and suppress persecution, bribery and despotic oligarchy and slavery once and for all in South Africa.*

Fred was, in his own phrase, "embodied" with the Donegal Artillery for the war in South Africa in March 1900. He had enlisted in February

1894 as a Second Lieutenant in the Mid-Ulster Artillery (Southern Division), based on Lord Ranfurly's estate in Dungannon. In July and August of the same year he travelled to Woolwich and passed "two stiff examinations in Artillery", as well as obtaining a Certificate of Proficiency from the Riding Establishment which stated that he could "ride sufficiently well to perform the duties of a mounted Officer". On 24th February 1897 he became a Captain with the Donegal Artillery. The military life held a great attraction for him; he was very much a soldier *manqué* and, with hindsight, regretted that he had not pursued a military career.[7]

As was to occur at the onset of the First World War, glamour and patriotism were attendant upon the volunteers for South Africa and Fred's fellow members of the Ulster Reform Club were sufficiently impressed in February 1900 to invite him to "a House Dinner to be given in his honour", when it was learned that he had been appointed second-in-command of a Service Company of the Donegal Royal Garrison Artillery.

Fred bade farewell to his family – his wife Nellie (Helen) whom he had married in West Kensington on 20th February 1896, and his two children, Naomi (born 1897) and Stuart (born March 1898) – on 19th March. The Artillery was entertained to dinner on 23rd March by the townspeople of Letterkenny (where the unit was based) and then marched through Derry to a public reception. It was perhaps a symptom of problems that dogged the British forces throughout the campaign that two men were court-martialled for falling down drunk. The Company left Derry by train at 6 pm and joined the Antrim Artillery at Portadown. Both units then travelled via Dublin to Queenstown (Cobh), where Fred was visited at the dockside on 25th March by his parents.

Whatever excitement and anticipation may have been felt by all concerned, it probably dissipated rapidly upon embarkation. *SS Umbria* departed the southern Irish coast at 12.30 pm on Monday 26th March, carrying 2000 men and around 120 officers (including 70 medical staff) – which was about 1200 in excess of its authorised complement. Fred recorded, possibly with relief, that there was not a single lady on board. Throughout the journey to Cape Town drill was undertaken every half hour, with regiments having to rotate as there was so little space on board. At least five men died before they arrived in southern Africa in mid-April.

By the time he had landed Fred's inevitable diary had already identified shortcomings in, and expressed reservations about, the conduct of the war, which he typified as a want of organisation and common sense. He noted that he had helped to kit out the unit's Colonel en route: "It seems that we are the only Company who had the foresight to bring any spare stores ... I requisitioned for 10% extra of all my stores, and got part, not all ...". At Maitland Camp on *terra firma* he sensed that "One would think we were on a picnic here", and he was to inscribe an identical opinion six months later.

A few days before he finally left the battle zone in June 1901 he noted a recurrent military failing: "We cannot get over the old Crimea system of sending out warm clothing for summer and light things for winter". From the outset he had revealed that supplies were badly managed and defended and, at the end of his service, he was probably even more convinced of the impiety of the whole conflict: "I was very much struck ... at the utter want of recognition of God throughout the whole business here ... Truly we are a stupid, happy-go-lucky nation, and only that the Lord Almighty seems to fight on our side, we should be wiped out".

St. Helena

His arrival in South Africa was marked by irritation, which accompanied him for the next fourteen months. The immediate onset of diarrhoea – which prompted "a great run on my Chlorodyne tabloids" – did not help, but he was greatly irked by the fact that, instead of heading for the front lines, he was despatched to escort 1100 Boer prisoners to St. Helena, where a prisoner-of-war camp had recently been established.[8]

The next five weeks were to prove a particularly unpleasant experience and provided Fred with a very jaundiced attitude towards the Boers, the British soldier and, in particular, the British officer class. The Boers were despised by the British, but they commanded respect as the war refused to end because the farmers were prepared to fight on against insuperable odds. In the final months of his own service, Fred expressed his admiration: "... we are simply chasing the Boers, and keeping a long way astern of them ... [they] can go where and when they like, and show us a clean pair of heels when it suits them".

Between the pages of his diary the Ulster Captain did not conceal his sadness that the captives he was guarding at St. Helena contained so many young boys and old men. Nevertheless, the fact that he and his men were forced to stay on board the boat with his prisoners was not eased by the disgust that the Boers displayed no propensity for basic hygiene. He considered that "they are far too well-treated and pampered ... Our own soldiers when in camp at Letterkenny do not get fed so well as these men do, and they get exactly the same as our fellows are getting at present, but nothing is good enough for them".

The Donegal Artillery officer did manage to make a visit to Napoleon's erstwhile home, Longwood, but otherwise spent uncomfortable weeks on the boat with his men and prisoners. *SS Bavarian* was a floating Petri dish: "The ship is in a most insanitary state – fever, influenza, and last night there as an outbreak of measles besides pneumonia".

Hospital conditions were appalling throughout the war and demonstrated that the British Army had no more learned the lesson in medical matters since the Crimean conflict than it had on supplies. One surgeon wrote candidly: "Believe everything you hear as to mismanagement and even incapacity and wilful neglect ... Certainly if I were ill or wounded, I would not care to be left to the tender mercies of the majority of men I have come across". Cholera was always a probability – everyone, including Rudyard Kipling, feared the water supplies[9] – but the most lethal disease, for which there was no known cure – was enteric fever. Fred witnessed a number of his men reduced to "perfect skeletons". In fairness, circumstances were not any better back in Belfast. 30,000 people had fallen victim to typhoid fever in the city in 1897, and during the campaign Fred was notified by an acquaintance that a mutual friend had died of the disease.[10] One of the 13,000-plus number who fell prey to the epidemic was one of the original pupils at Campbell College; Lieutenant Arthur Cowan – one of the sons of Sir Edward Cowan of Craigavad who, like Captain James Craig, made his living from the distilling trade – succumbed at Elandsfontein on 11th April 1902, only a month before the end of the war.[11]

Campbell College had been opened on the Belmont estate in East Belfast only in September 1894, but at least fourteen former pupils were to enlist for the campaign in South Africa, no doubt exhibiting the same idealism that was to take 126 of their fellow pupils to their death in the wider conflict of 1914-1918. The district around Vlakfontein in the Transvaal was to offer this handful of volunteers the full range of what war could devise, from the death in battle of Joseph Prentice on 27th July 1901, to the award of the Victoria Cross – only 24 days earlier in the same locality – to Second Lieutenant William John English. The latter, who lived in East Belfast for most of his life, and was to serve in both World Wars, was only twenty years of age; he returned to the College, only two years after leaving it, to "tumultuous applause".

As he arrived off Table Bay on 30th May 1900 on his return from St. Helena, Fred recorded his disillusionment after effectively nine weeks afloat: "I am sick of the sea, and very sorry I came out – I never volunteered for this job". He was clearly missing his family, and to while away the tedious voyage from the prisoner colony to Cape Town he had written to his first-born, "my own wee pet, Naomi":[12]

> *I had a letter from grandpapa [James Wright Crawford] in which he says my little darling is so much improved and so nice. Father [Fred] is so glad to hear this of his own wee daughter. Father hopes Naomi is good to Stuart and Mama. She must take great care of her little brother and Mama. Father is still in a great big ship. He brought a lot of naughty men over to a little island in the sea and left them there. They can't get away as the sea is all around them. And now we are coming back to a big country, where the naughty people are killing the soldiers of the Queen, but they must be punished for it, and Father has come out to try and help punish them … Do you often think of Father? He is always thinking of his little daughter and son and hopes they sometimes think of him …*

Fred was always a concerned father. Marriage was a topic he had discussed with his brother in their correspondence. Alexander had encouraged his younger brother by saying that Fred would make a good husband, and shortly after the latter's wedding he almost uttered a sigh of relief: "You are a married man at last".[13] On Friday 4th May, after less than seven weeks' absence from home, Fred – who carried a photograph of his children during the war – revealed: "It is hard to be so long without news from the dear ones at home; this is as bad as facing danger, hardships, and even much worse".

He counted the days of absence from his family, recording on 19th March 1901 that it was a year to the day since "I saw my dear ones last time". A few weeks later a raid brought them to mind again. By the close of 1900 he noted that "I am needed at home", probably for business reasons, as his father was disappointed that his son could not get back.[14] He was frustrated, complaining that, at this stage, "I have never been under fire yet, nor in action", and "I had never seen an armed Boer and there was not much kudos for us". It was only the third Christmas he had spent away from home and was "the most miserable year I have spent". He finally saw some action – ironically, as a Methodist, on Sunday 5th May – although it was not against Boer guerrillas, but against their womenfolk.

The British treatment of Boer women and children, who demonstrated scorn and resilience in the face of their enemies, became notorious. Concentration camps were invented to contain them in the most uncivilised, often inhumane, fashion. The camps were created to corral the non-combatants, following the policy of wholesale burning of farmsteads, which left them without shelter or food. It was a brutal policy of last resort for which Lord Roberts attempted to set regulations, but these made little difference. For many soldiers, it became a profoundly unpopular duty. In July 1900 Fred had spoken with a young lieutenant who had been ordered to burn the Boer farms:

> He said it was simply awful work, but it had to be done. The women and children prayed, begged, howled and screamed, cursed and swore and did everything to try and stop them. He said he felt it more than shooting prisoners would have affected him. He had to turn the little children with the women into the veldt ... it would make me ten years older in a few weeks, if I had to do it.

Fred's chance came ten months later. The captain was despatched ten miles along the railway line which he was guarding to a location whose place-name – Belmont (the site of Campbell College) – must have conjured up memories of home, to deal with rebels who were attacking the lines: "This place was a hotbed of rebels, so I settled I should go and surround the house, and take any men there prisoners, and blow up the house".

By the light of a full moon he travelled with a companion, and he managed to enter the house unchallenged. He found two women – a mother and daughter, aged about 22 – and then saw three young children. He recalled that he "felt the biggest scoundrel unhanged. I thought of two other little ones away in Ireland, and a kind of thickness seemed to gather in my throat". The two soldiers agreed that they did not have the stomach or heart to despatch the Boer family into the cold African autumn night: "We were both as pale as death". He informed the women that he was well aware that their brothers and sons were recognised at Belmont but, as there was no trace of Boer activity in the house, "I shall not interfere with you this time". He advised them, however, that any future evidence would result in the house being destroyed. Fortunately, a month later he was relieved of his local command and was preparing to leave for home.

Respect

The Artillery Captain's subordinates appear to have respected him, primarily because he gave them respect. There were occasions when he was unconvinced of their abilities. He recalled that, en route to St. Helena, "one man, while clearing his breech, pulled the trigger with the result that the carbine went off, and shot a man through the shoulder on the ship opposite"; nevertheless he acknowledged that they had no handling experience, and had not been properly trained.

He was appalled, but probably not surprised, by the amount of drunkenness amongst the ranks. He estimated that "seven out of every ten soldiers get drunk when they come out here", adding: "How I have longed for a few teetotallers, especially amongst the NCOs". Virtually all his sergeants "had quite enough drink" on the Twelfth 1900. He encouraged the temperance movement within the armed forces and even, at one stage, went so far as to "encourage total abstinence among both officers and men". Perhaps his most poignant observation on this problem was made as he entrained at the end of September 1900 for his command at the Orange River: "We passed a Canadian contingent tonight who are on their way home. One poor fellow fell out of the train and was cut in half, a sad ending after their cover through the war. The cursed drink was at the bottom of it".

As a Captain he acknowledged the adversity and problems which they faced, including the loneliness, boredom and inaction – he himself had been in South Africa five months before he wrote: "Here I am at last doing soldiering" – endless sandstorms, disease, idiotic but lethal orders from incompetent officers, scorpions ("every insect here seems to be able to bite or sting, and some do both"), countless white ants (which burrowed through everything "even lead bullets, to see what is on the other side"), and millions upon millions of locusts. Fred was overwhelmed at the self-sacrifice and courage of the ordinary British soldier at Spion Kop: "We should be proud to have such heroes amongst us, and also revere the memory of those brave men ... Every man who made his way up that terrible ascent deserves a VC or DSO. The charge at Balaclava was nothing to this".

As an officer he disliked having to sit on Courts-Martial, primarily as a consequence of his own highly-developed sense of personal inadequacy and self-reproach: "I hate being a judge. I feel it keenly when I have to assent to a man getting a heavy sentence, and I feel, so far as the moral aspect of the question of the sight of God is concerned, I am far worse, considering my opportunities than many of the poor fellows I have before the court, and I am not in a position to throw a stone at them".

His consideration for his men echoed that of Alexander the Great, who exhibited military prudence by suffering the same deprivations experienced by his men; on a route march through Cape Town in September 1900, officers were invited to a house for (non-alcoholic) drinks. Fred declined; "as I was in command, I thought it better not to go; besides, as the men were not getting anything to drink, I did not like to either".

Fred's concern for those associated with his command began before they had left Ireland – in correspondence with Lord Ranfurly, who was then in New Zealand, he urged consideration of pensions for men who were wounded[15] – and it continued well after the war in South Africa had ended. In 1911 he obliged a former rifleman under his command by vouching for him to the Paymaster at Victoria Barracks.[16] In February 1922 Fred wrote to his co-conspirator in the gun-running episode, Wilfred Spender, then Secretary to the Northern Ireland Cabinet (in a letter which also proudly announced that Fred had become a grandfather), asking if any assistance might be given to a former brother officer of the Donegal Artillery who had served in South Africa. Four months later Fred received a plea from another officer colleague named George Dobbyn who, by that stage, had returned from India to live in South Africa. The supplicant had earlier written from Peshawar, from where he had been compulsorily retired after twenty years' service on the sub-continent. He revealed that there were another 450 men in a similar predicament, and that they would find it difficult to find alternative employment: "It is a long way from the Donegal Artillery", Dobbyn added. He had returned to try and farm in South Africa, but in a phrase reminiscent of Alexander Crawford's early struggle to "make my tucker" in Australia, Dobbyn said it was "a bare livelihood" – although he was still resident there a quarter of a century later.[17]

Struggling to earn a living himself at that time, there was little of a practical nature that the former Captain could do, apart from seek favours from contacts, but his readiness to do all he could for those linked to his command was recognised by others. By chance, in October 1900 in Cape Town, Fred encountered the West Belfast MP Hugh Oakley Arnold-Forster. The latter had been appointed to the Land Settlement Commission and was en route to the Transvaal. He wrote to Helen Crawford to reassure her: "I daresay your husband will have told you that my wife and I had the pleasure of meeting him in Cape Town. I must tell you ... that we found him in excellent health and looks; in fairly fine spirits, and doing his work in a most soldierly spirit, and evidently with the regard and goodwill of his brother officers".[18]

Arnold-Forster, who remained MP for West Belfast until 1906, was to play a partial role in the reorganisation of the Armed Forces, as Secretary of State for War between 1903 and 1905. Fred's own belief that greater professionalism and better pay were needed to improve the performance of the Army was increasingly recognised. In November 1905 he seconded a motion at the Belfast Chamber of Commerce urging the Government to provide "an army sufficiently powerful to defend these islands against invasion and to repel aggression on the distant frontiers of the Empire".[19] Fred had written that: "There should be more men from the ranks among our Officers, and it would be better for the Army". His considered opinion was that: "The iron-bound system of seniority is a terrible mistake. Men in the Army should be promoted for their ability".

The South African War had been an acknowledged fiasco and restructuring of the Army was essential. Arnold-Forster initiated some of the proposals that led to the creation of the British Expeditionary Force, which required an officer cadre who earned its rank through merit and not seniority. The Officer Training Corps was designed to train young men, primarily at the Public Schools, who would train for Certificate 'A', which would enable them to enter the Army at Officer (Second Lieutenant) level. The first such school unit in Ireland was established at Campbell College, with Fred's gubernatorial encouragement. It was the only Irish contingent at their first camp in England (Farnborough, 28th July to 5th August 1910), which was graced by visits from the two leading military figures at the close of the Boer War – Lords Roberts and Kitchener.[20] Fred's enthusiasm for military training for contemporary youth was similarly evident in his involvement with the creation of the Young Citizen Volunteers on 10th September 1912.[21]

A Picnic

The part-time soldier and part-time starch manufacturer was unambiguous in his opinion that the real failings in the Boer War rested squarely on the over-stocked tables of the Officers and Generals. Even these, however, could be poorly prepared and unappetising. Fred's disdain at the menu when he was invited to lunch with his Colonel during the early days at Maitland Camp is barely disguised: "… tinned cocoa, milk biscuits and [misspelling every word except the second] patty de fois grass". As the Captain in the Donegal Artillery arrived in Cape Town, he demonstrated a subordinate's reserve: "I must remember I am now a soldier, and my first duty is to obey, and not criticise". This reticence soon evaporated.

He was prepared to accept that British Officers were brave, but it was the courage of the foolhardy. In August 1920 he paid a secret visit to T. J. Smith, Inspector-General of the Royal Irish Constabulary at Dublin Castle. To his own astonishment, bearing in mind the dangers that such men faced, Fred found it rather too easy to get close to Smith and said that he could have shot him had been of such a mind. "I remember when I was out in the Boer War in 1900", he chastised the policeman, "nineteen of the officers thought it was infra dig to take cover while their men were lying down firing at the Boers; they walked up and down in the open and disdained to take cover with the usual result that they were picked off one by one, and the men were left without officers ... The efficiency of a fighting force is dependent on its commissioned officers; if they are wiped out the force is rendered almost useless".[22]

From the outset in South Africa, the artilleryman was caustic about the mismanagement and misdirection of funds: "One would think that we are on a picnic here ... Champagne and all sorts of luxuries going up with rich officers – I expect at the expense of munitions of war". A few days later in St. Helena he complained that "the want of method and supervision displayed in the waste of public money annoys me, being a man of business". More bluntly, just before Christmas he wrote: "It is too bad to think that, after what we pay for our Army, it is useless". He believed that the English Officer preferred sport to military duties, an opinion expressed elegantly by the East Belfast author, St John Ervine, who encapsulated the Boer War as "The finest guerrilla troops in the world ... opposed by Generals who had been trained in the principles of expensive polo".[23] Another who remained unimpressed by the calibre of the British officer class was Captain James ('Jack') White [24] – and he was the son of Irish General Sir George White, whose tactical error led to the siege of Ladysmith, and who was effectively dismissed by Roberts!

Fred's sentiments about some of the Generals were also echoed by others, including those with whom he was to develop a close relationship either side of the First World War. Writing home from Orange River Colony in January 1901, Captain James Craig – future Prime Minister of Northern Ireland – claimed that: "Generals are just as much at sea as a Lance Corporal ... Everyone is pleased to see a number of fogies, Colonels and so on, going home".[25] Another Irishman, Henry Wilson, later rose to become a Field Marshal, but in early 1900 he was a Captain struggling to help relieve Ladysmith. He claimed that the fiasco over the latter was the result of "bad generalship ... our losses have been much greater than they ought to have been owing to bad generalship, and this on the part of several generals".[26] The gun-runner later came to admire Wilson for his post-First World War support for Ulster, but the latter was ultimately to disappoint Fred – who had arranged for the Field Marshal to inaugurate the Campbell College War Memorial in July 1922 – as a consequence of his assassination by the IRA only a few days before he was due to visit Belmont.

The Biggest Ass

If Fred was critical of most officers, he was vitriolic towards Generals, and his opinions presage those which were to be expressed about their conduct and lack of ability during the First World War – which was not entirely surprising, as many such as Haig and French, were to be veterans of both conflicts. He felt that those who had campaigned in India had earned a false reputation as they were only fighting "against coloured races without artillery ... the ones who had never been there [India] are utterly useless". Within a few months he summarised his feelings with disarming bluntness: "The British General as a rule is the biggest ass and fool it is possible to imagine. Schoolboys would conduct a snowballing match with more common sense and better strategy than some of them". He believed that the "worst feature of the whole affair [is] they delight in their ignorance".

His most pronounced scorn was reserved for those Generals who were actually despatched home because they were so incompetent. As Fred arrived in South Africa General Gatacre – one of those who had been to India – was travelling in the other direction. Fred felt that this was not before time, but he believed that "a long-suffering and stupid English people will as usual treat him as a martyr, and give him a snug billet at home". In order to avoid such a miscarriage of natural justice, Fred felt that a more terminal approach should be adopted: "If I had my way, there would be some Colonels, if not Generals, shot and more imprisoned for life".

Orange River Command

In November 1900, whilst in command at the Orange River, he was asked if he was going to arrange a salute for a General who would be passing by train. "Certainly not", he retorted, "we are at very important work [which was the construction of Fort Ulster] that must be finished at once, and I'll not stop even for a General". About six weeks later, another train approached; Fred felt that it should have been stopped: "It contained General C.., the greatest failure of the war, and one General at least that should be court-martialled". Four months later, he had changed his mind; amongst other observations, he commented on "alcohol Freddy (General C..) still retaining his command at Belfast, Ireland, instead of being shot as he certainly should have been". Evidently Fred was, for unspecified reasons, both familiar with, and unimpressed by, his namesake – Major-General Sir Frederick Carrington – who had enjoyed a wealth of experience in Africa, and who had held command of the Belfast District from 1899 to 1900.[27]

On 1st October 1900, after several hours delay as a result of uncountable numbers of locusts on the line, Captain Fred Crawford arrived at his new command at the Orange River [28] – perhaps the most appropriate location for an Ulsterman [29] – where he was in command of one officer and 50 NCOs (of both the Donegal and Antrim Artillery), based at Fort Munster (so-called because it had been constructed by the Munster Fusiliers) overlooking the railway bridge over the river. Fred was designated CRA Orange River Station, OC Fort Munster & OC Irish Artillery Militia Detachment, Orange River Station.

It was an unappealing destination, and Fred may have felt inclined to agree with Edward Saunderson's conclusion three years previously that: "England has no reason to envy the possession of [the Orange Free State]".[30] Although the artilleryman admitted that he was finally feeling useful as a soldier, he found the remote location lonely, oppressive and demanding: "Oh, I wish this miserable war were over and at an end. I feel now if things were managed right we could be relieved by Colonials and sent home". He seems, however, to have excelled almost instinctively in his role and it is probable that the experience of authority and command proved invaluable to him in later years when he was planning the gun-running, or helping with the organisation of the Ulster Special Constabulary .

Life was not made any more comfortable by the prevalence of unpleasant wildlife; on one occasion the fort was invaded by clouds of locusts which devoured everything thrown at them from the mess tent – porridge, bread and steak. The men were on parade at 3.30 am each day as they were much closer to the Boer units; the latter would occasionally cut the railway lines and Fred had to ensure that this damage was repaired promptly. He was heavily engaged with mining, but did once admit that, although he had been familiar with the employment of dynamite for many years, "I feel that Nobel's dynamite gives me worse headaches than the Scottish or British Dynamite Company's". A score of years later he was to admit that he had suffered considerable apprehension when forced to venture out to lay mines: "I felt very lonely and a far-from-home feeling took strong hold of me".[31]

In mid-October he commenced the construction of what was initially named Fort Ulster. He was highly praised during three inspections for this work and was told: "I have seldom seen a stronger position. It is impregnable and could resist an attack". In December the Commandant paid him the compliment of naming it Fort Crawford – it became more popularly known as Crawford's Death Trap (because of its threat to the enemy), although ultimately in May it was formally christened Fort Donegal (in honour of the Artillery unit).

It had effectively been completed by January 1901 around the time he was given the position of Officer Commanding, Orange River Bridge, and asked to take on the role of Adjutant of the Irish Brigade Division Militia Artillery, at 2s 6d extra per day, adding that: "I am in reality of Inspector of Fortifications and Defences in this command".

Home

On 3 June, shortly before leaving the region, he travelled to Kimberley in order to visit De Beers' mine. He indicated that he wanted to purchase some diamonds, but whether he actually did so is unrecorded. It had started to snow on 1st June and he was pleased to be relieved of command of the bridge a week later. He arrived in Cape Town on 14 June, and boarded the *Roslin Castle* (of the Union-Castle Line), acting as on-board Adjutant for the Donegal Artillery. As he sailed from Cape Town he paid homage to its natural beauty, and compensated for months of appalling cuisine: "I am afraid I astonished the waiter, as I ate solidly through the menu, all but two courses". A rather rough Canadian contingent on board found alternative uses for their provisions, and demonstrated insubordination by throwing potatoes at their officers. It was an uncomfortable journey home and he rechristened the boat the *Rollin' Castle*.

On 20th June he sailed past St. Helena where the Boer General Piet Cronje was now ensconced in Longwood. The Boer did not have too long to wait for release and his rather tasteless reconstruction of the Last Stand at Paardeberg at the 1904 St. Louis World Fair may well have been visited by those other Belfast businessmen, Samuel and James Davidson of Sirocco Works, who were there selling their ventilation equipment.[32] By a strange coincidence, another Boer General, Ben Viljoen, arrived at St. Helena in February 1902 on board the *Britannic*, on which Fred had been Sixth Engineer in early 1886.[33]

Fred arrived at Southampton on 8 July to be greeted by his parents and, taking the Fleetwood boat, was back at Letterkenny two days later to surrender officially his command. He travelled back to Belfast just in time to celebrate the Twelfth. Whilst his may not have been a spectacular contribution, it was an honourable one, and his reliability and trustworthiness appear to have been appreciated. He was mentioned in Lord Roberts' final despatch and was awarded the Queen's Medal with three clasps (for the Cape Colony, Orange Free State and 1901 campaigns), which he received in person from Edward VII at Marlborough House.

PLAYING SOLDIERS

For all the misery and ineptitude which he suffered, Captain Crawford clearly enjoyed the experience of soldiering; he admitted to Lt-Col. W.A.G. Saunders-Knox-Gore, a commanding officer, in 1908 that "There is nothing I have cared for so much in my life as my military work".[34] After his return to Belfast he eagerly retained his association with the Donegal Artillery, despite the inconvenient travel to its Headquarters in Letterkenny and training in distant, inhospitable locations such as Rosapenna, Finner and Dundalk.

In the long term it must have proved an unwelcome compliment to Fred that the complaints that he, and others, made about the mismanagement of the war in South Africa were actually heeded. Reforms were undertaken fairly promptly, and Fred probably viewed it ultimately as an irony that he received in October 1903 – as "a personal friend" – a letter from Arnold-Forster thanking him for all his efforts, concluding: "I cannot help hoping that, as a soldier, you will some day have reason to be pleased that you did so much to give me the chance of going on with my work at the War Office, but perhaps that is too sanguine a hope".[35] Fred must have been delighted at the opportunities presented by the Officer Training Corps to pupils at Campbell College; nevertheless, the changes came at his own expense, as the process of rationalisation and modernisation resulted in the demise of the Donegal Artillery! In August 1907 the Territorial and Reserve Forces Act transferred the Militia into the Army Reserve; the Royal Garrison Artillery units were incorporated into the Royal Field Reserve Artillery – the only two Irish units escaping this transformation being the Antrim and Cork Artillery.

Thus began a trail of copious and anxious, but ultimately unrewarded, correspondence from Fred's pen. Hoping to cultivate support for the salvation of the Donegals at the highest level, in March 1907 he asked Arnold-Forster to receive a deputation to clarify what his successor as Secretary of State for War, Haldane, "is going to do with the Irish Militia Artillery".[36]

Only a month earlier he had put in a request for promotion to an Honorary Majority. In October 1907 he reiterated the request "as I understand I am now fully qualified for this rank". He spent most of 1908 endeavouring to ensure that a fellow Captain, John Cochrane (who had held this rank with the Donegal Militia since 1891) was not elevated to Major; Crawford described the latter, who was awarded the DSO in the Boer War, as "a most undesirable officer to be associated with", and who "ought to have been posted a deserter in 1902".

Fred's elder son, Stuart, was married in April 1921 to Sheelagh Garvey in Ballina, and their meeting may well have been a consequence of Fred's relationship with his erstwhile Commanding Officer of the Donegals, Lt-Col. W.A.G. Saunders-Knox-Gore. The latter lived at Belleek Manor in the Irish town, and appears to have shown sympathy with Fred's search for promotion, but the imminent absorption of the Donegal unit clearly did not encourage the War Office to consider such promotions. On 9th April 1909 Fred bemoaned his misfortune: "It seems a pity after all my service to have to retire a Captain. The Reserve of Officers means nothing – no training and only called out in wartime". On 3rd May, however, he was writing to Saunders-Knox-Gore as 'Major Crawford'. He revealed that he had received notification that, being over forty, he must resign his commission or go into the Reserve of Officers, and reluctantly "I shall prefer the latter alternative". His entry in the Army List of 1910 reads: "Donegal Field Reserve Artillery (hon); Captain and Hon Major, Reserve of Officers".

The would-be soldier had mounted a valiant campaign to be appointed Commanding Officer of the Antrim Artillery, which was to survive. In April 1909 he wrote to Ballina, pointing that the Colonel of the Antrims – Sir Harry Stewart, formerly a fellow Captain in the Donegals – was retiring. Fred said that he was led to believe that neither the senior nor junior Major of the Antrims wanted the post, and "none of the other officers is eligible … so an outsider is bound to get it. We [the Donegals] will be disbanded after the next training and I am very anxious not to drop my military work till I get promotion".

The previous two years had been difficult for the family man and businessman, but by 1909 the sadness at his father's death in October 1907 had probably begun to abate and, although he had struggled to deal with the financial troubles on inheriting the company, after a couple of decades of uncertainty at Wilson Street he may well have been immunised against its ills. He launched into an impressive and sustained programme of lobbying. As a Donegal Militia colleague of Stewart (who lived at Fort Stewart in Ramelton), Fred appears to have made a calculated effort to cultivate the acquaintance. The two men were in correspondence as early as April and May 1908 when the importunate Captain clearly regretted not owning a more substantial farmhouse on his farm – known as Duff's Farm – at Islandmagee to offer to the retiring Stewart:[37]

> I have a cottage and farm of 45 acres [on Islandmagee]. I do not think you could go to a better place for health, but there are scarcely any houses on it ... and you would have difficulty getting one to accommodate your large establishment. My cottage is very small, otherwise I would have placed it at your service ... I am sorry it is not bigger as it is on the highest part of the island, and commands a lovely view including the Isle of Man, the Mulls of Kintyre and Galloway, the Mourne Mountains, etc ...

A year later (5th June 1909) correspondence about the impending closure of the Letterkenny base reveals that Stewart and his wife had been staying with Fred's family for about three weeks.[38]

Admitting that it was rather a long shot, in April 1909 he approached Saunders-Knox-Gore for his endorsement with regard to the command of the Antrims, and "when I put the special claims I have, if backed your support, I consider I have as good a chance as anyone else". His claims were, in fact, rather tenuous. In the same letter he admitted that he had previously been turned down twice for promotion (to Major) in the Donegals. He rehearsed his command prospectus in South Africa, emphasising that at least half of the Company he had commanded at the Orange River had been Antrim men. He added that he had been born in Co. Antrim, and that "I live within a 20-minute railway journey of Headquarters".

For a minor Belfast businessman, Fred could muster an impressive array of potential references. In April 1909 he was given encouragement by a sympathetic letter from Lt-Col. E.C. Wace DSO (formerly Officer Commanding, Royal Artillery). The letter agreed that Fred had given good service in South Africa and had been highly-regarded by Lt-Col. Eldred Pottinger, his Antrim counterpart (whose family hailed from East Belfast). Wace concluded: "If the Donegal Regiment had not been disbanded, I had every hope that in the ordinary course of events, you would have succeeded Col. Saunders-Knox-Gore in Command of that Regiment". Whilst Fred was clearly trying to court his contacts during these months, as an individual of considerable courtesy, there were few who would have denied him their assistance. Pottinger had suffered a lengthy painful illness in 1905, and his daughter wrote to Fred to acknowledge his solicitousness to reveal that: "You were the only man who had been with him in the Regiment in South

Africa who wrote us", adding that Pottinger was "very much attached to you".[39]

A few days earlier he had contacted Rt. Hon. Thomas Andrews of Comber (father of four notable sons, including the future Prime Minister of Northern Ireland, father of one of Fred's daughters-in-law), outlining his predicament: "I am anxious to get promotion and to do an annual training for some years yet. The only way this can be accomplished is by getting command of the Antrim Artillery … I know you have great influence with Lord Londonderry, and I feel sure in many ways he could give me a leg up". He also despatched an appeal to his old acquaintance and political mentor, Lord Ranfurly, urging his support; and he made a similar approach to Prof Sir John Byers of Queen's University (who was a fellow Governor at Campbell College) asking him to place Fred's name before Lord Aberdeen, Lord-Lieutenant of Ireland. The latter was an indication of the artilleryman's desperation, as the politician was a former close associate of Gladstone!

On 26th April he contacted Andrews again, revealing that no less a figure than Haldane "had promised to put my claims before the Army Council". He had, however, heard that the recommendation of the Commander-in-Chief in Ireland, General Sir Neville Lyttelton, carried the most weight and Andrews was asked to get Lord Londonderry to speak on Fred's behalf to Lyttelton. Three months later, an entry in the *London Gazette* officially announced the resignation of the Commanding Officer of the Antrims. This produced a flurry of further urgent appeals to Lords Ranfurly and Shaftesbury, Colonel James McCalmont (Hon. Colonel of the Antrims), Sir Francis McKnight (Chairman of Antrim County Council) and directly to the Marquis of Londonderry asking them to put his name prominently on Lyttelton's desk.

Despite his best efforts, Fred was notified on 20th August, by Lord Londonderry *inter alia*, that he had been unsuccessful. He responded ruefully that: "I may say in passing that had I known Colonel Southern was in the running I should not have sent in my application, but I was given to understand that he was not". This was somewhat disingenuous, as a few months earlier he had clearly hoped that Saunders-Knox-Gore would take the bait, when Fred endeavoured to rake up some rather trivial, antique 'dirt' on Southern: "He was in command of the battery of the 15th when the accident occurred in 1897, and it came out at the court of enquiry that he had been fooling around with a Kodak, trying to get snaps of firing".

The starch manufacturer was bitterly disappointed, but was resigned to the inevitable: "It seems a pity after my long service and experience I have to go at my age. I am not yet 47" – which in itself was mischievous, as he was writing to his correspondent the day before his 48th birthday.

By that stage the Donegals had been wound up – or down. He said "goodbye forever" to Letterkenny on 19th June 1909 and then drove to Dundalk for the final training camp. By early August he was informed that the Donegal camp had been cleared. On 29th October he moaned to Lord Lifford, his former Hon. Colonel – on whose estate the Donegals' camp may have been based, and who also proved a staunch opponent of Home Rule – that: "It is more than sad to think that the old regiment has been done away with ... I spent more than twelve happy years in it, but that is all over and I only have the General Reserve of Officers open to me now".

Nevertheless, as shall be seen, there was to be one last throw of the military dice for Fred Crawford to play at soldiering.

At one stage he had considered asking the Woolwich Mess "to hold our plate in trust and to hand it over to a Donegal Regiment if ever there is one formed", but the hope did not materialise and Fred rehearsed the procedure with the final Letterkenny occupants for the winding down of the camp: "... all money must first be paid into the hands of the acting quarter-master, and then it will be divided up according to the amount realised on each at the sale. Those who are entitled to a portion are Officers, permanent staff, sergeants and the Regimental fund ...".

Fred was clearly determined to retain some memories. It is not clear whether he purchased it, or whether he inherited it, but he was to bequeath several items of the Mess silver of the late Donegal Artillery to his children; this included two silver flower pots, two silver mounted wine jugs, and – probably most proudly of all – a silver bowl for the best battery shooting in the Donegal Artillery.

CREDENTIALS

Fred's rearguard action – if overwhelmed – reflected his enthusiasm, discovered late in life, for soldiering. The Boer War years demonstrated the imperialist credentials of one who believed that Britain had given birth to an Empire that was "a blessing to Mankind at large".[40]

Astutely, he forecast in 1901 that the mollification of the enemy, which paid dividends in South Africa, would be repeated at home, ultimately threatening the survival of Ulster. He observed presciently:[41]

> ... the authorities do not take the war seriously. The policy is the same as it has been to loyal Irishmen – smiles to friendlies and sops to enemies. The man who proposed to poison all the wells and rivers and all waters at the advance of the British is now placed by the same British authorities in a lucrative position ... What fools we British are ... Again, men who have done good service ... are now treated with less courtesy than those who are known to be rebels at heart. Ireland will be repeated as sure as I write this.

As he sailed past St. Helena on his way home he summarised his unhappy journey: "Shipboard to me now is very distasteful. I never wish to put my foot on another ship for more than a few hours in my life".[42] Almost thirteen years later he abjured this promise to himself, as he navigated the Baltic, North and Irish Seas on board the *SS Fanny*.

NOTES

1. The diary in PRONI is D/1700/3/2. The observation from Campbell College is in *The Touchstone*, Vol.2 no.10 (July 1902), 166-167. He addressed the Society on 25 March 1902.

2. D/1700/3/8, 23 May 1890.

3. D/1700/3/7, 13 March 1890.

4. Fred H Crawford, *Guns for Ulster*, (Belfast, 1947), p.9.

5. For Saunderson, see Alvin Jackson, *Colonel Edward Saunderson: Land and Loyalty in Victorian Ireland*, (Clarendon Press, Oxford, 1995), and his entry for Saunderson in the *Oxford Dictionary of National Biography*.

6. St John Ervine, *Craigavon: Ulsterman*, (London, 1949), pp.69-70.

7. A draft of a letter to Lady Ranfurly, possibly in the 1930s: D/1700/10. D/1700/10/1/396, letter of 29 April 1908 to Lt-Col. WAG Saunders-Knox-Gore; –/670, 21 July 1909, to his brother, Alexander. D/1700/3/10.

8. Byron Farwell, *The Great Boer War*, (Wordsworth Editions, Ware, 1999), pp.214, 420-421. Much of the general material about the war is taken from this, and from Thomas Pakenham, *The Boer War*, (Abacus, London, 2004).

9. Farwell, pp.242-246. Jad Adams, *Kipling*, (Haus Books, London, 2005), pp.132-133: "... disease cultivated by incompetence ... drinking water taken from the contaminated Modder River".

10. Fred was contacted by Janet, wife of Sam Cunningham of Fernhill, North Belfast: D/1700/5/13/4, 29 November 1900.

11. The main cause of enteric fever was probably poor food hygiene in Army camps. In 1906 a major survey was undertaken in India under the supervision of an Irishman, Lt-Col. Sir David Semple, who was to send both of his sons to Campbell College in that same year. Both sons were to die during the First World War. See Lt-Col. David Semple, *An Enquiry on Enteric Fever in India*, (Calcutta, 1908); the main problem was the detection and isolation of carriers, p.47.

12. D/1700/5/2/61, 28 May 1900.

13. D/1700/5/2/42, 24 April 1889; D/1700/6/1/7, 10 April 1896.

14. D/1700/5/13/6, 1 March 1901.

15. D/1700/5/13/2, 2 April 1900.

16. D/1700/10/1/883, 3 January 1911. He verified that William Godfrey (probably then a platelayer of 30 Egeria Street, off the Donegall Road) "was under my command in the late South African War".

17. D/1700/5/6/7 and –/16d, 20 February and 18 June 1922. Dobbyn had been a Lieutenant in the Donegals from August 1898. For Dobbyn in January 1947: D/1700/5/8/16.

18. D/1700/5/17/1/1, 22 October 1900.

19. George Chambers, *Faces of Change: the Belfast and Northern Ireland Chambers of Commerce and Industry 1783-1983*, (Belfast Chambers of Commerce, 1983), p.217.

20. For the development and role of the Officer Training Corps, see Keith Haines, *'Chevy' Chase ... a real Mr Chips*, (Ballymaconaghy Publishing, Belfast, 2005), pp.93-104.

21. Timothy Bowman, *Carson's Army: the Ulster Volunteer Force 1910-1922*, (Manchester University Press, 2007), p.25.

22. D/640/2/1, letter of 26 August 1920.

23. Ervine, p.57.

24. Captain Jack White, *Misfit: a revolutionary life*, (Livewire Publications, Dublin, 2005 – reprint of 1930 original), pp.19-20.

25. D/1415/B/24, 4 January 1901.

26. Major-Gen Sir C E Callwell, *Field Marshal Sir Henry Wilson: his life and diaries*, (Cassell & Co, London, 1927), I, 34.

27. His command, from 24 March 1899, included the nine counties of Ulster, plus Co Louth.

28. Details of this command are found in his diary: D/1700/3/2, with a useful summary in D/1700/10/1/144-146, drawn up in mid-1907, probably in support of his claim to be promoted to the rank of Major in the Donegal Artillery.

29. The humorous link between the Orange Free State and an 'Orange' Ulster was made by *Punch* magazine in relation to Sir Edward Carson in the years of the Home Rule Crisis; he was depicted in many guises in *Punch* cartoons, including that of a Boer farmer, Minheer Kaarson, the new Orange Free Stater: Joseph P Finnan, 'Punch's portrayal of Redmond, Carson and the Irish Question 1910-1914,' *Irish Historical Studies*, Vol.XXXIII, no.132 (November 2003), 440.

30. Saunderson papers at PRONI: T/2996/7/2, 17 November 1897.

31. D/640/11/2, p.87.

32. Pakenham, p.574. D/3642/A/2/2H.

33. Farwell, p.421.

34. Much of the following is taken from selected letters in D/1700/10/1/- between 1907 and 1910.

35. D/640/18/4, 26 October 1903.

36. It had been Saunders-Knox-Gore, Commanding Officer of the Donegals, who exhorted Fred to utilise the Arnold-Forster connection soon after the latter had become Secretary of State for War in 1903: D/1700/5/13/8, 3 December 1903.

37. The other family farm on Islandmagee, Milliken's Farm, which was inherited by Fred's brother was probably equally spartan. The stock of the farm was valued in 1907 at £45 at the time of James Wright Crawford's death, which was less than the sum owed (£50) to Sir William Whitla for "professional attendance" – see the Will of James Wright Crawford. Fred's family had known Stewart socially since their earlier days in the Donegal Militia: D/1700/5/11/3, 27 June 1901.

38. D/1700/10/1/399-400, 2 May 1908 and –/656, 5 June 1909. Between about 1907 and 1914 Fred lived at St Claire at Marlborough Park off Belfast's Malone Road.

39. D/1700/5/13/11, Katharine Pottinger to Fred from 17 Mountjoy Square, Dublin, 16 November 1905.

40. D/1700/3/8, 23 May 1890.

41. D/1700/3/2, 4 March 1901.

42. D/1700/3/2, 20 June 1901.

Pièce de Résistance

∞

Fred Crawford always fought shy of publicity and self-promotion; even after the fame which descended upon him in the years following the gun-running episode, he always emphasised that he could not have achieved anything without the assistance of others.[1] During the principal Unionist demonstrations in the years before the First World War, however, he was usually listed in the local press amongst those "on or near the platform".[2] One commentator was to describe him as "one of those exotics who seem to flash across the Edwardian stage as if it were a music-hall",[3] and Fred briefly acknowledged that he probably cut a picaresque figure when he referred to himself at sea in April 1914 as 'The Pirate'.[4]

Nevertheless, this was an image which embarrassed him and made him uneasy. For all that he became well-acquainted with the political, social and commercial élite of Ulster, and was on first name terms with members of the aristocracy, the man from Cloreen preferred an unheralded entrance. It was typical of him that, when invited to lunch by the Marchioness of Dufferin and Ava on 4th February 1911, he indicated that he would arrive without ostentation – catching the train to Helen's Bay and then cycling over to Clandeboye.[5] No-one would have been more incredulous than Fred Crawford if he had been informed, as he had stepped off the train in Belfast at the end of his visit to Australia at the close of 1892, that just over twenty years later he would have become one of the most celebrated and notorious figures in the north of Ireland.

One admirer commented extravagantly in July 1914 that "There are numbers of Irishmen who have done great deeds, but none will stand out more prominently in History than the man who made it possible for Ulster to resist ... and that man was Crawford".[6] Towards the end of that same year, Lilian Spender – the wife of the English 'blow-in' who helped Fred to organise the landing of the guns at Larne – showed herself a little more possessive, as she confided in her diary that she had had Fred's wife and eldest daughter, Naomi, to tea: "I would much rather have had the gun-runner himself, but he is now busy commanding the Army Service Corps here".[7]

Fred was to manifest a natural aptitude for the art of gun-running, and a conviction for its necessity, but the tensions which it created within and between the personal, professional and political arenas of his life should not be underestimated. There is no evidence that James Wright Crawford objected to his son's regular absence from the Works for the purpose of political campaigning during the 1890s and Fred allowed himself to be profoundly seduced by Unionist and imperialist philosophy at the turn of the century. The later testimony of Fred's brother reflects the family's pride in what he achieved: "I have always been proud of you, lad", boasted Alexander in July 1914, "but today I feel prouder of being your brother than I would have done if I were a brother to the King. I only wish our father, who has gone, could know what you have done and, if such a thing were possible, he would be proud that ever he was your father ...".[8]

Fred's own satisfaction at what he had achieved was echoed in his tolerance of the humour of his children. As the Twelfth parade passed Cloreen in 1914, he wrote to his fellow gun-runner, Captain Andrew Agnew: "The 'Boys' are just passing my house here as I write ... My eldest girl [Naomi] is full of mischief and she made a black banner and put a skull and crossbones upon it and under, in large letters, *Hello Fanny*. They placed this over our gate and Bob Wallace (the Colonel) took off his hat to it. He was sitting beside the Chief [Sir Edward Carson]. When he saw me he shook me by the hand as the carriage passed".[9]

Dilemma

Nevertheless, these proved to be very difficult years for the starch-manufacturer. He never managed to reverse the downward spiral of the family business and this only served to compound the uncertainty of providing for a wife and five children – born between the end of 1896 and March 1908 – as he explained to his brother at the close of 1908.[10] He was to admit much the same to James Craig only a few years later (c.1912), when he began to dedicate more time to the importation of arms. He indicated that:

> I have an old manager in my business who is too old to be left alone without my advice, and another youngster just come in who knows nothing about the business. I am not in a fit state to look after my interests with all this anxiety and absence from my business to look after these rifles and ammunition, and I must put more time and thought into it, as I find it is not prospering.

Rather plaintively, Fred continued: "I have five children and an aged mother to look after, and the business is all that stands between me and the Workhouse. You must let me off this work [i.e. importing guns] … I can't do it, James; my business, through neglect, is leaving me and I am making nothing". He suggested that the Ulster Unionist Council (UUC) should pay someone else "£1200 or £1500 per annum" to undertake the smuggling.

Craig – who was a stockbroker, and who had also inherited £100,000 from his father's whiskey distilling trade in 1900 [11] – believed, however, that there was no better man for the job than Fred and preyed upon the latter's ambivalence and irresolution. He admitted that "I know plenty who would undertake it at this salary, but no-one fit to carry it through", and the weapons' *aficionado* could offer no suitable alternatives. He rationalised the dilemma by reflecting that: "if Home Rule comes, we Protestants in Ulster will be gradually squeezed out, and in any case my business would go then", so he determined that he had to assume the responsibility. Whatever nobility may be ascribed to this, his business and family ultimately paid the price. Fred was far too ready to accept praise from Craig and Carson as full payment for his enterprise, and he noted in passing, almost with indifference:

"Needless to say I would not accept a penny of payment for anything I did, even though my business went to the wall".[12]

The late 19th century politicisation of Ulster was, in the language of those to whom it turned for hardware and ordnance, *zugzwang*: it was a development that Unionists felt was forced upon them, yet brought them no material advantage – only an obligation to seek survival. Fred had returned from Australia too late in the year to witness the substantial Ulster Unionist Convention on 17th June 1892, which had been held well within earshot of Chlorine, which emphatically rejected the notion of Home Rule. He later recalled that: "I threw myself heart and soul into the movement … Home Rule would sooner or later mean complete severance from the British Empire, and I was determined to do all in my power to prevent this, even by force if need be".[13]

The mainspring for this recalcitrance on the part of Ulster was commercial. If a man had a mind to do so at that time, he could, well within an hour, starting out from Alexander Crawford & Son, visit the largest shipyards, rope works, linen manufacturers and tobacco factory, and one of the largest engineering enterprises, in the world. The protection of such interests was one of the reasons why men such as Edward Harland, Gustav Wolff and George Clark entered politics. North and East Belfast were the most heavily industrialised parts of Ireland, and there prevailed the fear that this hard-won prosperity would be diluted, even dismantled, by a Dublin-based government. As Fred expressed it, less subtly: as the only prosperous province "we were to be bled and robbed of our hardly earned money to pay for Southern and Dublin lazy civil servants' fat emoluments for helping the Irish Home Rule Government to misgovern Ireland".

The sentiment was encapsulated by the 6th Marquess of Londonderry, who addressed the thousands gathered for the inauguration of the Willowfield Drill Hall on the evening of 16th May 1913 – which many may have regarded as a political, as well as an ecclesiastical, Ember Day. The aristocrat, indifferent to syntax, underscored the political justification for their actions: "This most important and most dangerous measure must, if carried, disintegrate the Empire"; and also the economic imperative for their resistance: "[it] must also bring poverty and misery to Ireland at the present moment enjoying the greatest prosperity it has ever known since the days of the Union".[14]

For all his unequivocal political commitment, as he sat "on or near the platform", absorbing the delirium of that Friday evening, one suspects that such a generalisation – particularly from an individual who had no experience of trade – would have been infuriatingly inappropriate to someone in Fred's circumstances, having suffered over five years of commercial hardship since he had inherited Alexander Crawford & Son. As will be seen below, his letters to his brother outline the virtually insoluble problems of the company. Whilst he rationalised that "Home Rule is upsetting everything", he must have recognised that the decline at Wilson Street Works was more entrenched and complex.

Helen Wilson

The one positive consequence of his political engagement was his personal engagement. The starch-manufacturer cum political campaigner appears to have first encountered his future wife when he was induced by the Earl of Ranfurly to canvass for the Conservative & Unionist candidate in the by-election at Brigg in Lincolnshire in 1894, or possibly during the General Election campaign of the following year.

Helen – whom Fred always called Nellie – Wilson was the second daughter of Robert Wilson of Acre House, Normanby-le-Wold in Lincolnshire, and was fifteen years the Ulsterman's junior! Her family appears to have been financially comfortable, as she was educated at the Francis Holland School in London and also acquired two years of further education in Germany. Fred's infatuation with the girl from Lincolnshire is apparent in a love-lorn letter, punctuated by some of the most charmless and unromantic imagery he could have conjured:

> *Every time I think of you my heart flops up and down like a churndasher. Sensations of unutterable joy caper over it like Spanish needles through a pair of tow-linen trousers … Visions of ecstatic rapture thicker than the hairs of a blacking brush … visit me in my slumbers … your image stands before me, and I reach out and grasp it like a pointer snapping at a blue-bottle fly. When I first beheld your angelic perfections I was bewildered and my brain whirled like a bumble-bee under a glass tumbler … Away from you I am as melancholy*

as a sick rat. Sometimes I hear the bugs of despondency buzzing in my ears, and feel the cold lizards of despair crawling down my back … If you cannot reciprocate my thrilling passion I will pine away like a poisoned bed bug …

In July 1895, at which time Helen was living in London, at the end of a lengthy political campaign trail in northern England, he wrote to her from Darlington. About a week later, by then in the Isle of Wight, Fred said that he was leaving to watch a military review in Aldershot, but indicated that he wished to visit her in London, and requested directions to her residence in West Kensington. At this stage he confided: "I do not forget your views on bi-metalism, and would like to hear them again", which may well be their personal code for wedding rings.

Later in August, whilst back in Belfast, he revealed that he would probably be visiting the company's agent in Nottingham, and he would run down to London to see her: "I often wish I could have fallen in love with someone in my town; being separated makes one so impatient … Till then I feel in love with all of a sweet, dear girl called Nellie Wilson".

They were married at St Andrew's Parish Church, West Kensington, on 20th February 1896.[15] It is impossible to know how many, if any, of his Belfast family and acquaintances attended the wedding, but Fred retained the list of wedding gifts which they were given, which included a Crown Staffordshire coffee set from future co-conspirator, Sam Cunningham and his wife, and six silver teaspoons from the long-serving employee at Alexander Crawford & Son, Ernest Knowles. One family doctor, Col. A.B. Mitchell of Mornington in Derryvolgie Avenue (who worked as a surgeon at the Royal Victoria Hospital) presented the couple with a travelling clock and case; a second, Sir William Whitla, who had made huge sums from the sale of his medical text-books, managed to struggle to a £5 cheque.[16] Both of the medical acquaintances were to receive substantial sums over the years for medical treatment to many members of the Crawford family.

Honeymoon

Three days before the wedding, at a cost of 8s 6d, the eager groom obtained a passport by which the Ottoman authorities were requested and required "to allow Frederick Hugh Crawford (British subject) travelling the Continent, in Asia and Africa, accompanied by his wife, to pass freely without let or hindrance, and to afford every assistance and protection of which he may stand in need".[17]

Carrying gold and silver, as well as notes of the realm – and two Baedecker guides – their first night of a ten-week honeymoon was spent in Paris. The journey does not always seem to have gone to plan, as many years later Fred noted in correspondence that: "Many a night on our wedding trip we had to put up with a single bed".[18] They then travelled via Marseilles to northern Italy, and down through Turin, Genoa and Florence before arriving in Rome. On Thursday 26th February he set aside any incubating Unionist fears of, or hostility towards, Catholicism, and paid 5 shillings for a tour of the Vatican.

From Naples they crossed the peninsula to Brindisi and followed the route he had last taken six years previously across the Mediterranean to Egypt. Arriving in Cairo on 5th March, they visited the Pyramids, before Fred paid out an astonishing £32 for a Nile cruise, on which they paid their respects to the ruins and sights of Luxor and Aswan (where he stumped up another £10 for entrance tickets). Later in March they retraced their steps to Cairo, where they visited the museum at Giza and Fred's favourite ostrich farm which had been part of his itinerary six years earlier.

The first fortnight of April was spent in the Holy land, with Easter Day passed in Bethlehem. By 19th April they had returned to Brindisi and travelled (probably by train) to Venice, where he appears to have chartered a gondola to their hotel. Their one full day in La Serenissima (Tuesday 21st April) encompassed a second gondola ride, a climb to the viewing tower of the campanile in St Mark's Square, a tour of the Doge's Palace and, rather bizarrely, the purchase of four small tortoises for 1s 6d. One week later, via Milan and Lucerne, they had returned to Paris.

Domestic reality

Fred's personal ledger for the honeymoon totalled the trip at £220–19s effectively a year's salary. It was no doubt a romantic and enchanting interlude for a young woman who may not have yet been out of her teens but, despite a personal account at the Bank Buildings department store,[20] the realities of life in Belfast – remote from all her family – must have proved unremittingly fractious and unfamiliar. She gave birth to five children over the next twelve years and her husband cannot have been at home as much as she may have wished. She was left with two very young children for fifteen months when Fred volunteered for service in South Africa and, on his return, he continued to pursue his military pastimes. Her husband became increasingly politically engaged, and both her parents-in-law were growing more frail, and the responsibilities of a struggling business devolved increasingly – and, after 1906, entirely – upon Fred.

In an age when infant – and even early adult – mortality was not uncommon, the fact that all the offspring of Fred and Helen Crawford survived to adulthood was an achievement. They were heir to all the prevalent diseases and afflictions of the period. Stuart almost died of influenza in 1907; the entire family was quarantined for five months in the summer of 1908 by an outbreak of mumps, and all the children endured whooping cough during the summer of 1910.

With regard to family illness, Fred was a chip off the old block, ever worrying about his children's health. In May 1908 he reported that Doreen "is a frail wee soul … [and] since she has had scarlatina she has been liable to all that is going around". During the previous year, when one of his daughters was caught biting her nails, he could not resist parental solicitude; he recommended the wearing of gloves, but his favoured solution was recourse to the traditional Crawford panacea: "You should ask Jesus to help you give up this habit. If you ask Him, He will help you to do it".

Naomi may well have been despatched to England partly to make it easier at home to deal with the final weeks of her grandfather's life. James W. had been failing for two years as a consequence of cerebral softening. His entire system had been affected since April 1907 by bulbar paralysis, and in October of that year he suffered shock as the result of a fall, from which he did not recover. He passed away on 26th October 1907, aged 75[21] – owing his neighbour, Sir William Whitla, £50 for medical attendance.

His wife, Madge, proved more resilient, despite being eight years older than her husband. In late 1906 she had felt so unwell that she did not leave her room for over two months and, in the weeks following her husband's death, she felt "very poorly". It was decided that she should continue to live at Chlorine, as "she would not be happy anywhere else", but Fred's comment to his brother at this time – "In case she passes away, I suppose you would like the house let furnished"[22] – was an indication of her fragility. In spite of this, she survived to hear of her younger son's gun-running escapade, dying on 18th January 1915 from senile decay and, ultimately, heart failure (with her elder grandson, Stuart, present). Madge Crawford was 91 years of age, and Fred was to emulate this longevity.

Several factors coincided to compound Fred's malaise over the months at the end of 1907 and in early 1908. He summarised this in a letter to Alexander in Australia on 19th March 1908: "… I have not been very fit this winter. Father's death was a great shock to me, and the business worry seems to have pulled me down very much. I had influenza before Christmas, and have not felt up to the mark ever since". Other contemporary correspondence reveals that all the family had suffered from influenza – Doreen on three occasions – and this added to concern over Helen Crawford, who was expecting their fifth child, named Adair, who arrived on 6th March 1908.[23]

Business Woes

Fred stated the obvious: that the arrival of another child "does not tend to keep down expenses" – a minor echo of his company's accelerating insolvency. Fred was fond of Old Testament imagery – he was to equate the situation in Belfast in 1920 to that in Jerusalem at the time of Nehemiah[24] – and one suspects that in 1908 he felt that his predicament resembled that of the Canaanites trying to obtain grain in the land of Egypt; in any case, as he wrote to his Alexander, following the release of probate of their father's will, he adopted the tone of the jeremiad: "Besides Father leaving me heavily in debt … wheat is now up to £9–5s a ton this season: this has slumped any prospective profit, and I expect a serious loss this season in business". Fred accentuated the inability of the Crawford dynasty to make money by revealing that they had also launched a subsidiary business in 1906: "The agent we had to try and open a laundry business was also a failure, expenses being much larger than returns"!

As has been seen in a previous chapter, the company accounts of Alexander Crawford & Son did not make for reassuring reading in the 20th century. The indications are that James W. brooked little interference in his management – poor or otherwise – of the family firm until he began to fail around 1905. Fred was to indicate that by late 1906 his father was "past all business, and the whole responsibility is now on my shoulders". The death of his father enabled him to take stock of the financial reality that faced the company, and he informed his brother in January 1908 that: "I knew poor old father was spending a lot of money a year or two before he died, but I had no idea I should be left so straightened (sic) as I am".

Fred continued the commercial struggle because others – family and employees – were dependent upon him, but 1909 proved to be "the worst year I ever knew in business". By mid-1911 the antiquated factory machinery required greater maintenance and expense and he notified Alexander that "business is just about three-eighths of what it was in your time".

Political Awakening

In this same letter, the businessman ascribed some of the difficulties in trading to the intensification of the Home Rule issue which, he claimed, "was upsetting everything". Fred may not have been a successful businessman, but neither was he naïve. At the very same time (May 1911) he replied to a correspondent who suggested that the best way to recover the West Belfast parliamentary constituency was to build more houses to accommodate sympathetic voters. Fred pointed out, realistically, that no-one in his right mind would invest in property whilst Home Rule was causing so much uncertainty and instability.

It was this determination to resist at all costs the establishment of a Dublin-based government that most impressed the English soldier – Wilfrid Bliss Spender – who was to play a significant role in the Ulster resistance to Home Rule. He observed that members of the aristocracy, such as the Duke of Abercorn and the Marquis of Londonderry, could face gaol and escheat for their principles; and that the whole of the Belfast business community was committed, despite the fact that political uncertainty and social disorder were a grave disadvantage to trading conditions.[25]

Fred Crawford was undeniably one of those most committed to placing political principle before commercial profit and it was always likely that – as he was on 30th January 1911 – he would be "unanimously co-opted a member of the Ulster Unionist Council".[26] By that time, Fred's political engagement stretched back for the best part of a score of years and one commentator has pointed out that, as a businessman, "Crawford had a sure sense of the patriotic occasion, and in a quite incredible way turned up at Chamber [of Commerce and Industry] meetings only when issues of patriotism, loyalty and politics were in the air".[27]

Work and travel meant that the first Home Rule controversy (1885-1886) had little impact upon Fred. Half a dozen years later he could not have proved more enthusiastic: "I returned home from Australia in 1892 and found Ulster in a fever of political agitation over the proposed [second] Home Rule Bill ... The political atmosphere was so charged ... that I threw myself heart and soul into the movement".[28]

Fred was always content to be servant to, rather than master of, Ulster politics; he had no aspirations to become a politician, once later ignoring a suggestion that he should enter politics. The voluminous Crawford archive does not contain any unambiguous political expression of adherence on the part of Fred's father, but the fact that he permitted his son extensive leave of absence from the company for political canvassing is a clear indication of his own sympathies. Father and son were, no doubt, confirmed in their opinions by the consistent anti-Home Rule agenda of the Methodist Church in Ireland.[29]

It was probably not a parallel which occurred to Fred – on the contrary, it was one from which his personal piety and insecurities would have shied away – but, like Jesus, as a young man in his early 30s, he finally identified the specific path chosen for him by God. In Fred's case, this was the preservation of Ulster's rightful place amongst the elect of the British Empire which – as he indicated in his Boer War diary – he believed was the aegis created by God to bring fairness, freedom and justice to all people. This was the dominant motif reiterated by all leading Unionists over the next thirty years; for instance, in 1922, Ronald McNeill (later Lord Cushendun) equated " a regime of Nationalist and Ultramontane domination" with the loss of freedom.[30]

Ulsterman

Within a few days of his return from Australia at the end of November 1892, Fred opened a devotional diary, the focus being his despair at a relapse into sin: "God help me to withstand the evil one. I am so weak. Oh God, I want to live for Thee. Help me to start afresh".[31] There are indications that, during the long, lonely voyage home from visiting his brother, he had reflected upon the exhortations contained in Thomas à Kempis's *The Imitation of Christ*, which he had borrowed from a fellow passenger on the outward journey, which had impressed him. A recurrent theme of this work is the control of one's desires, the inner struggle of the individual to withstand the relentless temptations provoked by an unsleeping Devil.

Fred's own weakness in the face of temptation is voiced repeatedly in echoes from the 15th century work [Book I, chapter 22]: "How great is the frailty of Man … Today you confess your sins; tomorrow you again commit the very sins you have confessed … we can easily lose by carelessness that which, by God's grace and our own efforts, we had hardly won". At the start of 1893 Fred lamented, in a clear personal reference: "I think the most exquisite torture is remorse, when a person finds the resolution of perhaps years' standing suddenly collapse … and he finds himself just where he was three to five years ago. The wakening to this fact must be as near a foretaste of Hell as can be got in this world … God have mercy upon one, a sinner".

James Wright Crawford's own fear of mortality was also articulated by the German monk [Book I, chapter 23]: "Each morning remember that you may not live until evening, and in the evening do not presume to promise yourself another day"; and in the opening days of 1893 Fred prayed: "Oh God, let me live so that I can be of some use", and restated this at the close of the year: "May I live for something worth living for". In the same entry in the diary he admitted that "ever since childhood, Thou, Oh Christ, hast guided and guarded me is a special way". He believed that this had been incontrovertibly demonstrated one Friday in September 1893 when he had prepared to descend the company's new well by a special seat and discovered as he "swung out over the shaft 120 feet deep [that] I found I was sitting over eternity, and I may as well say Hell", suspended only by a few strands of fine twine. He believed that God had shown "His goodness in saving my life today" [32] – and one suspects that on the morning of 25th April 1914 he knew what had been God's purpose for him and that he believed that he had fulfilled his destiny.

Nevertheless, not all of Thomas à Kempis's advice proved congenial to Fred. The monk recommended [Book III, chap.36]: "do not engage in bitter controversies", but this was taking self-denial a stage too far for the Ulsterman. In 1893 he joined the Ulster Loyalist Union, forming a life-long friendship with its President, the Earl of Ranfurly, whom he later described as "my political father".[33]

Fred attended meetings at Northland House in Dungannon (Ranfurly's family home) during that year, primarily to deal with matters attendant upon Gladstone's introduction of a second Home Rule Bill (which did pass through the Commons). The aristocrat was evidently taken with the commitment and enthusiasm of his new recruit, although he did baulk at Fred's alleged plan to kidnap the Prime Minister in Brighton – whence he travelled almost every weekend – and to transport him to a remote Pacific island until he reversed his policy.[34] If this legend were true, one suspects that it was the projected cost of £10,000, rather than the principle, to which Ranfurly objected.

The tale has been repeated by historians and even by *The Irish Times* in its obituary upon Fred's death. There is, however, no reference to such a plot amongst the voluminous Crawford archive and it first seems to have seen the light of day in Ian Colvin's 1934 biography of Lord Carson.[35] Even twenty years after the event, Fred was still reluctant to engage in publicity about the gun-running episode and his co-operation with Colvin was probably patchy, as the latter seems to have readily resorted to imagination and invention. In 1893 even Fred is unlikely to have wanted to spend £10,000 on such a singular project; twenty years later this sum would have purchased several thousand rifles. Why, as Colvin states, Fred would have suggested supplying "an axe for felling palms" to a near 84-year-old is also unclear. Other details in the biography indicate that Colvin never actually met Fred and that his grasp of factual material was tenuous.[36]

Fred Crawford adopted an unequivocal militaristic opposition to Home Rule from the outset: "From the very first, I came to the conclusion that our resistance, to be successful, must eventually come to armed resistance ... I knew that mere words were useless ... I was determined to do all in my power ... even by force if need be". The most recent study of the Ulster Volunteer Force (UVF), has shown that "the drilling and arming of 1910-14 was built on earlier precedents" during the first and second Home Rule controversies[37] – and much of this was the result of the activities of the man from Chlorine. He established what was ostensibly a gymnasium club, but later admitted that "instead of gymnastics we drilled in the different halls" and on Lord Ranfurly's estate from where "we used to march in company formation to the square in the town [Dungannon] where we were dismissed in regular military style". It was probably such activities which persuaded Fred to enlist within the ranks of the more formal military regime of the Mid-Antrim Artillery early in 1894.

The ardent Unionist later recorded that: "My first move was to get in touch with a man named St. Aubin, a gun merchant in London". The latter was offering German Mauser repeating rifles for sale, delivered to Belfast for 18 shillings each. Fred admitted that his modest salary only enabled him to purchase a sample, and that he imported this "with some difficulty". He then began to bring in further weapons "disguised as cart axles", all of which proved invaluable creative practice for the more substantial deliveries he was to arrange early in the next century.

Fred also discovered around 1913 that the response to the employment and bearing of arms reflected the nervous attitudes he experienced twenty years earlier, which he treated with both bemusement and contempt. He records that even the Orange Order "looked at me askance" when he offered them rifles and that James Musgrave – who, with his brothers, established the foundry in East Belfast – was rendered speechless at Windsor when he offered a sum of money for a prize and Fred countered that it would be more useful if this were directed at the purchase of rifles! It may be surmised that there was some vengeful humour in Fred's original suggestion that the bulk order of UVF rifles be landed in Belfast via the Musgrave Channel, which was named after Sir James![38]

Ignoring the indifference of the older generation, Fred started a secret society which he called Young Ulster. The membership requirement was the ownership of one of three types of gun – a Martini rifle, a USA cavalry Winchester rifle, or a .455 revolver [39] – plus one hundred rounds of ammunition. He established several rifle clubs, including a 600-yard range on the Ranfurly demesne. So popular did these become that eventually the authorities at Dublin Castle banned the unauthorised importation of Martini ammunition, as it became evident that it could not all be used legitimately.

Never discouraged, Fred resorted to manufacturing his own ammunition in the pigeon loft above the stables at Chlorine where his father housed his ponies and phaeton. "I supplied a number of caretakers of halls and sextons of churches with a lead-melting ladle and a bullet mould", he later recalled, and he employed his father's transport to travel round each week to gather bullets. He claimed that the birds watched himself and five co-conspirators fill six hundred cartridges each night on the Malone Road. Ranfurly made a visit one night, and was sufficiently impressed to stay until 1.30am.[40]

As a resistance fighter, Fred was never one to underestimate the enemy and took it very seriously when he was warned, on 16th January 1894, that John Morley, the Chief Secretary for Ireland, had issued warrants for the arrest of himself and Ranfurly, whom he (Morley) had "marked down as the two most dangerous men in Ulster". Although the warrants were never executed, Fred had all incriminating evidence removed from the family stables within the space of two hours.

Political Campaigner

Evidently taken by the passionate and varied talents of his new armourer, in late 1893 the Earl recruited Fred for more prosaic political purposes – electioneering. In November Fred travelled to Berwick-on-Tweed – the constituency of the Liberal pro-Home Ruler, Edward Grey. He spoke in ten communities which, well over a century later, are still small villages and one can only assume that Ranfurly was testing Fred's promotional skills. Afterwards he spoke in Kentish Town (London) and spent the weekend at the aristocrat's home in Woking, "his Lordship being even nicer in his own home than out of it". It is quite likely that Ranfurly – who was Hon. Colonel of the Regiment – sponsored Fred's application to the Mid-Ulster Artillery as reciprocation; the would-be soldier later recalled the Earl's "thoughtful kindness to me ... how he gave me free use of the library of Northland House and its grounds, and in every way possible he tried to show the Officers' Mess that I was a friend of his, which was a great advantage to me".

In November 1894 Fred was despatched to canvass in the by-election at Brigg. He held meetings every evening for a fortnight and contributed to the success of the Conservative candidate, who won by a mere 77 votes – although this victory was reversed at the General Election held the following year. Fred was asked in February 1895 to take charge of an electoral division in England or Scotland during that latter campaign. He demurred because of his lack of experience, but clearly his integrity had been recognised: "I can trust you, and the men with enough experience I cannot trust", explained Ranfurly. Fred agreed on condition that he was not engaged, at that time, in military training.

He was appointed 'Captain' of the Irish Unionist speakers and workers for the Northern Division [41], bounded by Bradford and Berwick, and Newcastle and Whitehaven. Whilst probably distracted by his encounter with Helen Wilson, he appears to have worked exceptionally hard throughout the campaign. He notified Nellie that "we, on the whole, have been pretty successful in the North", and the Irish Unionist Committee was sufficiently grateful for "his exertions and successful management" to conclude that his "skilful direction of the forces at his disposal largely contributed to the triumphal return of the Unionist Party".[42]

His obvious talents as a political operative resulted in him being appointed, between 1895 and 1897, as Hon Secretary of the West Belfast Registration Association. He was enough of a realist to recognise the problems attached to the retention of this constituency, and to acknowledge the capable machiavellianism of the Nationalist endeavours to capture it: "It … required the Unionists to have a majority of 600 on the Register to hold their own against the clever and unscrupulous tactics of the Home Rulers. At one election the Nationalists voted all their dead men and, at another, when the Unionists were on their guard against a repetition, the Nationalists voted the Unionists' dead men".

The MP for the constituency between 1892 and 1906 was Arnold-Forster, with whom – despite the latter being a Liberal Unionist – Fred developed an amiable working relationship, which was acknowledged when the Member notified his resignation: "Among the pleasantest recollections I shall carry away", he penned in March 1904 to Fred, "will be that of your unfailing friendship, and of your courage in action and your excellent good sense in council". Fred remained Hon. Secretary of the West Belfast Committee until 1906 when, although still anxious to "buckle on the old armour" for Unionism, he resigned as a consequence of his father's ill-health and his own increasing responsibility in Alexander Crawford & Son. In 1907, after the loss of the seat to the Nationalist, Joe Devlin, he expressed in correspondence the opinion that the Unionists had been cheated following recent revisions of the constituency. He finally resigned as a member of the Committee at the end of 1910, believing that new blood was required if ever the seat were to be recovered.[43]

Fred, however, continued to be politically active. On 19th March 1907 he visited London as part of a Unionist delegation to visit the treacherous Arthur Balfour, leader of the Conservative Opposition.[44] This had nearly been postponed as a consequence of the death on 10th March of Sir Daniel Dixon, MP for North Belfast. Fred acknowledged that a by-election would mean "work for all", but a month later was able to express satisfaction "on the great victory we have obtained in North Belfast". The victor was (the future Sir) George Clark, of the Workman, Clark shipyard, who was a leading Unionist figure and, a few years later, was to chair the secret arms sub-committee which helped to co-ordinate Fred's gun-running escapade. Fred made it clear to one correspondent that the North Belfast election "was fought on the question of the Union, and the Union only. There were no side issues as far as Mr Clark was concerned".[45]

Ronald McNeill acknowledged that, for a few years either side of the turn of the century, the issue of Home Rule had faded into the background but, by the close of 1906, the starch manufacturer was growing increasingly concerned. In 1904 he had rocked the becalmed boat by publicly asserting in the Ulster Hall that "Home Rule is not dead and is only in a state of suspended animation … You people of Ulster must not be lulled into a false sense of security".[46]

On 14 December 1906 Fred wrote outlining his alienation towards Balfour, the erstwhile Conservative Prime Minister, who had resigned at the end of 1905, allowing the Liberals to accede to power with a large majority: "At one time all Unionists in the north of Ireland trusted Mr Balfour completely", recalled Fred. "When he allowed out the Dynamitards, the Orange working man was suspicious; when he started his Catholic university campaign, all the Unionists here distrusted him, and when he was a party to the appointment of Sir Antony MacDonnell [as Permanent Under-Secretary for Ireland, in 1901] every true Unionist here thought him a traitor", and – adding as much insult as he could muster – "what is more, they still think worse of him than they did of Gladstone".[47]

In the same letter Fred blamed the appointment of MacDonnell for the increasing defection of the working class from the Unionist cause: "The old Unionist enthusiasm is dead among the masses here". They had transferred their allegiance to "the labour and socialist programme" and, two years later, Fred was still touting the same interpretation: "There is a lot of apathy in the north since Balfour appointed Sir Antony MacDonnell. We find it hard to get the working man to realise that Home Rule is once again a living issue".

The Belfast dock strike in the middle of 1907 revealed Fred as rather out of tune with social movements of the early 20th century, and his antipathy towards socialism continued at least into the early 1920s.[48] The dockers, eventually led by the fearsome Jim Larkin from Liverpool, sought improved working conditions and their dispute led to them being locked out of their workplace on 9th May by their employers. The latter feared not so much the dockers' action, but the revolutionary syndicalism they suspected it represented. MacDonnell actually believed that the employers were as much to blame for the rising tension over the next few weeks, but the Under-Secretary and his master, Augustine Birrell (Chief Secretary for Ireland), were obliged to make a more emphatic and punitive response when the police in Belfast showed signs of mutiny in late July. Eventually, the Nationalist Joe Devlin became involved against his better judgement – he was not enamoured of Larkin – and a riot followed in the Lower Falls on 11th August, which left Birrell with no alternative.[49]

Birrell had never impressed Fred from the time of his appointment at the end of 1906: "he stated … he was the right man to take over the duties of Chief Secretary for Ireland because he was unprejudiced. He had never been in Ireland in his life and he knew nothing of her politics. He also stated Ireland had not been so prosperous or contented for 300 years as she then was", Fred wrote in 1920. "What a testimony to the utter incompetence of the man his ten years of misrule showed … One will have to go back very far in history to find an equal in any statesman for crass stupid misrule".[50]

On 20th August 1907, in a letter to Major Doyne, a colleague in the Donegal Artillery in Letterkenny, Fred rather myopically interpreted recent events as "a political move on the part of a section of the Nationalists to discredit Belfast, connived at by Birrell …It would have done very well for Birrell if the police had not mutinied … He was very glad to have the whole affair patched up as quickly as possible". Fred expressed relief to Doyne that the rioting had occurred in the Catholic part of the city, which "branded the whole thing as a Nationalist movement". He also suggested that Larkin may well have been the grandson of one of the Manchester Martyrs – Irish Nationalists executed in 1867 – but this was not the case.

Fred indicated that he had been personally threatened at this time "because of the political work I had done in West Belfast", but he interpreted the strike as "a political plot to ruin Belfast trade". He claimed that Nationalists were envious of the prosperity of Protestant Ulster, and "want to ruin us, and this is one move in that direction". He was, however, clearly unsettled that "a lot of Protestants" – that is, the working classes – had been "duped".

Home Rule

By 1910 the menace of Home Rule was squarely back on the Ulster agenda. Alarm bells had been rung by one sentence in a speech by Asquith, the Liberal Prime Minister, on 10th December 1909 that: "the Irish problem could only be solved by a policy which, whilst explicitly safeguarding the supreme authority of the Imperial Parliament, would set up self-government in Ireland in regard to Irish affairs".[51] The concern was exacerbated by the two General Elections at the start and close of 1910, which left the balance of power in the hands of John Redmond's Irish Nationalists. With the Liberals prepared to accommodate the latter and the prospect of the Parliament Act (passed in 1911) effectively eradicating the usual House of Lords rejection of any Home Rule Bill, the political landscape suddenly looked very bleak for Ulster Unionism: "the last constitutional bulwark against Home Rule was bound to go".[52]

The Ulster Unionist Council had been established early in 1905.[53] Since its inception Fred had responded to occasional invitations from Dawson Bates, its Hon Secretary, to attend meetings. In 1911 the membership was augmented to 370 and, on 30th January 1911, Fred was co-opted "unanimously" to the body.[54] In February of the previous year they had exhorted Sir Edward Carson to accept the leadership of the parliamentary party. Carson was not readily moulded to party politics; he was too eclectic in his opinions to suffer a party Whip. The foundation of his political philosophy was "the sanctity of the Union of Britain and Ireland" and he, as much as any Unionist politician, most vociferously articulated their integral role in the British Empire.[55]

Fred was to form a very close relationship with the man he always referred to as The Leader. In the early 1920s the Ulsterman regarded the Dubliner as "the guiding spirit and leader of the Ulster Unionists. Without his leadership, Ulster could not have held out as she did". Carson reciprocated the sentiments, telling Fred, in all sincerity, that "I have no more valued friend than yourself".[56]

Carson made it clear from the outset – as he wrote to James Craig – that, in return for his leadership, he wanted "to satisfy myself that the people [of Ulster] really mean to resist. I am not for a game of bluff and, unless men are prepared to make great sacrifices which they clearly understand, the talk of resistance is no use".[57] Fred Crawford was the one who most unambiguously appreciated this. After the General Election of January 1910 he resigned from the West Belfast Unionist Association, and by the end of the year – as he informed one correspondent – was "engaged in other political work which will take up all my spare time".[58]

CRAIGAVON

In an attempt to reassure Carson of the commitment of Ulster, a massive demonstration was organised at Craig's home, Craigavon, off Circular Road in East Belfast, on Saturday 23rd September 1911. Fred attended all UUC meetings of the Demonstration sub-committee.[59] The occasion probably exceeded expectations. The crowd was variously estimated at between 50,000 and 100,000, and the *Belfast News Letter* encapsulated its character: "It was in very truth a man's meeting – a great assembly of the manhood of Ulster, gathered together for a solemn purpose, and the spirit of earnestness manifested was in keeping with the seriousness of the occasion".

In the eyes of the UUC the tangible passion of the assembly had to be sublimated; solemnity, decorum and discipline were regarded as paramount. In common with Carson and Craig (and others), Fred – both before and after the First World War – always gave a high priority to the need for Ulstermen to demonstrate personal restraint in order to manifest the worthiness and justice of the cause. Consequently the parades from Donegall Square to Craigavon were not to be spontaneous or unregulated, but organised through the Orange Order and the Unionist Clubs, two of which (West Belfast and Smithfield) Fred hosted at his Wilson Street Works.[60] The press reported that, despite the parade taking two hours to pass any point, "excellent order was maintained throughout". It had been raining in the morning, but divine favour was displayed – and it may be that the journalist's choice of noun was deliberate – as "the sun gained the ascendancy".

Fred did not march on this occasion; he was one of those "on or near the platform", and had accepted an invitation to lunch at Craigavon with Sir Edward. The Craig's menu offered a varied selection,[61] although someone may have thought it ill-advised to include 'chaudfroid of pigeon'; blowing hot and cold was precisely what Carson did not want and, in any case, there was a reasonable chance that the pigeon was actually rook, prolifically available, and shot less than a mile away on the Belmont estate of Campbell College.

One speaker articulated the Unionist spirit, asking all Loyalists across the Channel to "aid Ulster in its determination to remain as at present under the Imperial parliament, an integral part of the great British Empire". Fred will have heartily applauded such sentiments but, being on the platform, he may have been one of the few who could actually hear what was being said, at what was described as the biggest open-air demonstration ever witnessed in Ulster.

Carson uttered words that have entered Ulster lore, offering to "enter into a compact" with Ulstermen to "defeat the most nefarious conspiracy that has ever been hatched against a free people … We must be prepared, the morning Home Rule passes, ourselves to become responsible for the government of the Protestant Province of Ulster". The occasion was effectively designed to assess whether Ulster had the stomach for such extreme action; it was probably the case that the verdict had already been determined, for the menu for the lunch named the event "The Arming of Ulster"!

Carson resided at Craigavon from 23rd to 26th September, as he was attending the crucial session of the UUC on the following Monday. He signed the Visitors' Book, appending the understatement: "An historical visit".[62] It is not without significance that Fred, who consistently avoided the limelight in all his political actions, never autographed his presence on the Circular Road.

Emboldened by the success of the demonstration, delegates of the UUC assembled on Monday at their office in Mayfair in Arthur Square and determined, in language that was an early echo of the Solemn League & Covenant one year hence, to resist Home Rule and to form a Provisional Government to run the affairs of Ulster. Fred was recommended, along with Colonel Robert H. Wallace and others, as part of a Special Committee. By the end of the year they had persuaded Belfast Corporation to rent them the Old Town Hall in Victoria Street (at a cost of £500 per annum) as a central office.

Balmoral

By October the UUC was already planning a further mammoth demonstration for Easter Tuesday, 9th April 1912 – which, by coincidence, proved to be only two days before the third Home Rule Bill was introduced to Parliament. Originally destined for Ormeau Park, Fred (on 12th January) reported that he had arranged to lease the Showgrounds at Balmoral from the North East Ulster Agricultural Association for £75 – the cost per demonstrator proving an enormous bargain.[63]

Detailed arrangements for the occasion – including the parade of at least 100,000 Ulstermen; admission of the public; co-ordination of the railways, trams and police; and the route of the procession – were made at the Old Town all on 4th March. A large flagstaff was to be erected, "and the largest possible Union Jack [to] be provided for the same". Fred was placed on the catering Committee and set the tone of the day by insisting that no intoxicants were to be sold in the grounds.

Not only was the magnitude and organisation of the event impressive, but so was the discipline. The emphasis upon respectability, by which Fred set such great store, was apparent from the outset when he and others determined that "Morning dress and silk hats had to be worn" when greeting Bonar Law at noon on Easter Monday at the Midland Railway Station. McNeill later boasted that, at Balmoral, "there was no drunkenness, no noisy buffoonery, no unseemly behaviour". The decorum and piety of the occasion was illustrated by the opening of the proceedings by the Archbishop of Armagh and the Moderator of the Presbyterian Church in Ireland.

Even Brigadier-General Count Gleichen, who had arrived at the end of July 1911 to command the British forces in Belfast declared the occasion "most impressive", although the *Belfast News Letter* revealed that the Orange Orders and Unionist Clubs had been drilling for weeks in order to attain orderliness and precision. Bonar Law, who boasted Ulster Presbyterian ancestry and who brought seventy British MPs in his wake, made an appropriate and impassioned speech asserting that "you have saved yourselves by your exertions and you will save the Empire by your example". Carson also spoke, urging the multitude to swear: "Never, under any circumstances, will we have Home Rule".[64]

Two days later the Home Rule Bill was introduced to Parliament, but Carson refused to be dismayed or disenchanted and, on 14th April, wrote to Lady Londonderry that: "The whole proceedings at Balmoral seem like a dream; it was the most thrilling experience I have had or will have". A day later he contacted Fred in similar vein: "It was the finest sight I have ever witnessed, and has been a great encouragement to me".[65] It was perhaps Bonar Law who best reflected the ultimate mood of those two days. He attended a debate on Home Rule in the Royal Albert Hall in London and told his colleagues who were returning to Belfast "to tell their friends, in no uncertain voice, that the Government last night declared war against Ulster". If those men travelled home that same night across the Irish Sea, they were more fortunate than some, as – several hundred miles away – Thomas Andrews, son of a UUC member, and many others did not survive the sea to fight for the cause.

Bonar Law became quite adept at articulating *le mot juste* to express the mood of Ulstermen. In February Winston Churchill had been run out of the province and, as if to rub salt into the wound, a large Unionist rally (said to total 40,000) was held in July at his birthplace – Blenheim Palace – where the Conservative leader foretold that: "I can imagine no length of resistance to which Ulster can go in which I should not be prepared to support them".

Ultimately others became far more implicated in keeping Ulster part of the Empire, but such a statement echoed the increasingly impetuous and impatient mood in the province. The *pièce de résistance*, literally, of the Home Rule theatricals was Ulster Day – 28th September 1912 – when a quarter of a million men [66] signed the Solemn League & Covenant to declare that: "Home Rule would be disastrous to the well-being of Ulster, as well as the whole of Ireland, subversive of our civil and religious freedom, destructive of our citzenship, and perilous to the unity of the Empire" and that they would refuse to recognise, and would resist the authority of, a Home Rule Parliament.

This was the *terminus ad quem* of the talk of resistance. Many of the opponents of Unionism, including most particularly Joe Devlin, had openly expressed the opinion that much of what was said was that nightmare of Carson – bluff. Paul Bew encapsulated the consequence of Ulster Day, however: "By such a public demonstration, the

Unionists deliberately left themselves without any room for dignified retreat. Contingency plans for the direst doomsday scenarios had to be drawn up by the local leadership".[67]

Few, if any, understood the implications better than Major Frederick Hugh Crawford, who was appointed to the Committee of twenty-six figures – which included James Craig, John Miller Andrews, George Clark and Col. Robert H. Wallace – for the organisation of Ulster Day. Fred was appointed to the Bonfire, Decoration, General Holiday and Procession sub-committee.

The day after Fred's 51st birthday, Ronald McNeill recorded in the Visitors' Book at Craigavon that there was "a quiet discussion of grave affairs".[68]

Notes

1. He also acknowledged this privately to others. He wrote to Captain Agnew, who had been on the *Fanny* with him: "I know another name ought to be bracketed with mine. You did your work like a man": D/1700/5/17/1/28, 13 July 1914.

2. That is, he was a prominent participant; for example, at the inauguration of the Willowfield Drill Hall in East Belfast, *Belfast News Letter*, 17 May 1913.

3. Richard Killeen, *A Short History of the Irish Revolution* 1912-1927, (Dublin, 2007), p.8.

4. In correspondence with Samuel Kelly and Richard Cowzer: D/1700/5/17/1/15, 17 April 1914.

5. D/1700/10/1/899, 3 February 1911. Much detail in this chapter is derived from this source – a Works' correspondence book of Alexander Crawford & Son, which covers the years 1907 to 1911 – and it would be tedious to cite each individual reference.

6. D/1700/5/17/1/49, 24 July 1914.

7. D/1633/2/19, 30 November 1914.

8. D/1700/5/17/1/41A, from Alexander Crawford in Geraldton, Australia, 19 July 1914. Fred had written to him from Brussels to outline the events of the gun-running.

9. D/1700/5/17/1/28, 13 July 1914.

10. D/1700/10/1/515-516, 26 November 1908.

11. St John Ervine, *Craigavon: Ulsterman*, (London, 1949), p.568. The biographer claimed that Craig "died comparatively poor", as his political activity had caused

his personal fortune to dwindle to £27,000. Fred would have settled for less!

12. Details of this are taken from D/1415/B/34, pp.74-76.
13. Fred H Crawford, *Guns for Ulster*, (Belfast, 1947), p.9.
14. *Belfast News Letter*, 17 May 1913.
15. For much of the above, see D/1415/B/34, p.107. D/1700/5/2/53-56, –/62.
16. D/1700/3/11.
17. D/640/19/5.
18. D/1700/10/1/895, 24 January 1911.
19. D/1700/3/11.
20. D/1700/5/17/1/139, 26 December 1916.
21. D/1700/8 (death certificate). D/1700/10/1/192, –/206, –/216.
22. Despite the friction between father and son, James Wright Crawford left Chlorine to his elder son.
23. He was born at St Claire in Marlborough Park South, the rented accommodation which the family occupied from 1907 to 1914.
24. D/640/11/2, 6 September 1920.
25. Ian Maxwell, *The Life of Sir Wilfrid Spender 1876-1960*, (QUB Ph D thesis, 1991), p.52.
26. He was notified by the Hon Secretary, Dawson Bates: D/640/18/6, 1 February 1911.
27. George Chambers, *Faces of Change: the Belfast and Northern Ireland Chamber of Commerce and Industry 1783-1983*, (Belfast, 1983), p.217.
28. Crawford, p.9.
29. *Northern Whig*, 14-15 March 1912; Fred sponsored one of the resolutions made at the meetings in the Exhibition Hall and Sir William Whitla chaired one session in the Ulster Hall. D L Cooney, *The Methodists in Ireland: a short history*, (Columba Press, Dublin 2001), p.99. Methodists in England were, however, pro-Gladstone and Home Rule.
30. D/1700/3/2, 15 April 1900. Ronald McNeill, *Ulster's Stand for Union*, (London, 1922), p.14.
31. D/1700/3/10, 18 December 1892.
32. D/1700/3/10, 9 January, 12 January, 15 September, 24 December 1893.
33. Crawford, p.10. D/1700/10. D/1700/3/10. Fred christened his elder son (born 8 March 1898) Stuart Wright Knox Crawford. Fred wrote to the Earl, then at Government House in Wellington, New Zealand on 26 June 1898 to notify

him that he had christened his son Knox – the Ranfurly family name. The latter replied that he was pleased, "but why you should require two of them, I don't know. Stuart is also a family name with us": D/1700/6/1/8, 13 August 1898.

34. ATQ Stewart, *The Ulster Crisis*, (Faber & Faber, London, 1967), p.90. Fred's obituary in *The Irish Times*, 6 November 1952.

35. Ian Colvin, *The Life of Lord Carson*, (London, 1934), Vol.II, 360-361.

36. He twice refers to Fred as "a little man" and in his presentation of the Larne gun-running story confuses the two Hamburg characters of Spiro and Schneider – and calls them both, inaccurately, Schmidt: Colvin, pp.357, 362, 365, 367.

37. Crawford, pp.9-12. Timothy Bowman, *Carson's Army: the Ulster Volunteer Force 1910-1922*, (Manchester University Press, 2007), pp.16-18.

38. D/1415/B/34, p.79. It was the Channel by which the diversionary *Balmerino* arrived in Belfast on the evening of 24 April 1914: Stewart, pp.200-201.

39. The latter probably constituted Fred's membership. On 20 June 1881 (aged 19) he had obtained Licence no.57 for a gun, rifle and ammunition to be held at Chlorine Villa; on 11 February 1891 he acquired another licence for a revolver: D/640/19/1-2.

40. A large amount of this home-made ammunition was found as late as 1952 in the loft over the stables by one of Fred's sons and grandsons. Although this loft features on the inventory of Cloreen after Fred's death (D/1700/10), the ammunition does not!

41. The appointment was made by the Irish Unionist Joint Committee based at Westminster.

42. D/1700/3/10 (notes appended to his devotional diary). D/640/18/1-2. D/1700/5/2/53. D/1700/10/1/90-91.

43. Crawford, p.12. D/640/18/4-5. D/1700/10/1/12-13, –/191, –/855.

44. Patrick Buckland (ed), *Irish Unionism 1885-1923*, (HMSO, Belfast, 1973), pp.202-203, 278-280.

45. D/1700/10/1/76, –/78, –/90-91 (March and April 1907).

46. Crawford, pp.14-15.

47. D/1700/10/1/514, 25 November 1908. MacDonnell was a Catholic with self-confessed Nationalist leanings. His brother was also Home Rule MP for Queen's County, later Co Laois.

48. D/640/11/2, p.30 (written in September 1920).

49. Jonathan Bardon, *A History of Ulster*, (Blackstaff Press, Belfast, 1992), pp.427-430. Mark Radford, 'Tampering with Mutiny: the 1907 RIC agitation in Belfast', *Due North*, Vol.I no.4 (2001), 30-32.

50. D/640/11/2, pp.33-34.

51. McNeill, p.21.

52. Geoffrey Lewis, *Carson: the man who divided Ireland*, (London, 2005), p.76.

53. Its Standing Committee comprised 200 members: 100 from local Unionist Associations, 50 from the Orange Lodges and 50 from amongst MPs and co-opted individuals.

54. D/640/18/6, 1 February 1911.

55. Lewis, pp.51, 60.

56. D/1415/B/34, p.123. D/640/14/2, 6 May 1921.

57. T/3775/2/1, 29 July 1911, cited in Lewis, p.76.

58. D/1700/10/1/855-856, –/881.

59. D/1327/2/7.

60. Fred belonged to the Balmoral & Malone Unionist Club. They had been founded in 1892 at the time of the second Home Rule Bill.

61. D/1415/E/13.

62. D/1415/D/1.

63. D/1327/2/7.

64. McNeill, pp.80-89. Major-General Lord Edward Gleichen, *A Guardsman's Memories: a book of recollections*, (Edinburgh/London, 1932), pp.362-363. RJQ Adams, *Bonar Law*, (London, 1999), p.103.

65. D/640/23/1, 15 April 1912.

66. A similar number of women signed the Declaration.

67. Paul Bew, *Ideology and the Irish Question: Ulster Unionism and Irish nationalism 1912-1916*, (Clarendon Press, Oxford, 1994), p.110.

68. D/1327/2/7. D/1415/D/1.

The Ark and the Covenant

Early in 1909 a young man, who completed his education at Campbell College shortly after Fred Crawford had become one of the newly-inaugurated Board of Governors in 1898, found himself trapped in the siege of Tabriz in northern Persia (now Iran). Arthur Moore, after graduating from Oxford University and election as President of the Oxford Union, became a journalist, and was sent to cover the civil war that had erupted in Persia. After three months of deteriorating conditions in Tabriz, on 1st April 1909, Moore joined the Constitutionalist (or nationalist) forces, helped to drill them and, on 19th April, led the final sortie of the siege against the forces of the Shah.

The British consul in Tabriz, with whom Moore had been residing, recorded that: "This crisis Moore, to whom, as to Cato, the losing side offered an irresistible attraction, chose for adhering openly to the nationalist cause ... at this time, if there was a row on, as a good Irishman he felt bound to be in it". A few years later Fred was to make much the same observation about Irishmen to Carson.[1]

Sir Arthur Hardinge, the previous Minister in Teheran, would not have been surprised at Moore's action; in 1905 he had written to the British Foreign Secretary, noting the similarity between the Irish and the Persians:[2]

> *It is very little use to argue in the daylight of pure reason; you have to enter, in both cases into his peculiar sympathies, to make large allowances for the shams and vanities on which he lives; and you will do more by a little cordiality, a little gush and, I would add, a little blarney, than by the most serious sustained reasoning.*

The British Foreign Secretary was the Fifth Marquess of Lansdowne, one of the largest Anglo-Irish landlords who – despite having been fag-master to Conservative Arthur Balfour at Eton – had started his political career as a Liberal, but had converted to become leader of the Unionist peers. He also happened to be married to a younger daughter of the Duke of Abercorn – whose family were personal acquaintances of Fred.

Ulstermen were (and are) probably less inclined to gush and blarney than their fellow Irishmen – indeed, Ronald McNeill specifically described them as "laconic of speech, without gush" [3] – but Moore did exhibit one quality which Fred would have admired: the willingness to take on a seemingly lost cause and to be involved in a good fight. It was, however, a trait not shared by all Fred's Ulster Unionist colleagues:[4]

> *Though for a long time back I recognised that sooner or later we in Ulster would have to fight to prevent being put under a Parliament in Dublin, I was more determined than ever to get arms in, as we all knew the Liberals had no love for Ulster. But I felt as Noah must have done all the time he was building the Ark – very disheartened by the apathy shown by our people about arming.*

Fred's militant outlook attracted a certain amount of mirth and raillery: "I preached my gospel of physical resistance till some of my friends seemed to think I was 'beside myself', and used to slap my pockets when I went into the Ulster Unionist Standing Committee and say 'Well, Crawford, have you any rifles about your person?'".

As has been seen in the previous chapter, Fred had been keen on obtaining arms to challenge Home Rule from the mid-1890s. In 1904, at the Ulster Hall, he continued to warn against a false sense of security: "I predict that Home Rule will never be killed until we show any British Government which brings it forward that we will resist it to the death, even with arms, if necessary".[5]

Fred was unambiguous and unvarnished in his political opinions, but proved more circumspect in his actions. McNeill relished conspiracy and, in the period of the Home Rule Crisis before the First World War, was regularly in attendance at Craigavon, and – unlike Fred – took a great delight in signing the Visitors' Book. He adopted an ambivalent attitude to Fred, pointing out that "every movement has its Fabians and also its Hotspurs … Major Crawford had more of the temperament of a Hotspur than of a Fabius", but acknowledged that when it came to the question of importing guns Fred was level-headed and astute; he "possessed qualities of patience, reticence, discretion and coolness which enabled him to render invaluable service to the Ulster cause in an enterprise that would certainly have miscarried in the hands of a man endowed only with impetuosity and reckless courage".[6]

Historians and other commentators have outlined a timetable that shows Fred to be engaged in the sourcing and importation of guns for about eight years from 1906 until the celebrated landing at Larne in April 1914.[7] This is erroneous, but the mistake is a consequence of Fred's own comments. In his memoir of his gun-running escapades he states quite specifically that he placed advertisements in European newspapers in 1906-1907 "asking for tenders for 10,000 second-hand rifles and two million rounds of ammunition", when the Liberals had been returned to power. He says that he gave his address as 'H. Mathews, Ulster Reform Club (to be called for)', and that he received several useful and informative replies, "but some of the Committee demurred at my action, and so I sent in my resignation as Hon. Secretary".[8]

Whether or not this error with regard to the date was deliberate or simply forgetfulness on the part of the gun-runner is unclear, but it was most certainly incorrect. He himself admitted when he was compiling the recollections after the First World War: "It is very hard to keep writing correctly as to when each event happened after the lapse of eight or nine years; those days were so crowded with excitement and incidents that I can only remember some of them, and not always in the order in which they happened".[9] With a substantial overall majority at the 1906 General Election, there is no indication that the Liberals were inclined to revitalise the embers of Home Rule; however, the Liberals and Unionists could not be separated at two elections in 1910 and, as reward for their support, the substantial Irish Nationalist party made the inevitable demand. It was in the final weeks of 1910 that Fred played his initial gun-running gambit.

That Fred's memory was faulty is made evident by the fact that, despite the fact that he claimed he had resigned the post in 1906-1907, he was still Hon. Secretary of the Ulster Reform Club in 1910. At this latter date, in his capacity as Hon. Secretary he contacted a number of individuals – including Thomas Andrews junior, who did not prove forthcoming – to ask for donations to alleviate the debt that had been accrued by the West Belfast constituency as a result of its efforts to challenge the Nationalists.[10] Even if Fred had been reinstated after a resignation in 1906 – which did not happen – his conspiratorial sagacity would never have allowed him to utilise the same cover name and address only three or four years later.

The Hon. Secretary claimed that "some of those with a little more courage came to me, and tried to get me to reconsider my decision, but I was firm. I felt that the timorous persons would only hamper me, and told them that I would be doing much more dangerous work in the future". It was also at this time (23rd December 1910) that he resigned from the West Belfast constituency committee "as I am engaged in other political work, which will take up all my spare time".[11]

'Political' Work

This "political work" was in reality the importation of arms and ammunition for the Ulster cause – over two years before the formation of the Ulster Volunteer Force (UVF) – and the unanimous co-option of Fred to the Ulster Unionist Council (UUC) a few weeks later on 30th January 1911 was probably a foregone conclusion.

Tuesday 22nd November 1910 effectively marked the initiation of the Ulster gun-running campaign. It may well be fair to conclude that very few would ever have heard of Frederick Hugh Crawford if it had not been for the events of the next forty months, but the surviving correspondence indicates quite clearly that these activities were not the singular obsession of an obscure Belfast starch manufacturer. It was, however, only three months since Fred had finally been notified that the Letterkenny militia camp, for which he had so much affection, had finally been cleared, and it may be possible to argue that his dedication to – and even fanaticism for – the gun-running was his way of proving to the British military authorities that they had unwisely dispensed with his talents and commitment.

On 22nd November a man who did not exist sat down in the offices of Alexander Crawford & Son and posted a general request to four arms manufacturers in England, Germany and Austria: "Kindly state if you could supply for immediate delivery 20,000 Military Rifles with and without bayonets, and one million rounds of ammunition to suit, and price of same. Rifles need not be very latest pattern; second-hand ones in good order preferred". Before the end of the month the Hon. Secretary of the Ulster Reform Club, as one of his final duties, had sorted to his own mail-box four replies requesting further information. There was probably little application to starch manufacturing in Wilson Street on Thursday 1st December, as 'H. Mathews' dealt with a considerable amount of correspondence.

One of his letters that day was addressed to 'Charley' – probably Col. Harold Richard Charley, whose family had been in the linen trade since 1822. On 13th May 1910 Charley had been appointed Adjutant to 5th Battalion Royal Irish Rifles (also known as the South Down Militia), and he joined its Commanding Officer, Col. Bob Wallace – another close acquaintance of Fred – at Downpatrick.[12]

It is not clear what Fred expected from the Charley interest, but he wrote to say "I called with your people here but they did not seem inclined to go in for the job". He revealed, however: "I have made enquiries from BSA and LSA[13] for second-hand rifles, such as the War Office have just discarded. I have also replies from two continental firms, but none seems quite what my committee want. I want a military smallbore rifle, second-hand because cheaper than new". He continued in his letter to Charley: "If you can do anything for us and to your own advantage at the same time, why all the better. We look upon you as a good Ulsterman and better than some weak-kneed ones I know". He then revealed why he was engaged in so much correspondence that day: "The Committee meets tomorrow to discuss this serious question. The Committee consists of the leading men in this part of Ulster, and men who have practically unlimited means to carry this thro'".[14]

This was a propitious time to be purchasing second-hand rifles, as

European armies were discarding old stock as they acquired the latest models for the anticipated war. As correspondent for *The Times* in St. Petersburg in 1913, former Campbell College pupil Arthur Moore witnessed the modernisation of the Russian Army – primarily at the exhortation and intervention of their French allies. One of Fred's fellow gun smugglers, Robert Adgey, indicated that the 88 Steyr Mannlicher model was readily available, as the German Army acquired the newer 98 pattern.[15] The Vetterli rifle, of which so many seem to have been imported to Ulster, had been withdrawn from the Italian Army as early as 1887.[16] Fred informed Charley that he regarded Martini-Henry rifles as too antiquated, but from the Steyr company in Austria he sought a quotation for their Mannlicher rifle; and from Deutsche Waffen und Munitionsfabriken in Berlin he wanted the latest pattern of Mauser rifles "to be delivered to an Irish port". He notified the London Small Arms Co. that he required Mannlicher, Mauser or Lee Enfield stock "all of one kind", and from their Birmingham counterpart he sought "6900 Metfords with 14,000 to follow in four to six months". He indicated that no references would be given, but that terms would be cash on receipt of documentation.

In case none of these enquiries proved fruitful, Fred simultaneously placed an advertisement in six European newspapers – *Le Temps* (Paris), *L'Etoile Belge* (Brussels), *Frankfurter Zeitung, Neueste Nachrichten* (Berlin), *Pester Lloyd* (Budapest) and *Der Zeit* (Vienna): "Wanted, 20,000 good second-hand small bore military rifles with one million rounds of ammunition for same".

In his recent work on the development of the UVF, Timothy Bowman indicates that "the drilling and arming of 1910-1914 was built on the earlier precedents of the first and second Home Rule Bills", and that rifles had been used during the drilling of 1886 and 1893.[17] There were certainly guns available in Ulster from those days, but they lacked the uniformity and quantity needed by the second decade of the 20th century and would have been no match for the better arms being provided to state armies. There is no evidence that worthwhile quantities of rifles or guns were being imported until the second half of 1911.

Importing

It is beyond question that Fred's advertising for weapons was undertaken with the full approval of the UUC; there is no way in which Fred could have financed such quantities on his own initiative.[18] He later recorded that: "My heart rejoiced when an Inner Committee was formed to look into the question of physical force"; this committee authorised his acquisition of specimen rifles from the Continent and this helped to weed out those whom Carson regarded as bluffers. Others supported him; James Craig's brother, Charles (MP for South Antrim), declared at a public meeting in Antrim in March 1913 that it were better that £10,000 was spent on rifles than on mere talk and pamphlets.[19]

Many talked of resistance in Council meetings, but after one session Fred "asked them to step into another room ... I had the weapons [samples] laid out with fixed bayonets, and when they saw the cold steel and rows of cartridges, and the very businesslike look of the rifles, some of my friends protested they had no idea I really meant this sort of thing". Fred observed that some started to get cold feet; some resigned, but "I was truly thankful as they were only a hindrance and brake on all my efforts".

Similarly, Fred was irked by the non-committal approach offered from England. He recalled that he was once asked to meet at the 1900 Club in London a group of Englishmen who professed concern for Ulster. The kindest description he bestowed upon them was that "They were such a harmless lot of old gentlemen", but he regarded the group as nothing more than "a big Gasbag" as, although "they could send over men in great numbers", they declined to help obtain arms and ammunition. Fred retorted that he did not want "a rabble of unarmed men to house and feed and look after". He said that he already had large numbers of enthusiastic Ulstermen, who were "of much more use than strangers who would not know the country and, as the war will be a guerrilla war, it is essential that the combatants on our side should know Ulster and her people". The UUC representative rattled them by stating that if they were not prepared to provide finance or arms they might as well dissolve the group. "None of them seemed to realise that Ulster meant it when she said she would fight".[20] Asquith, the Liberal

Prime Minister, was of much the same mould; he did not deny that there was a problem but, taking Ulster as a whole, it had "17 Unionist MPs and 16 Home Rulers, figures which showed the misleading character of the pretence that Ulster would die rather than accept Home Rule".[21]

Fred and Wallace tested sample weapons on a range – probably at Downpatrick – and the UUC recommended the purchase of 1000 rifles. At this stage, Fred adopted the alias of W.H. Jones, but used his Works' address (14 Wilson Street) for communications. By April 1911 he had received a case of rifles from two firms, but a further order, which may have been placed four months previously, was clearly proving problematical. Eventually, on 8th April, Fred contacted George Grotstuck at Brehmstrasse in Berlin and made it clear that delivery of their order was "very urgent". He wanted the 1000 "long sticks" delivered immediately (500 to Belfast and 500 to Dublin) and settlement would be made at the quayside. At the same time he wrote to James Craig in London, but the Easter break delayed a reply by over a week.

The stockbroker was undoubtedly becoming very edgy, nervous of both being detected, and of criticism from supporters. Employing a non-too-subtle code, Craig wrote to Fred on 20th April bemoaning a waste of "four valuable months".

> Personally I am strongly of the opinion that the fishing rods should be got in at once and as secretly as possible. Month after month goes by and we … run daily the risk of being asked point blank at a mass meeting: 'Does Ulster mean business?' Even if ten are got through we can confidently say 'Yes'. My great fear is that the game will be up before anything is done … I am convinced that unless a steady supply is started we will be caught like rats in a trap.

Fred responded from his Works on the following day saying that the delay was "not our fault". Resorting to their coded language, he indicated that if they had had the 'essential' [the money], the grand [= 1000 rifles] would have been delivered before then. He posted off an order and a cheque for "a mille", but said more money could have harvested a twelve-fold supply. He added that £6000 would have provided "all the fishing rods including lines and hooks [which probably meant bayonets and ammunition] we want".[22]

On the day that he wrote to Grotstuck and Craig – 8th April – Fred also contacted Lt-Col. T.V.P (Patrick) McCammon of Woodville in Holywood to indicate that the delay was also making him nervous, but revealed that "the necessary is practically guaranteed" by the Unionist Standing Committee – although there had been some debate as to whether the ordinary funds of the UUC were available for the purchase of arms. It was an irony that six years later, almost to the day, McCammon would lie dead on the fields of France as a result of conflict with the Germans, having travelled in April 1911 to Berlin "to see if he could speed [the rifles] up, but without avail".[23]

Fred was made of sterner mettle. In June 1911 he took his wife and two eldest children to see the Coronation of George V before travelling on to conduct business with Blattmann AG, who were in the starch trade, in Wädenswil near Zurich. He determined to travel north to Berlin to visit the obstructive arms supplier. He accused the company of being "a pack of swindlers", and of divulging their arrangement to the British Government. He promised that he would continue to pursue the matter and he felt that justice was served when the representative of the company was later shot dead in Central America as a result of a further dubious arms deal.

Fred then travelled west to Hamburg to meet the man whom he came greatly to admire – Bruno Spiro. The latter was the son of Benny Spiro, the founder of the company Waffen, Munition und Militär-Effekten (founded in 1864), with offices in both Hamburg and the German capital.[24] It is quite probable that Spiro responded to one of Fred's newspaper advertisements, as by early January 1911 the arms-seeker had placed a sample order. On 19th January Fred informed the weapons' salesman that "The box containing the two rifles has arrived safely, but the cartridges have not yet come to hand". Recognising the dangers of such correspondence, he asked the German to send all future communications under a plain cover, on plain paper, and simply signed BS, to one of Fred's many aliases: W.H. Jones, 14 Wilson Street, Belfast.

On 22nd March the latter wrote to Spiro in Hamburg confirming that he had placed an order for 1000 magazine carbines, late Italian Government pattern – which he indicated was "practically a sample order". He also requested the price "with or without one hundred rounds of ammunition for from 10,000 to 20,000 [rifles]".[25]

Fred and Bruno Spiro established a friendship and trust which developed into mutual admiration and which long survived the vicissitudes of the Anglo-German conflict of 1914-1918. It is unlikely that, without Spiro's co-operation and assistance – which often placed himself in danger of arrest – Ulster could have adequately challenged the threat of Home Rule. There were those at the pinnacle of Ulster Unionism who subtly acknowledged this.

Carson developed considerable affection for Craigavon, the home of Craig, and always appended a comment in the Visitors' Book as he departed. Occasionally this revealed a sense of humour, as in July 1914 when the situation was becomingly increasingly tense: "Wanted by Bonar Law – and perhaps the police"! On 6th June, whilst inspecting the West Belfast Regiment at the home of James Cunningham, Glencairn in North Belfast – which, to Mrs Spender's regret, was not graced by the presence of the principal gun-runner – Carson recognised some of the cargo Fred had landed at Larne. As he signed out of Craigavon later that day, he added the Latin phrase *Dum Spiro, Spero*, which strictly translates as 'While I breathe, I hope'. The use of upper case was probably deliberate on this occasion, as he usually penned such foreign language phrases – such as *immer derselbe* ('always the same') – in lower case. One suspects that, on this occasion, at such a delicate political juncture, Carson really meant: 'As long there is Spiro, there is hope'.[26]

Spiro had other contacts in Belfast. He was acquainted with Robert Adgey, a pawnbroker who had studied the gun trade. It was the German who introduced the two Belfast men, who became firm friends, Adgey becoming one of Fred's principal agents in the importation of guns about 1913 and 1914.[27] It is evident from Adgey's memoir that Fred was far from being the only gun-runner in those few years leading up to the First World War.

Adgey also revealed the wide range of weapons being brought into Ulster; he himself imported several thousand hand-guns both for personal use and for many clubs which sprang up. The Earls of Kilmorey and Leitrim each imported quantities of rifles. Not all deliveries reached their destination and being caught would certainly risk incarceration. Fred could not help commenting to an acquaintance, a few days before the declaration of war against Germany that: "I have been appointed to an important command here in Belfast already, and now I am an officer in the Reserve doing duty with full Army rank and pay. Strictly speaking I ought to be in prison for what I have done, but instead the above is the fact".[28]

Adgey echoed Fred's belief that "The police did not count for so very much, but Customs Officers had their heads screwed on". Quite often successful gun-running was the result of doing the obvious. Adgey summarised the philosophy: "They [officials] did not always see the things they were looking for, although sometimes they were very visible". Regular shipments were made to those who imported such goods as shop-fittings, ironmongery and general hardware – but with alternative loads. Large barrels used for bleaching powder – but accommodating 50 rifles or 8000 rounds of ammunition – were shipped to bleach-works in Belfast and Derry. The main destinations tended to be the larger companies, farmers or landowners, as they had the facilities and space to store weaponry. Adgey also concurred with the starch manufacturer's sentiment, offered to the 'Gasbags', that it was necessary to rely upon those familiar with Ulster. Those who smuggled arms benefited from many sympathisers within the Royal Irish Constabulary, the Post Office, the Customs service, as well as the docks and quays.

Fred's increasing expertise gave him an intuition for danger. Close to the outbreak of war, Carson was offered 100,000 German 98 pattern rifles and ammunition; the suppliers said that they would deliver anywhere – and suggested Belfast Lough. When Adgey was sent over to England to investigate, he was informed that they were available at one-third of the usual price. It was a tempting offer, but Fred recognised that, after all the struggles they had experienced for piecemeal loads, this was too good to be true – and refused to contemplate touching it.

The owner of Wilson Street Works developed a good personal and professional relationship with Bruno Spiro from the outset. When he first visited the Hamburg offices, he revealed the dishonest and untrustworthy tactics of Spiro's competitors. The German indicated that such actions were not uncommon and purchased the original order from the Unionists and recovered the rifles himself. Fred was delighted that Ulster only lost £20 on the entire transaction and he never expressed anything but praise for the arms salesman thereafter.

Under the nom-de-guerre of W. H. Jones and the business alias of John Ferguson & Co, Shipping Agents, whose name-plaque he attached to one of the Wilson Street entrances, Fred began to import thousands of rifles (primarily Vetterlis) from Hamburg. These were brought into the Works, repackaged, then taken down to a yard behind the offices in Mill Street. During the night they would be loaded into cars and distributed up to 100 miles distant. Fred noted that "the first few thousand rifles were all sent to the districts where the Nationalists were strong and the Unionists weak".

He was well-aware of the axiom that, in Ulster, everyone else knows what you are doing – all that is lacking is the evidence! Fred harboured grave suspicions about the Ancient Order of Hibernians (whom he described as the forerunners of Sinn Fein). When they hired a loft as a ballroom next to the yard where he conducted the packing, Fred suspected that they had an inkling of what was happening and, as it would have been very easy to raid his premises via their window on to the stable roof, every time he had more than 100 rifles in store, he maintained an all-night guard until they had been distributed.

The police were certainly alert to his extra-curricular activities and he recorded that there were two or three detectives watching his yard for over two years. His relationship with them remained quite civil and sociable – except with one overly inquisitive detective who regularly spied through an observation hole at the rear of the Works. On one occasion, knowing the detective's habit of appearing there when a vehicle arrived, Fred waited with a grey eye pressed to the observation point. It took the detective ten seconds to realise what he was staring at but, when he did, he did not stay to witness any further events!

There were other dangers experienced at Wilson Street. One night during this period, Fred was awoken at Marlborough Park South by one his carters, informing him that there was a fire at Wilson Street adjacent to where the rifles were stored. Fred dressed and raced down town on his bicycle. The fire had been dowsed by that stage, but so had the rifles. Fred needed to move them, but was concerned that the sacking in which they were bound would be easily torn and the contents discovered, and suffered many an anguished moment until he succeeded in removing the public, the firemen and the police from the premises. He and three employees privy to the secret contents then transferred the Vetterlis to one of the old unused wells in the yard. He placed a platform 50 feet down the shaft, and covered and disguised the access. A few months later he realised that the enclosed damp atmosphere was causing them to rust, and so he and his employees had to work several nights to clean them.

In 1911 Fred began to import rifles and ammunition from Hamburg, designated as zinc crates and nails. Almost 700 of the first thousand arrived safely in heavy crates, but one load of 300 or 400 was intercepted. Thomas James Smith, Chief Commissioner of the RIC, would not release them, as they were consigned to the fictitious John Ferguson & Co. As there was no prohibition against despatching the goods, Spiro requested that they be returned to Germany, stating that there had been an error on his company's part. He then re-shipped them back to Ulster via West Hartlepool.

By July 1911 they decided to start using Leith (near Edinburgh) "as questions were being asked in some other places".[29] Rifles and ammunition were despatched on boats belonging to the Antrim Iron Ore Steamship Company, which left the harbour usually every Thursday, and, at the end of July, Fred reported that: "The business has become very satisfactory so far, and we hope it will continue to be so". He was, however, to be disappointed and on 6th September W.H. Jones requested of Hamburg: "Do not send any more goods at present. Customs have stopped last six at Leith". At night his men managed to switch the boxes for ones filled with furnace ash from the starch works' boilers, but they were betrayed by an observant barmaid. The original boxes were seized by the authorities, but again, following the admission of another 'error' by Bruno Spiro, they were returned to Germany. Another 400 rifles were also later intercepted at Newcastle-upon-Tyne.

There were occasional minor victories, which reveal that starch manufacturers were not always stuffed shirts. Fred was greatly amused by the fact that the Commissioner of Police was, on one occasion, to travel from England on one of the vessels of the Antrim Iron Ore Steamship Company, which was carrying a further consignment of rifles. "I did not lose them this time", smiled the smuggler.

He also took considerable pleasure in relating the tale of two Customs officials in 1913 on board Lord Leitrim's ship, who could not understand how a whole case of rifles mysteriously disappeared at sea. For all the efforts that Fred made to import guns into Ulster, part of his psyche genuinely hoped that they would never be used and there is no evidence that the man who handled thousands of weapons ever fired one in anger at another human. He was, however, as we have seen, greatly irritated by the apparent indifference of the British Government, which he felt did not treat the Ulster scene with sufficient gravity. He arranged for five cases of one hundred rifles each to be despatched to the north of Ireland. Four of these loads were sent via Glasgow, Manchester, Liverpool and Fleetwood, and were promptly seized by the police and displayed at the Belfast Custom House.

As Fred recalled: "The seizing of them caused an enormous sensation in Belfast and all over England and Scotland – just what I wanted. Questions were asked in the House of Commons and the Government had at last to admit that a very grave conspiracy was on foot to get large quantities of arms into Ulster". Fred was well aware that the Government had allowed the arrival of the consignments in order to try to discover the identity of the conspirators.

The fifth load, however, remained a mystery to the authorities. It had been despatched for Portrush on board the small steamer, *SS Ganiamore*, belonging to Fred's old military acquaintance, Lord Leitrim, which travelled each week from Glasgow, via Portrush to Mulroy Bay in Co Donegal.[30] On this occasion two Customs Officers joined Captain Morrison on board. It proved a rough night and the two officials suffered sea-sickness and took shelter in the Captain's chart room. They failed to notice that a case of rifles, which had sat prominently on the deck, being lowered overboard off Ballycastle, where it was picked up at daylight. Fred said that after their recovery, the rifles were then "well-oiled"; one suspects that their superiors felt that this equally applied to the myopic employees!

ULSTER DAY

At the UUC meeting at the Old Town Hall on 27th August 1912, Dawson Bates was asked to engage the Ulster Hall for 26th and 28th September. The latter date was to become known as Ulster Day, and there were further meetings early in September at which it was decided that there would be a simple, singular motto that would encapsulate their aspirations: "We will not have Home Rule".[31]

It was hoped that there would be an emphatic turn-out of Ulstermen on Saturday 28th September to sign the Solemn League & Covenant and, to that end, Carson had stood (on 19th September) on the steps of Craigavon to enunciate the fundamental document.[32] For ten days prior to the landmark day there were several other Unionist demonstrations around the province, addressed by an impressive array of British Conservatives, including Lord Salisbury, F.E. Smith, and one of those whom Fred had informed at the 1900 Club that he could do without his help, Lord Willoughby de Broke.[33]

As usual, despite the enormous crowds, a disciplined and sacrosanct demeanour was expected from all. The Churches had been consulted about the Covenant and, whilst there was general approval, the new Moderator of the Presbyterian Church, Rev. Henry Montgomery, advised that it should relate only "to the present conspiracy to set up Home Rule in Ireland", and not bind future generations.[34] In the Ulster Hall that Saturday morning a recent Moderator, Rev. Wm. McKean, delivered a sermon reminding those present that the threat was a challenge to Protestantism and the Empire, but that "We are plain, blunt men who love peace and industry".

The latter's message clearly struck a chord with the Moderator's family, for nearly forty years later at Campbell College Speech Day (July 1951) his son, then Chairman of the Governors, still believed that the school prepared young men "to play a noble part in the service of the Empire".[35] Fred was well-acquainted with both Moderators, who had put six sons (between them) through the school in its early years. Fred was given the crucial role on Ulster Day of ensuring the smooth running of the signing and the maintenance of good order. Inevitably, his organisational skills served him well and so confident of his arrangements was he that he attended a Board of Governors' meeting at Campbell on the night of 26th September.

Dr Stewart described the celebrated gun-runner as "the commander of the Praetorian Guard in bowler hats who escorted Carson on Covenant Day",[36] and Fred and his complement of 2500 stewards – carrying only batons – appear to have performed excellent service. Fred stood in line behind T.R. Nixon of Glenbrook, Cliftonville, to sign Sheet 99 of the Covenant. He signed himself as 'Major Frederick Hugh Crawford of Chlorine Gardens [although at that time he was still resident at Marlborough Park South] and of the U[lster] C[ouncil] City Hall Guard 2500'. The legend is that he signed the Covenant in his own blood. The tale certainly gained early currency – one London-based Ulster Unionist mentioned this in a letter to Fred himself on 13 July 1914 – and it has since been repeated in several works.[37] The relevant sheet, however, provides no evidence that Robert Bradley (14 Glencollyer Street), behind him in the queue, had to wait and witness this. Fred does not appear to have denied the story, but he was not a man prone to histrionic public actions and, if he did compose his signature in his own blood, it may perhaps have been in private on the individual copy of the Covenant which he owned.[38]

A few weeks later on 13th November there was uproar in the House of Commons when Asquith made it clear that Home Rule would be pushed through by use of the parliamentary guillotine. Ronald McNeill struck Winston Churchill on the head with his copy of Standing Orders and Sir William Bull (with whom Fred made arrangements for the use of a depot at Hammersmith) called Asquith a traitor. This effectively removed any reservations Ulster may have had with regard to establishing a Provisional Government to manage its own affairs. Before the end of the year Fred had initiated the process of purchasing batons, which would be partially used for drilling the ranks of the UVF. Similar ones had been manufactured for controlling the public on the day of Churchill's unpopular visit on 8th February 1912 and had been carried by the marshals on Ulster Day. As the political deadlock intensified, the UUC approved a new baton which Fred passed to one of the Herdman family for potential carving in hardwoods such as laburnum or hickory, but now boasting the arms of Ulster and the ominous legend UPG (Ulster Provisional Government).[39] He ordered 400 of these, of which he later said: "I need scarcely say that they were good silencers"![40]

Maxims

It was probably in these final months of 1912 that Fred endeavoured to import half-a-dozen Maxim (later called Vickers) machine-guns. The conspirators had felt it necessary in the preceding months to quieten their gun-running activities and Fred sensed that a new approach would be worthwhile. He believed that a couple of Maxims mounted on an armoured lorry was worth 500 foot-soldiers. Again, there were dissenting voices on the Ulster Council which demurred at "these dreadful engines of death", but eventually he was given permission to negotiate for six of the latest pattern at £300 each.

Dr Stewart believed that Fred visited Vickers House in London in the summer of 1913.[41] As we have seen, the arms smuggler's own chronological accuracy is suspect, but late 1912 seems more likely. In June 1913 Fred suffered the indignity of having several thousand rifles confiscated from his John Ferguson & Co. depot in London. This was located in stable yards adjoining the Windsor Castle Hotel at Hammersmith. The storage had been arranged through Sir William Bull – who was MP for Hammersmith, and Chairman of the London Unionist MPs from 1910 to 1929 – and his brother-in-law, Captain H.A. Budden, who had married the sister of a titled Unionist MP.[42]

The guns were seized on the premiss that they contravened gun-making legislation; they could have been reclaimed at a charge of £2 each barrel. As this was more than the Unionists had paid for them initially, Fred declined the invitation, particularly as it would also have given away the identity of those involved. He was, however, to get Spiro to reclaim the bayonets and these eventually entered Ulster via Larne and Bangor in April 1914.[43] What probably annoyed Fred more than the loss of the weapons was that he was usually a good judge of character, but was later to discover that he had been betrayed by the alcoholic, debt-ridden Budden.

The transportation of the Maxim guns was effected partly through Hammersmith and it is very unlikely that the shrewd arms smuggler would have been tempted to approach anywhere near this depot after the loss of the above load – particularly as the authorities were keeping a watch on the place. Fred also quite clearly recalled that the relevant visits to England and Hamburg to obtain the Maxims were undertaken in December, when it was still dark in the early morning. This makes it more probable that his venture occurred in late 1912, as by the last third of 1913 Robert Adgey claimed to have sourced a large amount of weaponry in Britain, which included 100 Maxims.[44] If this were the case, there was no need for Fred to be going to the lengths which he did to smuggle a mere half-dozen of the machine-guns into Ulster.

Fred presented himself to Mr Owen of Vickers as an American, John Washington Graham. He professed interest in the latest model of Maxim, which he acknowledged to himself was a great improvement on the type he had used in South Africa. He did, however, make one recommendation to improve the speed of the elevation of the gun, which Vickers adopted themselves. Fred tested one of the Maxims and paid for it, but made it clear that he would be unhappy if the British Government were informed of the transaction, maintaining the fiction, apparently believed by Owen, that they were destined for trans-Atlantic action during the current Mexican Revolution. Fred fostered this impression further by requesting six manuals in Spanish.

The Ulsterman ordered a modification of the standard packing (a case each for the gun, tripod and ammunition) so that it resembled cases for band instruments. At Euston station he bluffed out a request by an "inquisitive beggar" of a weighman to open the boxes, and eventually accompanied them safely to Belfast. He had, however, ordered five additional guns and had to plot their transportation.

In the meantime, a certain Hugh Mathews renewed his acquaintance with Bruno Spiro. In Hamburg the latter offered Fred a surreptitious trial of a machine-gun he had for sale, at £50 cheaper than the Maxim. Fred was taken, to his own amazement, to the Military School of Musketry about six miles outside the city, where they were met by a senior NCO, who assured them that there were no officers on the site. After the first trial, the NCO returned in an agitated state, dismantled the gun and urged everyone to race for the gate. They sped off in their car and Spiro explained that the site commandant had not actually left the School that day and had become intrigued by the sound of firing. Fred admitted to the German that he liked the gun, and that it was cheaper than the English version, but that on this occasion he would stick with his original purchase, as it would be easier to acquire ammunition and spare parts for the Vickers gun.

He returned to England to collect the other five Maxims and at this point had the initials UPG engraved on each gun – which coincided with the application of the legend to the batons (late 1912). By showing Owen the catalogue of the cheaper German guns, he negotiated a £200 'commission', which he claimed greatly pleased Craig, the Ulster paymaster. He also stunned Owen by tendering Bank of England notes for £1000 and £500 in payment.

Fred travelled to Woolwich in a lorry at 5.30 one dark winter morning. After loading the fifteen cases, he set off on what appeared to him to be an unsettlingly slow journey for Hammersmith during which "It seemed to me that everything that moved got in our way and blocked us wilfully". Five cars were loaded up and each set of cases was despatched for a different port – Liverpool, Fleetwood, Heysham and Stranraer for Belfast and one via Greenore in Co. Louth, which was delivered to Narrow Water Castle in Carlingford Lough. Fred accompanied one via Reading and Liverpool. "The whole five guns arrived at their destination without mishap", noted Fred with relief and four of them joined the original one under a lean-to roof of the Manager's office at the Wilson Street Works, in company with 600 Vetterli rifles and bayonets and 200,000 rounds of ammunition.

Even if the British Government seemed to demonstrate insouciance towards the realities in Ulster, by early 1913 the imminence of Home Rule and the constant – if intermittent – importation of weaponry, created a volatile mixture. Grass-roots opinion and intent was difficult to regulate and, as the months passed, "T.J. Smith, the highest-ranking police officer in Belfast, admitted to Birrell that violence was being prevented only by the firm grip Devlin and Carson had on their respective followers".[45]

Ulster Volunteer Force

Various groups such as the Unionist Clubs and Orange Lodges had been drilling during 1912, but this was for the broader purpose of a disciplined turn-out at the demonstrations and reviews rather than for any sinister localised purpose.[46] In early 1913 the UUC, anxious that potentially anarchic forces did not undermine their moral advantage, formed the Ulster Volunteer Force. The Regulations of this body[47] stated that it was "to raise and enrol a Force of men at once for the self-preservation and mutual protection of all Loyalists, and generally to keep the peace". Membership was restricted to those who had signed the Covenant and – particularly important – all Volunteers had to sign a declaration that they were willing to obey Superior Officers.

The provision of experienced officers was to prove a problem for the UVF. Timothy Bowman has shown that UVF battalions were commanded by men with no military expertise – nine out of fourteen battalion commanders at the Balmoral review on 27th September 1913 had no military rank. Some were simply prominent local businessmen, such as Fred's acquaintance, George Clark, the shipyard owner. Bowman lists 132 UVF officers with military training, including eight Officer Training Corps (OTC) cadets.[48] This latter figure may well be an underestimate.

Queen's University had established the first OTC in Ireland in late 1908, but this was followed closely by the first school contingent at Campbell College in 1909 – which remained the only one in Ulster until after the First World War. Pupils were trained in military skills – such as drilling, signalling and marksmanship – and received Certificate 'A', which entitled them to join the British Army at officer level. A number of these enlisted in the UVF and, as a consequence of their military training, became Company or Half-Company Commanders. Other former pupils from Campbell also joined the ranks of the UVF, such as James Davidson, the heir to the Sirocco Works, but – like George Clark – he had no military background. Another former pupil, Henry Ouseley Davis, was to join the UVF HQ Staff at Craigavon. Davis had left the school before the inauguration of the OTC but, in common with a small proportion of Campbell pupils, had passed through Sandhurst and adopted a military career (joining the Royal Dublin Fusiliers in 1906).

As a member of the UUC and the Campbell College Board of

Governors, it is likely, as political circumstances became more tense in 1914 and the Ulster Provisional Government needed to improvise, that Fred sought to exploit the advantages of the Belmont estate, which was only a mile from Craigavon. On 26th March 1914 Davis approached his alma mater to ask the Governors (including Fred) if the building might be adapted as a hospital in the event of civil war.[49] Agreement was given, on the undertaking that no military stores were brought on to the premises and that any damage sustained would be repaired at the expense of the UPG. One of the others from the College who may well have been consulted about this possible use of Campbell College was the school doctor, Dr Richard Whytock Leslie, who featured on the Medical Board of the UPG.[50]

In retrospect the significance attached to the opening of a modest Drill Hall may appear extravagant. Nevertheless, if the British Government and public were to be persuaded that Ulster was serious about its resistance to Home Rule, the rank-and-file Ulsterman had to be engaged. To persuade the latter that they were valued, a Drill Hall was inaugurated with all the pomp and ceremony that Unionism could muster at Willowfield in East Belfast on 16th May 1913. Earlier that Friday Fred had attended a Standing Committee with Carson at the Old Town Hall to discuss "further steps to be taken in order to defend the rights of Irish Loyalists threatened by Home Rule".[51]

The leading figures did not arrive on the Woodstock Road until just after 7.30pm – by that stage thousands of local people had gathered for the occasion. There were also representatives from North, South and West Belfast, and most of the principal Ulster Unionist characters turned out for what was undoubtedly regarded as a seminal event. These included R.J. McMordie (of Cabin Hill) – East Belfast MP and Lord Mayor – and aristocratic figures such as the Duke of Abercorn and Marquess of Londonderry, who chaired the occasion. The speeches all emphasised the threat to the Empire and, despite the late hour, Carson spoke for 75 minutes, enthusing the multitude by waving the personal Covenant that bore his signature. Bearing in mind that, as was usual at such gatherings, the vast majority of the crowd could not hear a word of what was declaimed, their patience was remarkable. The

Unionist leadership recognised, however, that ultimately the patience of the ordinary volunteer was not limitless.

One of the features of the Drill Hall was a 50-yard rifle range, not too dissimilar to the one boasted by Alexander Crawford & Son; but, whereas a rifle was not a rarity on the latter premises, it was not a ready commodity at Willowfield. Volunteers were to become weary of drilling with replicas and, for all the impressive turn-out of 12,000 well-drilled men at the Balmoral review of the Belfast battalions of the UVF on 27th September 1913, the lack of arms can only have encouraged those who believed that the paramilitary posturing was really only bluff.

It was on that latter date Lord Abercorn noted in the Craigavon Visitors' Book: "Ulster Week: was present at establishment of Provisional Government". Events had been moving inexorably towards such a move during the second half of the year and, although Carson inscribed his predictable *immer derselbe* on 11th July (1913), this was clearly not the case. General Sir George Richardson noted that he was there "to assume command" of the UVF, and Chief of Staff, Colonel Hacket Pain, was there "to help the Commander".[52]

Balmoral

The review at Balmoral, at which Carson inspected the fourteen Belfast battalions of the UVF, was yet another triumph of management and spectacle, with 12,000 Volunteers on parade. The four South Belfast battalions (2800 men) set off from their designated assembly points at 2.30pm, all under the "supreme command" of Major Frederick Hugh Crawford "mounted, like the other regimental commanders". As he entered the arena he was greeted with hearty cheers.[53]

These men expected that their efforts and personal sacrifice of time and commitment would be reciprocated; as Fred later reflected: "We had all promised those faithful men of all ranks in life who had drilled and worked so hard to be ready for the crisis that, when the time for action would come, we would supply them with weapons wherewith to defend their rights and themselves".[54]

By the close of 1913 the issue of obtaining guns became paramount amongst the Unionists. In the final months of that year the police and

Government spies were evidently more active and Fred maintained a reasonably low profile. There was some correspondence with Bruno Spiro in August and, in early October, the starch manufacturer spent two weeks visiting Blattmann AG on company business. Whilst in Wädenswil, as W.H. Mathews, he wrote to the Hamburg supplier about some goods being returned – which were probably the bayonets from Hammersmith. He revealed that "the place is being watched by detectives and your people will be asked questions". Fred suggested that Spiro act as surreptitiously as possible, as "the Government here is most anxious to get a clue where these came from".[55]

Volunteers

Others were starting to volunteer. William Johnston, eldest son of Samuel Johnston, who ran the Glen Printworks at Newtownards, was sent in August 1913 by his father to run the Manchester base of the family business. He volunteered his services to the gun-runners, and over the next year he smuggled into Ulster three million rounds of .303 ammunition and 500 rifles in bleaching powder barrels padded with farina. His two brothers, who also worked for the family business, had both attended Campbell College and served the UVF in Newtownards; the middle son, Elliott, was a Half-Company Commander. He later became a Captain in the 13th Battalion Royal Irish Rifles (Co. Down Volunteers), was awarded the Military Cross and became one of thirteen pupils of his former school (including James Davidson) to die on the opening day of the Battle of the Somme.[56]

By the close of 1913 there were many constraints on the importation of rifles into Ulster. George Clark agreed to try but, for all the facilities he may have had at his disposal as the owner of a large shipyard, "all ports were so closely watched that at the end of twelve months he had only succeeded in bringing in some 300 rifles without bayonets".

Reading the memoirs of Robert Adgey, Fred Crawford and others, the impression is given that thousands of rifles were imported between 1911 and 1913; however, Fred bewails the fact that at the close of the latter year the UVF could only boast 10,000 weapons. In November 1913 it became evident that the allocation of rifles to the various battalions "fell far short of the number required for training, let alone arming, the Volunteers".[57] Bearing in mind that Fred's figures can be suspect – he claimed that the UVF totalled 200,000 Volunteers, which was probably double the true figure – it is difficult to be certain of the reality. Late in 1913 Wilfrid Spender, who was on the UVF HQ Staff at the Old Town Hall and was its Quarter-Master General, inadvertently allowed Lord Northcliffe to see the UVF arms register, and the latter admitted that it was nowhere near as impressive as he had been led to believe. Spender would not have disagreed; in his private account of the gun-running episode, he accepted that, at the start of 1914, "there were only a few hundred arms available and the importation was less than 100 per week".[58] The reports of T.J. Smith, the Commissioner of Police, who had inadvertently accompanied one delivery of arms into Ulster, came to much the same conclusion.[59] Count Gleichen was also unimpressed.

Gleichen

Brigadier-General Lord Edward Gleichen had taken up his Irish Command in Belfast at the start of August 1911; he was GOC of the British troops in the city. Gleichen had been one of those unfortunate enough to be trapped in Ladysmith during the Boer War as a result of the erroneous tactics of Ulster's General Sir George White. He made an ascent in a balloon above the town, but did not consider using the opportunity to escape! White died in 1912, and was buried at Broughshane during Gleichen's command in Belfast.

As a grand-nephew of Queen Victoria, Gleichen could never fathom the Belfast working-classes. He was once surrounded by half-a-dozen waifs asking 'Wah's tarm?' "Eventually I discovered that these infants wanted to know what o'clock it was … the lower classes in Belfast were decidedly not attractive; but all the same they must have had a hidden sense of the beautiful, for they were always stealing our flowers".[60]

His elevated social status, however, allowed him access to the Ulster élite and, despite what were obviously difficult social moments, he made an effort to maintain good relations with those who became heavily involved in the development of the UVF. Social engagements provided an opportunity for both the Ulstermen and the military representative of the British Government to keep a close eye on the other.

Gleichen was invited to Craigavon in January 1913, but regretted it (as did F.E. Smith the following August) because, as he noted in the Visitors' Book, he was "heavily rooked by Mrs Craig who knows too much about auction bridge".

Gleichen confessed that he was impressed by the spectacles performed by Ulstermen, but he does not appear to have been too concerned by their alleged weaponry. He was aware of the seizures which had occurred in 1913, adding that he was told "that none of the real ones had yet been seized". He revealed an alleged figure of 50,000 rifles in the province; he said that he was prepared to believe this, but added a note of disdain: "These rifles were converted Lee Metfords taking Government ammunition".[61]

Herein lay the problem for the UVF. The Lee Metfords had effectively been phased out of the British Army before the Boer War. Also no-one, it seemed, wanted to use the Vetterlis. The arsenal gathered by the Ulstermen was too antiquated and lacking in uniformity to enable satisfactory training, distribution of ammunition, and confidence in use. Whilst the UVF may well have challenged any opposition from the RIC, it would prove no match for the concentrated military might that Westminster could muster.

Effectively, Gleichen's last duty in Belfast was on 24th July 1914 – before he found himself, rather unexpectedly three weeks later, riding down the lanes of France on the front lines – as Chief Guest at Campbell College Speech Day. He may well have appreciated the irony and humour of the occasion, for there sitting on the front row, probably exhibiting an air of quiet amusement, was none other than recent Public Enemy No.1, the individual who – only three months earlier – had done more than anyone to ensure the survival of the Ulster cause: Frederick Hugh Crawford.

Even at that late date no-one was aware just how lethal Europe was to become over the next four years. Nevertheless, during the summer of 1914 the political scene in Ulster had become increasingly destabilised following the successful passage of the Home Rule Bill in May, which defied the prediction of the *Belfast News Letter* from two years earlier. It had then portrayed Ulster people as "patriots of the finest type, and it is inconceivable that the British nation will ever permit any political party to put into force legislation which would rob these Loyalists of their birthright. To do so would be to make loyalty a crime".[62]

As Ulstermen had found themselves effectively branded criminals, the illegal bearing of arms made little difference to them. On the day after Campbell College's Speech Day, only a couple of miles distant on the Newtownards Road, some of Fred's handiwork was on display. Three thousand men of the East Belfast UVF paraded; on show they had two Colt machine-guns and one Maxim. These were men from all walks of life. Men who had just completed a long shift at the shipyards joined captains of industry (including Sir William Ewart) and members of the professions: "a practising barrister who had discarded wig and gown for a khaki cap and tunic, and who had relinquished a quill for a Mauser".[63]

As one historian has commented: "The success of the Larne gun-running had increased the possibility of conflict between the Government and the UVF in the summer of 1914".[64] In acknowledgement of the growing political fragility, Birrell had visited Ulster in June, and probably found circumstances worse than he anticipated. He recognised that Carson was running out of options and that the UVF was tired of constant drilling. The arrival of the rifles at Larne made the situation more friable – and, indirectly, the Chief Secretary for Ireland gave Fred his due. In communication with Asquith he stated that "the great smuggling coup" reflected great credit upon its organisers and he confessed his admiration: "as plotters, they beat us hollow".[65]

Notes

1. D/1700/5/13/20, 10 December 1916: "You know Irishmen as well as I do and better, and how they like to join a shindy no matter what it is about".

2. Keith Haines, *The Looted Paradise: the life and times of Arthur Moore*, (Ballymaconaghy Publishing, Belfast, 2004), p.62.

3. Ronald McNeill, *Ulster's Stand for Union*, (London, 1922), p.43.

4. D/1415/B/34, p.1.

5. Fred H Crawford, *Guns for Ulster*, (Belfast, 1947), pp.14-15.

6. McNeill, pp.190-191.

7. McNeill, p.19. ATQ Stewart, *The Ulster Crisis*, (London, 1967), pp.90-91.

8. Crawford, p.16. D/1415/B/34, p.1. Mathews was, of course, his mother's maiden name.

9. D/1415/B/34, p.22.

10. D/1700/10/1/808, –/812, 15 and 24 June 1910.

11. D/1700/10/1/881.

12. For Charley, see James W Taylor, *The 2nd Battalion Royal Irish Rifles in the Great War*, (Four Courts Press, Dublin, 2005), pp.211-213.

13. Birmingham Small Arms Co. and London Small Arms Co.

14. D/1700/10/1/860. This last word is a useful way of authenticating a document by Fred; he invariably spelled 'through' as 'thro''. The other related correspondence is D/1700/10/1/854, –/857-859.

15. R.J. Adgey, *Arming the Ulster Volunteers 1914*, (Belfast, post-1952), p.57.

16. Timothy Bowman, *Carson's Army: the Ulster Volunteer Force 1910-1922*, (Manchester University Press, 2007), p.144.

17. Bowman, pp.16, 18.

18. D/1415/B/34, p.18 seems to indicate that James Craig sought out 'subscriptions' from amongst the businessmen of Ulster, whilst James Cunningham dispensed the actual sums: Adgey, p.20.

19. McNeill, p.147.

20. D/1415/B/34, pp.25-28.

21. León Ó Broin, *The Chief Secretary: Augustine Birrell in Ireland*, (London, 1969), p.54.

22. D/1700/5/6/1. D/1700/10/1/917, –/927, –/930-932, –/939-940.

23. D/1415/B/34, p.4. McCammon died on 28 April 1917.

24. Stewart, p.259 n.6

25. D/1700/10/1/918, –/920.

26. D/1415/D/1. Ian Colvin, *The Life of Lord Carson*, (London, 1934), Vol.II, 401, cited in Stewart, p.219. D/1633/2/19, 6 June 1914.

27. Adgey, pp.11, 18-19.

28. D/1700/5/17/1/53, 31 July 1914. Sometimes the imported quantities were very small: Bowman, p.141.

29. D/1415/B/34, pp.6-7. D/1700/5/17/1/2A-2G, July to September 1911.

30. For fuller details: Stewart, pp.93-96. Crawford, pp.19-20.

31. D/1327/2/7.

32. D/1415/D/1.

33. In fairness to de Broke, despite the fact that one historian described him as "not more than 200 years behind his time", he demonstrated a solid commitment to Ulster's plight: Stewart, p.73. George Dangerfield, *The Strange Death of Liberal England*, (Stanford University Press, 1997), p.47.

34. Patrick Montgomery, *Following Father's Footsteps in Flanders*, (privately published, Belfast, 2005), p.24.

35. Keith Haines, *Neither Rogues nor Fools; a History of Campbell College and Campbellians*, (Campbell College, Belfast, 1993), p.239.

36. Stewart, p.91.

37. D/1700/5/17/1/31 (Michael J F McCarthy in Wimbledon). McNeill, p.123. Colvin, II, 359.

38. He presented this to his first school, Methodist College, in February 1939: D/1700/5/6/60.

39. D/640/20/1, 10 December 1912. The batons were essentially truncheons about two feet in length.

40. D/1700/5/5/90, 16 December 1934.

41. Stewart, p.88.

42. For this episode: D/1415/B/34; Bowman, p.141; Stewart, pp.94-95. The sources give different quantities of confiscated rifles. Fred stated that there were up to 6000 or 7000; Bowman p.141 claimed that there were only 4500. Adgey p.17 believed that there were 2000 and that, a few months later, he and William Hunter 'liberated' the bayonets – but Fred was quite categorical that Spiro reclaimed the latter. The titled MP may have been the Earl of Farnham, but I have been unable to substantiate this.

43. The bayonets stayed in storage for some time, and Fred settled the account early in 1914: D/640/26/2-4.

44. Adgey, p.20.

45. L W McBride, *The Greening of Dublin Castle: the transformation of bureaucratic and juridical personnel in Ireland 1892-1922*, (Washington DC, 1991), p.178.

46. *Belfast News Letter*, 10 April 1912. Bowman, pp.19-24.

47. D/640/24/1.

48. Bowman, pp.95-97.

49. Campbell College became no.24 General Hospital during the Second World War.

50. D/1327/2/12. Haines, *Neither Rogues …*, pp.106-112.

51. *Belfast News Letter*, 17 May 1913.

52. D/1415/D/1.

53. *Belfast News Letter*, 29 September 1913. Stewart, p.78, states that Fred led the West Belfast battalions; however, Fred's personal correspondence indicates that he commanded the South Belfast Regiment: D/1700/5/13/17, 4 October 1913. See also D/640/11/2, p.67, 8 December 1921.

54. D/1415/B/34, p.70. Major R McCalmont echoed this sentiment: Ian Maxwell, *The Life of Sir Wilfrid Spender 1876-1960*, (QUB Ph D thesis, 1991), pp.64-65.

55. D/640/26/1. D/640/28/1-5.

56. Stewart, pp.99-100. Letter from a niece of William Johnston to the author, 17 November 2000. Haines, *Neither Rogues…*, pp.130, 133.

57. Crawford, p.27. Stewart, p.104.

58. D/1763/6.

59. Maxwell, pp.58-59. Spender recorded that "My duties comprised the supply of equipment, arms and ammunition, the organisation of transport and the supervision of communications": D/1763/6.

60. Major-General Lord Edward Gleichen, *A Guardsman's Memories: a book of recollections*, (Edinburgh/London, 1932), p.352.

61. Gleichen, pp.365-366. The Lee Metford used the .303 calibre ammunition.

62. *Belfast News Letter*, 10 April 1912.

63. *Belfast News Letter*, 27 July 1914.

64. Maxwell, p.74.

65. Ó Broin, pp.84-85, 94-95, 99-102.

A Box of Cigars

∞

As has been stated earlier, if ever Frederick Hugh Crawford recalled the day in September 1893, when he had hung virtually by a thread over the shaft of one of the wells at Alexander Crawford & Son, and felt that Heaven had preserved his life for a purpose,[1] that moment came on the night of 24/25th April 1914.

It is stretching parallels too far to endow the voyage of *SS Fanny* with the characteristics of a Viking saga, but there are echoes of episodes from such tales as *King Harald's Saga*. The *Fanny* was a Norwegian vessel which was to sail the very same waters of the north-western Baltic and Kattegat that Harald Hardrada, King of Norway and pretender to the English throne, had done 850 years previously – past the island of Laeso, beyond the point of Skagen (or the Skaw) and into the North Sea. As had Harald, Fred sheltered in the lee of the islands, took advantage of a sudden fog and negotiated his way past awkward protagonists. The principal article of faith that both Harald and Fred had in common was their attachment to the notion of an Empire.[2]

By early 1914 the self-styled Ulster Provisional Government clearly believed – both in relation to the British Government and its own Volunteers – that unless it possessed the martial means to sustain its aspirations, its bluff would be called. On Saturday 17th January the Chief Staff Officer of the Ulster Volunteer Force (UVF), Col. Hacket Pain, sat down at his desk in the Old Town Hall and penned a letter to a Belfast starch manufacturer. Its destination was only one mile distant, but it proved the inspiration to one of the most momentous events in Ulster's history. Hacket Pain notified Fred that General Richardson, Commanding Officer of the UVF, was asking Carson to call a conference on the arms question at the Old Town Hall at 10.45 am three days later, "when your attendance is especially requested".[3]

A Single Delivery

Fred – as Director of Ordnance of the UVF – was requested to itemise the status of the number and distribution of weapons already in Ulster, as Carson was being asked "to define the future policy in regard to the importance of arms". It had become necessary to decide what level of further importation might be required and Fred was asked "whether you would be willing to undertake the full arrangements for this importation if the Leader authorises it", and to frame a plan of action and assess its chances of success.

The large single delivery of almost 25,000 rifles which arrived at Larne in April 1914 was very much the *chef-d'oeuvre* of Fred Crawford, and his fame – or notoriety – is based almost exclusively upon this episode. It is equally evident from his memoirs that he was reluctant to become involved in it. He revealed that he had believed for some time that "I could not do anything more by smuggling" and the very jejune results achieved by George Clark only confirmed his belief. Within two days he had replied to Hacket Pain that "I much prefer having nothing to do with further importation of arms and ammunition on business and family reasons". He had not, however, abandoned his conviction that "the only thing to do was to run the guns into Ulster in one large consignment", and, if he were to be cajoled, he laid down a lengthy list of stipulations to be presented to what was, in reality, a session of the secret arms committee of the Ulster Unionist Council (UUC).

Dr Stewart assessed[4] that the latter, in addition to Fred, comprised General Richardson, Col. Hacket Pain and Captain Wilfrid Spender – all of whom were integrally involved on the staff of the UVF; George Clark, shipbuilder and the original chairman; James Craig and James Cunningham, who were engaged in the financing operations; Richard Cowzer, who worked for Cunningham; Frank Hall; Dawson Bates (Hon. Secretary of the UUC); solicitor Alexander McDowell; and ship-owner and later philanthropist Samuel Kelly. At least six of these had existing or future links with Campbell College;[5] and six of these rebels against the Crown were to receive knighthoods!

In his reply to the committee, Fred indicated that there were 3000 Lee Metford rifles in Birmingham, which were paid for, but not delivered; he recommended that these should be sold at cost price to the British League, who could store them, and this may also help to mislead the authorities. Additionally – although the figures which he supplied were only approximate – they had in Hamburg 4600 Vetterli rifles and one million rounds of ammunition, plus 4800 bayonets (reclaimed from Hammersmith), which were awaiting despatch.

With regard to possible purchases he offered alternative proposals. The less preferred option was another 20,000 Italian rifles and two million cartridges which, with £2000 for additional expenditure, would probably cost around £33,000. Although this was cheaper than the alternative, he felt it more dangerous, as the Vetterlis "are carefully watched by our Secret Service, as only Ulster is buying them". Much more expensive, at almost twice the price, was the same quantity of Mausers and ammunition, which could probably be landed in six weeks and would have the advantage of greater secrecy. He argued that there was no point in striving to import a lesser quantity of weapons.

Fred stated that, if the arms committee were agreeable to his submission, he would want the entire funding available "before I make a definite move". His obligation would be to get the load alongside the quay, but others would be responsible for its distribution. He added that all small-scale imports by others should be deprecated, as it would only draw the unwelcome attention of patrol boats and naval craft, and that no-one else should be engaged in negotiating for weapons. For his own protection he insisted that he receive written instructions and that only one person should have the authority to interfere with or to vary these instructions. He concluded by stating that: "I believe this [plan] to be quite feasible and can be carried out".

The seasoned smuggler attended the meeting at the Old Town Hall. He rehearsed his proposal and added that he felt the best option was to travel immediately to Hamburg to see if a deal could be arranged with Bruno Spiro. He would then purchase a steamer, load it up "and transfer the rifles to a local steamer in some estuary in an out of the way place in Scotland". If the plan sounded simple, it evidently set nerves jangling, none more so than those of General Sir George Richardson, who perhaps felt he had most to lose. Walter Long MP, who was generally on the periphery of Ulster politics, left Craigavon a couple of days later in boisterous mood, commenting that it was a "Grand meeting ... Marching to Victory"; Carson was a little more restrained with his pen: "Grave but encouraging. Fear not".[6] Certainly all of them could have faced charges of treason, which is no doubt why Fred did not receive the written instructions he requested from the Committee. The possible consequences were so unthinkable that agreement could not be reached at this stage and Fred discussed the idea further with a sub-committee on Monday 2nd February, when it was finally agreed that he should visit Hamburg.

Hamburg

At this meeting Richardson seems to have argued that it would be preferable to land the guns in England. Fred disagreed, and he wrote after the meeting to say: "I feel fully convinced if the rifles are once landed in England openly, you will never get them out again". He firmly believed that his plan was "the only one that will be satisfactory" and suggested that, with himself and Craig in attendance to air their views, Richardson could talk it over with Carson and a sympathetic Lord Roberts (who was to pass away at the end of the year). The struggling businessman reiterated that: "I prefer, for family and business reasons, not to undertake this work", but said that he was happy to go along with anything agreed by Carson. Fred notified Richardson that he could be contacted via his office until Thursday evening, but he did not hang around to be further delayed and set off for Scotland the following day (3rd February).

Engaged upon an act of recidivism, Fred clearly knew how to blur his trail. He travelled to Dundee via the boat to Ardrossan, as ever shadowed by a detective – a companion to which he was to become accustomed over the next few months.[7] He visited the offices of Andrew J. Kirk, chemical agents in the Scottish town, one suspects on ostensibly legitimate business. In Dundee Fred also felt it incumbent upon him to address fears and reservations evidently expressed by James Craig about the venture:

> You and I have so far seen eye to eye in the matter we are interested in at present. I have been giving your scheme a great deal of thought and, the more I turn it over, the less I like it. You have to consider our own men and how exasperated they will be if they do not get what they want. Even should my scheme fail, it will show them that their leaders were fully alive to the situation and that they did all in their power to fulfil their promises ... I do not think there is more than one chance in ten ... of it being a failure and, if it were carried thro', what a moral effect (sic) it would produce not only with our own men but in England and Scotland.

On the evening of 4th February he took the train from Edinburgh to Darlington, in order to contact Major F. T. Tristram who had been instrumental in shipping large quantities of .303 ammunition to Ulster by means of the legerdemain of his Pioneer Cement Works – which is still extant – at Haverton Hill on the Tees.[8] The sympathetic English Territorials' officer had clearly just returned from Belfast and wanted to discuss details of a shipment destined for Coleraine. Fred indicated to Tristram that "I am at present an object of interest to the authorities". Both of them were justified in their caution, for in June the smuggling operation was dramatically uncovered. A large quantity of ammunition (150,000 rounds) was discovered by accident and Tristram felt obliged to contact Fred later to apologise. Fred was to accept it generously as the fortunes of war.[9]

On Friday, Fred took the opportunity at the Royal United Services Institution to catch up on some correspondence. In a letter to Captain Ricardo of Sion Mills, one of the leading UVF figures, he confirmed his reluctance for the mission on which he was engaged: "I only wish someone else who could do the work would do it. I have too much in hand at present to take this up. However, there is no use growling. I suppose I have got to do it". Over the next three months Fred's available time for family and commercial matters was rather erratic.

The recipient of his other letter from Whitehall was Lord Carson and it was typical of Fred that, amongst all the distractions and stressfulness of those days, he should take time out to congratulate his Leader on his impending 60th birthday (9th February): "I hope before your next birthday you will see Ulster freed from all anxiety for the future as the result of your labour. I believe now is the time to strike the last great blow".

He indicated to Carson, and to his other correspondent and fellow conspirator, Richard Cowzer (who worked for James Cunningham, at the latter's offices in Ocean Buildings in Donegall Square), that he expected to be away about a week. He notified Cowzer that his contact details would be W. H. Mathews, c/o Benny Spiro, Adolphsbrücke, Hamburg – but that 'Mathews' was not to appear on any envelope.

Fred spent a couple of days in the German port discussing three proposals made to him by Bruno Spiro. One offer was of 30,000 Russian rifles with ammunition and bayonets – although the latter were without scabbards. Fred was always insistent that any rifles he purchased boasted bayonets. His arms committee pointed out that the absence of bayonets reduced prices, but Fred's riposte was that "a man with an empty rifle but no bayonet was a more or less harmless creature". He argued that "the day of the bayonet was not yet passed", and believed that the First World War proved his thesis. Bruno's second offer was for Vetterlis with bayonets, for which he had Ulster's one million cartridges in store, but Fred was weary of obsolete Italian rifles.

The arms committee would have preferred Fred to take one of those alternatives, but its representative was adamant that Spiro's third offer was by far the best, despite being nearly double the price of the others – 15,000 new Austrian and 5,000 German Army rifles, which utilised the standard Mannlicher ammunition which was readily available in the United Kingdom and America.

On the assumption that his colleagues would accept his recommendation, Fred also made tentative arrangements about the packing of the consignment with a shipping agent named Friedrich (Fritz) Schneider and the whole delivery was initially agreed at £51,272. The purchase of a steamer – at a cost of £3,500 – to transport the arms had also been discussed; the vessel would be retained by the smuggler at the end of the voyage, or it would be sold as quickly as possible if returned to Hamburg. Spiro added that "it is not impossible to have everything ready by 30th March if your definite order will reach me inside ten days".

Fred returned to London via Flushing around 12th February and collected mail for W. H. Mathews at his *poste-restante* at Charing Cross. He reported to Carson and Craig and explained why he had selected the third option: "One point I emphasised very strongly, viz the moral effect (sic) of our men being armed with the most modern rifles of the latest improvements". They concurred and Craig found the money, although Fred added: "how, I do not know".

From London Fred wrote to his German supplier, indicating that he was pushing their choice, and confirming their arrangements, but – always determined to seek a bargain – he asked if Spiro might agree to an overall sum of £50,000. Ever mindful of security and the intrusion of inquisitive officials, he posted his letter to Hamburg to the arms dealer's secretary, Frau Elsa Kanzki, at her home at Pöseldorferweg 17 in the city.[10] Fred had returned home to Belfast by 14th February, via Birmingham. At home he received – in his guise of Robert Smith – further contractual details from Spiro's organisation. The German expressed some irritation at the rounded-down figure of £50,000, but did agree to split the difference on any packing costs above £500.

Fred placed the details before his fellow plotters, but had to write to Hamburg on 18th February to say that: "I am still trying to get our people to accept [the preferred deal]. Of course, the amount is so large that they hesitate" – which was probably a genuine comment, but one which contained another bargaining gesture. Fred and Bruno Spiro came to trust each other implicitly and to develop a very close working and personal relationship, but both of them always acted in a cautious professional manner. It is difficult to know whether Spiro sensed that the Ulstermen were stalling to obtain a better price but, if so, he was not to be outmanoeuvred. He sent a couple of letters on 16th and 17th February which revealed – probably quite honestly – that an established American customer was interested in purchasing the same arms.

On 21st February 1914, a dismal Saturday characterised by mist and thick fine rain, the Spenders – given tickets by George Clark – went to watch the launch of the late *Titanic's* sister, the *Britannic*. They returned to their home in Adelaide Park (off the Malone Road) via the Old Town Hall, where Craig "was looking very grave". It may be that Fred had broken the news to him about the American intervention in their purchase but, somewhere in Belfast that same day, W. H. Mathews communicated once more with the north German port. He asked the arms dealer to hold off as long as he could, as the Ulstermen did not want to have to fall back on one of the other rifles. He also asked Spiro to tell Schneider that a ballast of coal was preferable to that of salt, which would "spoil the other stuff". On 24th February the arms dealer corresponded with Robert Smith, saying that he was procrastinating with the Americans: "I quite see your difficulties, and I should like to do my best to help you".

The Bravest Man

Fred, however, was by that stage probably en route to Hamburg to finalise the deal. In London he called on Carson at his home (5 Eaton Place) and emphasised unambiguously that "once I crossed this time to Hamburg there is no turning back with me, no matter what the circumstances were, so far as my personal safety is concerned, and no contrary orders from the Committee to cancel what they have agreed will I obey". He said that he would never renege on his promise, even if it cost him his life. He made it clear that he would only go if Carson gave him a categorical assurance that he was "willing to back me to the finish in this undertaking", even though he ran the risk of imprisonment. Fred recalled the barrister looking "stern and grim", but the latter rose and promised: "Crawford, I'll see you through this business even should I go to prison for it", adding "you are the bravest man I ever met".

Fred had admired Carson since he had donned the mantle of the Unionist leadership four years previously; from this point on, he became extravagant in his political and personal devotion to the Dubliner: "from that moment my soul was knit to his, even as Jonathan's was to David, and I loved him as a leader and as a man". His affection for Carson could be expressed in unusual ways; in July 1914, in the wake of the gun-running episode, Fred thanked his Leader for a framed portrait: "I shall treasure it more than any other in my possession" – and intimated that he would hand it down as a family heirloom.

Such sentiments had expanded into grandiloquence by the close of Carson's active political career. In May 1921, three months after Carson had relinquished the Unionist leadership, Fred wrote to "My dear old Chief" to congratulate him on his elevation as Baron Carson of Duncairn:

> There is only one man I have implicitly trusted … during three or four years of the political stress Ulster passed thro' prior to the War, and that man is yourself. Tho' I bid you goodbye as my Political Leader, I shall always have that love and devotion for you that a son has for his father. I look upon the confidence, trust and friendship you have imposed in me as the greatest privilege God Almighty has permitted me to enjoy during my lifetime. I shall ever hold these sentiments towards you while you live, and revere your memory when in this sphere your work is completed.[11]

On 26th February 1914 a resurrected John Washington Graham of New York arrived on a very brief visit to Hamburg to finalise details of the order and transportation of the goods. Including £3,500 for the purchase of a steamer and nearly £1,300 for packing costs, Fred agreed arrangements for the payment of almost £62,500.[12] He paid £9,000 whilst in the city, and agreed the transfer of £15,000 when he returned to London. A second payment of £15,000 would be made, and Spiro would be handed a further sum on 30th March "provided the goods are packed ready for sailing" and arrangements would also be made to transfer the full settlement when Fred had joined the rifles in the steamer. The total order was 20,000 Austrian and German rifles, plus two million rounds, 4600 Vetterli rifles plus one million rounds held in store and 4800 bayonets.

The arrangements worked well. Although occasionally Fred feared having to be overdrawn at the bank, the representative at the Union of London & Smith's Bank at Sloane Street, Mr Nind, proved collaborative and James Craig ensured that all payments were covered promptly. Spiro did, however, specify one caveat: "I am not responsible for seizure on the high sea"!

15,000 Austrian Steyr (Mannlicher) rifles arrived at Hamburg in a special freight train of double-bogie wagons, labelled for Galveston, USA, to join the Mausers and Vetterlis already in store. All future packaging was addressed to the Texan port or to other ports in Mexico and Central America. Fred's arrangements for packing were detailed and laborious – and consequently expensive. The arms committee was "aghast" at the cost, but Fred was insistent that his method was essential for rapid and tractable transfer at sea and upon arrival at a port in Ulster.

Secrecy and security aside, the packing proved to be Fred's main headache. He had each Mannlicher and Mauser rifle wrapped in paper with a bayonet and 100 cartridges, and then tied in twine; likewise each Vetterli with 200 rounds. Five rifles were then packed in straw and sewn tightly in sacking cloth and thick cord. Each bundle weighed approximately 75lbs (or 35 kilos). Fred was to express irritation at the dim-witted character of the packers, which necessitated him making several return journeys to Hamburg to supervise progress, all of which attracted the unwelcome attention of the German police, but ultimately Schneider kept his part of the deal and the rifles were ready for loading by the agreed date of 30th March.

These proved extremely stressful weeks for the prospective gun-runner, the arms dealer and the shipping agent; Fred later observed that: "No-one will ever realise what all the worry and anxiety meant to Spiro, Schneider and myself. Schneider [described elsewhere as 'a stout man'] was eventually worn to a shadow". It is not surprising that, over the next few weeks, there were occasions when Fred was to become tetchy and abrasive.

Although the sale made him a good profit, even Spiro voiced his reservations about the likely chances of the success of the mission and had warned Fred from the outset that such an operation was bound to be discovered because it was too conspicuous. Fred enquired of Spiro what was the largest consignment he had previously despatched: "He said two or three thousand"! The Ulsterman, most probably trying to convince himself, replied: "My chances were good just because it had never been tried before. It was the very audacity of it that gave me confidence that I could carry it through". Inevitably, appeals were made to higher quarters: "I believed that our cause was just and I believed in God Almighty".

This agency clearly proved responsive and reliable. During March Fred travelled between Belfast and Hamburg via varied routes, as he knew that he was often trailed by detectives; the conspirators were constantly under the surveillance of the British and German authorities, and a British consular official in Hamburg actually sent the Foreign

Secretary [Grey, whose constituency Fred had impertinently canvassed in late 1893] a cable, half way through the voyage warning that "*SS Fanny* was British-owned and carrying guns".[13]

As Fred travelled backwards and forwards, he made a conscious effort to keep Belfast informed of developments, especially when he was unexpectedly delayed abroad. The intermediary with the UUC was Richard Cowzer, who was asked to take enclosures for such as Richardson and Spender the short walk down Chichester Street to the Old Town Hall. Later in March he would have found both these men, in company with many of the UUC and UVF leadership, encamped at Craigavon. There had been rumours of the impending arrest of a number of individuals and of the threat of military action against the province; Lilian Spender recorded seeing two warships in Belfast Lough on the first day of spring. Craigavon effectively became an armed camp in late March and early April – so much so that even Spender was held at the gate for twenty minutes at midnight one night when he had forgotten the password.

His wife noted the amusement generated by the fact that the Dorset Regiment, en route from Victoria to Holywood Barracks, had marched past Craig's home and, having been saluted by the UVF guard (in civilian dress), returned the salute. It should be borne in mind, however, that this march past was probably intended to emphasise the Government's military presence in Belfast, and even to be intimidatory, as Circular Road must have been a deliberate diversion on the part of the Dorsets; whether they marched along the Holywood Road or the Old Holywood Road, Craigavon was not on their direct route.[14] Fred always felt gratified that this UVF guard was armed with rifles that he had earlier imported, "not to fight in a rebellion but to fight to retain their right to be loyal to the Crown, King and Constitution".[15]

Helen Crawford endeavoured to fill some lonely hours by holding an At Home one day in March,[16] attended by Mrs Spender who commented on two or three "really musical individuals", whilst Fred spent much of the month occupied with the purchase of a suitable vessel, and landing site, for his Mannlichers, Mausers and Vetterlis.

SS *Fanny*

Her husband had become anxious at the start of that month. He had evidently discussed the possible purchase of a ship with Schneider at the end of February and now, in correspondence about one of the instalments paid for the guns, he urged Spiro to "Tell Schneider I shall supply him with a Captain and Chief Engineer for the steamer, and tell him to try and mark down a steamer as soon as possible. My people are hurrying me. I must be up to time". Spiro replied that he was seeing the shipping agent that afternoon (5th March), but also revealed that "the goods" had not yet arrived in Hamburg. On the following day, as John Washington Graham, Fred again made clear his anxiety that all the packing and loading should be completed by the end of the month.

Within a few days Fred arrived in Hamburg in search of a vessel. He knew that it would probably prove relatively easy to hire suitable deckhands and firemen on the continent, but he needed the assurance of reliable and trustworthy officers. He had approached Mr Brown, the Managing Director of the Antrim Iron Ore Steamship Company, who loaned him the services of the burly Captain Andrew Agnew, whom Fred described as "a fine specimen of the British Mercantile Marine officer".[17] The latter hired a Captain Nichol, as his Mate, and a Chief and Second Engineer named Calderwood and Boyd. Agnew met Fred on 8th March and made final arrangements. Four days later the four crew members took slightly differing routes via London to Cologne. They then caught a train to Hamburg arriving at 9 pm on Saturday 14th March, to be met on the platform by the leading conspirator and Fritz Schneider.

With information garnered from some discreet newspaper advertisements, the shipping agent provided Fred with a list of potentially suitable steamers and the erstwhile marine engineer decided to examine two – both moored in Norway. One was a Russian ship, based at a port in the south of the country; the other was the Norwegian-owned *SS Fanny*, berthed further north in Bergen.[18] Leaving Nichol and Boyd in Hamburg, Fred, Agnew, Calderwood and Schneider set off to inspect the steamer.

Departing at night – making their first contact with the Kiel Canal in the dark – they reached Fredrikshavn in north Denmark in the late morning of 16th March and boarded a boat, later caught in thick fog, bound for Christiania (now Oslo). Following a pleasant journey by train they arrived in Bergen late on St. Patrick's Day.

Wasting no time, they approached Erik Rusten, the owner of the *Fanny* early the next morning. Fred, Schneider and Calderwood used their marine and engineering background to assess the vessel, which was still discharging coal after a rough journey from Newcastle-upon-Tyne. Although it could only manage a speed of eight knots, Fred's *alter ego*, wealthy American John Washington Graham believed it would serve its intended purpose and offered Rusten his asking price, so long as the sale was made on the spot and that a number of necessary repairs were made. Fred wanted to sail her under the Norwegian flag and he took out a mortgage on the ship, but registered it in the name of the man who had owned it prior to Rusten.

66-year-old Marthin Falck, who captained the *Fanny*, had once owned her. His father had been a ship owner, and Marthin had been a ship's captain since at least the age of 28,[19] but a string of bad cargoes with the *Fanny* had obliged him to sell her to Rusten. Fred regarded it as advantageous to utilise the captain and his officers, who had experience of the vessel's idiosyncrasies, so he hired them. They, in turn, proved more than delighted that the new American owner raised their wages by half.[20] They were told that the vessel would initially be used for pleasure, mainly fishing, and then they would be heading for Iceland to collect a general cargo destined for Hamburg.

Fred was keen to return that night (18th March) to the German city with Schneider, so he spent the afternoon making his arrangements with Agnew for a rendezvous. Falck, who would have enjoyed up to half a century's familiarity with the Baltic waters, was asked to suggest the best location to unload a cargo from lighters on to the *Fanny*, and it was agreed that the rifles would be brought to the bight off the island of Langeland, opposite Svendborg (on the island of Fyn), about four miles from each shore. In his own later account of events, Fred's memory proved faulty, as he specifically states that he told Agnew to "meet me … on the Monday three weeks from the present date", but in reality the arrangement was for the original date of 30th March.

Agnew remained in Bergen to load the *Fanny* with stores and equipment, to make all final payments and to arrange for the ship's papers to be forwarded to Schneider at Mattentwiete 24, Hamburg – a street that runs down the water's edge. The Ulsterman added another 100 tons of coal to the 43 tons which were left on the vessel when they bought it, and purchased supplies for a possible two or tree months at sea. Clearly the final arrangements made with Fred had been a little rushed because, as the latter took the train from Bergen to Hamburg, via Christiania and Göteborg, he rattled off three letters with further requests and instructions. These included plenty of fresh water, a signalling lamp, and fishing tackle, as they would have plenty of time to use this, and it would supplement their stores. In the event, the fishing gear proved enormously helpful to Agnew. The crew had become convinced that they were expected to run a blockade, and were on the point of leaving; the arrival of the fishing gear from the chandler enabled Agnew to convince them that the *Fanny* was destined purely for a pleasure trip.

One of the features that may have insinuated something more sinister to the crew was that Fred asked Agnew to ensure that the slings could bear a one ton weight, as they would have to load 260 tons of cargo at Langeland. One of the ironies experienced by Agnew during the five days he was in Bergen, before he sailed on 24th March, was that Falck unwittingly read aloud all the news from Ulster in the press! After they sailed, Falck said that they knew the *Fanny* was destined for some secret mission, but that they believed it to be an escapade related to events in France.

Although the new owner had originally indicated that the ship was destined for Iceland, at 4pm on 24th March the vessel set sail for Denmark. Four days later, as they reached Thoro point, as per Fred's instructions written from the train, and much to Falck's evident distress, Agnew began to disguise the ship, painting out the name of the *Fanny* on the port and starboard bows and the stern, primarily so that those bringing the rifles to meet her off the Danish island would not discover her name. Agnew arrived off Svendborg at 2.30pm on the Saturday: "As the time was near when the crew would find out what our business was, I took the opportunity to let them know what we were about to load. I had to pay them well for the part they were about to take, but I made it conditional on them playing their part well. Captain Falck was the hardest to please, but even he was satisfied". They spent a warm Sunday at rest, awaiting the arrival of the lighters carrying the guns.

Fred returned to Belfast via Flushing and London about 22nd March during the most turbulently political week, when circulating rumours were making even the leading UUC figures apprehensive; the Lord Mayor of Belfast, R. J. McMordie, even chose that week to pass away! In an endeavour to cover all eventualities, and to create diversionary lines of communication, Fred contacted Tristram in Darlington asking him to send any correspondence or telegrams that he received to James Cunningham (at Ocean Buildings), adding: "Things are moving rapidly now". He wrote to Spiro and indicated that "The situation has altered since I left here – but you can expect me not later than Saturday 28 inst".

Fred cannot have seen much of his family during that week. Within the claustrophobic atmosphere of Craigavon disagreements were aired about the wisdom of continuing the gun-running. The exhortation of Carson and Craig to proceed prevailed, but there was much debate about where the landing should occur. Fred and Wilfrid Spender spent many long hours deliberating this. General Richardson – who appears to have lost every argument he started – preferred Belfast, as he felt that it offered a better chance of military control, but Fred and the UVF Quarter-Master general favoured other options, particularly Larne. This dispute had still not been finalised when Fred departed Belfast on 26th March. The arrangement was that, when Fred had sailed the *Fanny* into a remote western Scottish loch, he would place a pinhole in a map to identify his location, and post it via "a private business firm" in Belfast. After the guns had been transferred, the *Fanny* would then proceed to Iceland, and collect a cargo of salt and fish destined for Hamburg.

Fred arrived at Hamburg's eight-year-old Hauptbahnhof on 28th March to be met by Bruno Spiro and Elsa Kanzki, for whom the Ulsterman developed a great admiration – he described her as "one of the cleverest ladies I ever met". Spiro, probably more so than Fred, was well-aware that in Germany prison, unlike a verb, came at the start of a sentence; they all got into a car, drove a mile, then walked quickly through a large building and climbed into another car, which drove off at speed. After some miles they parked and walked a short distance to a private house where Fred deposited his bags, and then went to a restaurant for a meal. Later they met Schneider in Spiro's office, where Fred was informed that the rifles had been loaded on to two barges, which were awaiting a suitable tide around midnight to head towards the Kiel Canal. The four of them then retired to another restaurant for supper. Fred's memoir relates that, whilst at his meal at 11.30pm, he heard a distinct voice repeat to him, three times, "Go with the tug tonight and don't lose sight of those rifles till you hand them over in Ulster".

Despite the protestations of the other three, Fred immediately abandoned the plan for himself and Schneider to catch the train to Kiel to meet the barges and, as Schneider collected his bags, someone was sent to pick up Fred's belongings. These included a pair of Zeiss binoculars, stationery, chequebooks, a photograph of his family, a .38 Colt automatic pistol and – rather unusually for a non-smoker – a box of cigars. On a bitterly cold night, at the dock gates, Fred and his agent were taken along a gangway of floating logs to the tug. At 2am they started down the Elbe estuary and spent an uncomfortable night, before reaching the Brünsbuttel entrance to the Kiel Canal. Here he encountered an echo of the *Titanic*, a manifestation of Anglo-German rivalry that was rapidly bringing Europe to the very brink of war – the *Imperator*, launched in 1913 and briefly the world's largest liner, in port from a trans-Atlantic voyage.

The Ulsterman and the German, who five months later would officially be enemies, travelled effortlessly along the Kiel Canal. They flew a black flag, which reminded Fred of the Jolly Roger, for which privilege they had paid an extra 200 marks (£10). All other ships had to give them right of way in the narrow stretches of the sixty-mile Canal, and Fred admitted that "It was rather ridiculous to see great Atlantic liners and other big foreign ships having to tie up, while our bit of a tug with two lighters passed them". As they arrived at the eastern end of the Canal Fred was justified in his decision to travel with the cargo. A rather officious port official boarded the tug, claiming that he had heard it was carrying rifles. Schneider admitted that the man was likely to cause trouble. Fred had noted that, from the outset of the plan, "it was hinted that the Palm Oil flowed pretty freely during the squaring up of everything" – all paid ultimately by James Craig – and that this was another of those occasions: "I was in as big a hurry to be off as a hen on a hot griddle" and, for 100 marks, the jobsworth accepted that all was in order.

Fred was relieved to head for the open sea: "To think that I had actually got this cargo of such nature, packed as it was, which took so long in being done, out of Germany without being discovered was itself an achievement of very considerable satisfaction and relief".

Nevertheless, Fred's sudden change of plan during the last thirty minutes of 28th March presented problems. He had expected to be in Hamburg until at least the following day, before travelling on to Kiel, where he was to "pick up a cable addressed to a fictitious name, giving me final instructions to act upon". In Belfast Spender was troubled: "On the morning of the day selected, information was received from London which convinced our advisers that it was inexpedient to make this attempted landing at this time, and I was instructed to communicate to Crawford to that effect".

It was decided that the adoptive Ulsterman should travel to Dublin to send a wire which, as Fred was unable to return to Kiel, he never received. Spender was a courageous individual – he had, after all, named his daughter Daffodil – but he must have been gripped by grave disquiet in the Irish capital: "As I returned to Amiens Street station I saw on the headlines of the newspaper that a mysterious ship called the *Fanny* had been captured by the Danes in the Baltic, and it was supposed to have arms for Ulster".[21]

Notes

1. D/1700/3/10.

2. M Magnusson & H Palsson (trans), *King Harald's Saga: Harald Hardrada of Norway*, (Penguin Classics, 1966), pp.84-85.

3. The principal sources for the events of this chapter are Fred's own account in D/1415/B/34, which is condensed into Fred H Crawford, *Guns for Ulster*, (Belfast, 1947), and D/640/22/1-4. See also ATQ Stewart, *The Ulster Crisis*,

(London, 1967), pp.105-129, 176-212.

4. Stewart, p.197.

5. Fred was the longest-serving Governor of Campbell College, and sent his two sons to the College; James Cunningham was a brother-in-law of the first Headmaster, James Adams McNeill; Alexander McDowell had been involved in organising the defence of the latter during his legal *cause célèbre* in 1896-1897, when sued for slander and libel by the staff of the College; Samuel Kelly was one of the very first pupils when the school opened on 3 September 1894; George Clark sent one of his sons to the school; and Wilfrid Spender was later also a Governor.

6. D/1415/D/1. Staunch Ulster supporter, Major-General Sir Henry Wilson – then Director of Military Operations at War Office – also visited Belfast at the end of January 1914 and commented that "there is no doubt of the discipline and spirit of the men and officers" of "the Ulster Army": Maj-Gen Sir C E Callwell, *Field Marshal Sir Henry Wilson: his life and diaries*, (London, 1927), Vol.II, 137.

7. Additional material is taken from D/640/22, –/26, –/27, –/28 and D/1700/5/17/1/-.

8. For Tristram's operation, see Stewart pp.100-102.

9. At the same time, Tristram congratulated Fred on "the magnificent success of the Larne gun-running": D/1700/5/17/1/63, –/65C, 16 & 20 August 1914.

10. She continued to live at that address until her death in 1959: Stewart, p.265.

11. D/1415/B/34, p.35. D/640/7/13, 2 May 1921.

12. Fred later claimed that all this money was raised outside Ulster: D/640/30/2, 10 December 1936.

13. Timothy Bowman, *Carson's Army: the Ulster Volunteer Force 1910-1922*, (Manchester University Press, 2007), p.142.

14. D/1633/2/19. Stewart, p.157.

15. D/1415/B/34, p.76.

16. D/1633/2/19, 18 March 1914.

17. At this time Agnew lived at 150 Mountcollyer Street, but in his later years he resided on the Antrim Road.

18. Additional information on this episode is provided by Agnew's own account of events: D/1415/B/36.

19. I am most grateful for the information on the Falcks to Trine Bogenes of Fjaere, the birth-place of the Falck family.

20. Calderwood was sent home directly from Bergen, via Leith; and Nichol and Boyd were later repatriated from Hamburg.

21. D/1763/6.

A non-manifest Manifest

∞

Spender's gloom and pessimism was not unwarranted. In the light of the contemporary euphoria and elation which followed the landing of the rifles at Larne, and in consequence of the legend that has flourished around it, it is forgotten – as Spiro warned Fred – that the odds were stacked against the success of the venture. Rumour became congenital to the episode; all parties were attempting to communicate from a variety of locations (often on the Continent and whilst at sea), over long distances, whilst at the mercy of the vagaries of a simple postal system. With personal reputation – and, ultimately, freedom – at stake, it is scarcely surprising that many in Ulster were afflicted with cold feet and endeavoured to abort the enterprise.

Having invested so much time, effort, stress and personal sacrifice in the project, such a pusillanimous response by his colleagues outraged Fred Crawford. He had not undertaken it for his own glory and self-aggrandisement, but because: "We had all promised these faithful men of all ranks of life, who had drilled and worked so hard to be ready for the crisis, that when the time for action would come we would supply them with the weapons wherewith to defend their rights and themselves".[1]

During the three-and-a-half week mission, however, even Fred was to suffer occasional bouts of doubt and despondency. At such times he resorted to the only course of action available to him – genuflection before the Lord: "The strain of this responsibility was almost more than I could bear, but I trusted in God … and I realised that in the past He had never really let Ulster down, though she had come through some very dark days during the last two hundred years". Fred survived a number of very close shaves and resolved a number of seemingly impossible problems, that it is hard not to believe that – for the month of April 1914 at least – God was an Ulster Protestant!

As well as to God, Fred gave the praise and credit for the success of his saga to others who had assisted him. He tended to deprecate his own role; as one correspondent wrote a year later: "Of course such a feat could not be the work of one man. It was the work of a Province favoured by Providence, and the combination, organisation and discipline were marvellous. But in any great job of the kind there must always be some central figure and someone who made it 'go'. Even your modesty can hardly deny that place".[2] If that were so, Fred still did not undervalue the contribution others such as Andy Agnew. Later reports acknowledged this generosity: "The late Andrew Agnew … shared in the risks of the adventure and Fred Crawford saw that they shared in the gratitude of the people of Ulster".[3] On the occasion of Fred's death, two of Agnew's children wrote to Helen Crawford to express their gratitude for her husband's acts of kindness towards both their parents and to add that Fred always remained a very faithful friend to the family.[4]

Disguise – as in the repainting of the funnel of the *Fanny* – was integral to the ship's evasion of detection. The only personal concession that Fred appears to have made, apart from the re-adoption of an American accent, was the removal of his moustache, which he had sported for at least thirty years. He had adopted many aliases and the same was to apply to the *Fanny*. Despite a voyage of less than a month, the ship has passed into Ulster lore, yet for the majority of that period it actually travelled under the names of other girls: *Naomi*, *Doreen* and *Bethia* – Fred's three daughters.

LANGELAND

Fred and Schneider on board the tug found the now nameless *Fanny* at its station early on Monday 30th March. Fred's method of bundling the rifles together paid dividends in the ease of transfer from the lighters to the *Fanny*. The two gangs made good progress, but they wanted to knock off at dark. Fred offered them double wages if the job was done that night and loading was completed before midnight. Despite Marthin Falck's assurance that he had recommended the location because there was no chance of detection, a large number of boats witnessed their activity and in the early afternoon they received a visit from a customs official from Svendborg, who enquired as to why they were loading so far from land.

He asked to see the manifest, which indicated that they were bound for Iceland with a general cargo and coal. Fred allowed his intuition – which was to flee – to be overridden by the Norwegian captain, who handed the ship's papers to the maritime official. At 6pm the latter returned with the Harbour Master, "with a face exactly like a ferret", who examined the load in the three holds. He indicated that he would have to contact Copenhagen, but would return with the ship's documents by 8am the following morning. Fred knew that the officials were well aware of the nature of his cargo and was extremely apprehensive: "I was pretty sick after all our work for months past to be caught like a rat in a trap". His nervousness was not eased the following morning at breakfast when Agnew pointed out that their alleged port of call – Iceland – was actually seeking Home Rule from Denmark, and that the Danish officials must have assumed that that was the destination of the rifles! Fred was rather irate at Falck's casual attitude on the previous day, but conceded that the Norwegian had not known what cargo he was collecting off Langeland when he had suggested the location.

It was agreed that Schneider should leave with the tug at daybreak. He was given some correspondence to take to Spiro, and also for Fred's associates in Belfast, which included the map of the Scottish coast now marked with a pin-prick. After the German had departed at 5am, Fred decided to wait until 8am – "to put the port officials in the wrong". In normal circumstances he would have had to pass in full view of a torpedo station at the entrance to the bay. He had, however, on the previous day, gone to his knees in the cabin and "in simple language told God all it meant to Ulster". His prayers were answered, for on Tuesday morning, on the last day of March, a gale was blowing and there was sufficient fog to disguise their departure – although they were now "technically pirates".

The North Sea

Travelling south of Langeland and into the open sea, they anchored that evening in German waters and removed the metal letters 'WT' from the funnel. Fred's night was spoiled by the revelation of the Chief Engineer that they had only enough engine oil to last them three days. Next morning was 1st April – and Fred had trouble appreciating any joke.

The next few days witnessed much improvisation. The *Fanny* was repainted "in such a way as her own mother (so to speak) would not know her". Fred re-christened her with the name of his youngest daughter – *Bethia* – and redesignated her home port as Anvers (or Antwerp). He composed a number of letters to Spiro; one of these enclosed an advance to Falck's wife, and a cheque for £56 to be forwarded to Erik Rusten which was pay for the crew, to be sent to their families. He also urged Spiro to recover the ship's papers by any means possible as "we are outlaws till we get them and cannot put into any port".

He also wrote letters to Wilfrid Spender and James Craig introducing Schneider, and praising the work he had done for Ulster. Rather inexplicably, Fred must then have altered his intended rendezvous on a whim. Schneider had only left that morning (31st March) with the map of Scotland and the identifying pin-hole; yet in his letter that same day to Spender, Fred stated, without explanatory comment: "We hope to reach Lundy Island about Saturday 11th April, DV; Poste Restante, Lee Side, Lundy Island, Bristol Channel will be my address" – although this correspondence was never to reach its destination. These letters were posted in Trelleborg, on the southern tip of Sweden, where they went for the engine oil. Fred anchored a few miles offshore and Agnew took one of the ship's lifeboats – renamed *Ada* for the purpose – with Falck and two of the crew to the town, where he also obtained bunting to run up a Belgian flag.

Swedish newspapers indicated that the now infamous rifles were destined for Ulster: "the fat is in the fire and we shall have to be very cautious". Whilst Fred became despondent at the problems which arose, he ultimately came to believe that Fate was acting on his behalf. He realised afterwards that if he had been able to visit Kiel, to collect Spender's wire, he would have had to abandon the voyage to the British Isles. From Trelleborg he directed the *Bethia* initially towards the eastern Baltic but, at night, changed direction past Copenhagen and into the North Sea.

"Just about this time", Fred recorded, "I got an attack like malaria, brought on I presume by worry and anxiety, not being able to eat properly". As the seas became rougher he probably also suffered seasickness. The ship's bunker coal began to diminish, but without the ship's papers Fred was not prepared to risk calling at a port. He then realised that they had emergency coal on board, although it would have been a very tedious and onerous job, in the gale, to transfer it along the deck. Fred utilised his knowledge as a marine engineer, realising that he could gain ready access to the spare coal through a plate in the bulkhead. The Chief Engineer denied that it could be removed, but Fred indicated that, despite being ill, he would do this personally, which would cost the engineer some of his bonus. Two hours later the problem was resolved. Further into the North Sea the gale intensified and the glass of the starboard lamp was accidentally smashed, which caused problems with other vessels. They did not have a spare green lens, and on 7th April Fred determined to put into Great Yarmouth.

Agnew was despatched to the shore with the Mate and another seaman to acquire a spare starboard glass which, despite the late hour, they managed to do. Fred was surprised and relieved that the *Bethia* was not visited by port officials but, as the crew arrived at their boat, Agnew was asked by two customs officers why he was not returning to his ship. Fred had posted letters at Trelleborg to notify the Ulster Unionist Council (UUC) that he wanted to change the rendezvous, originally off the Scottish coast, for the transfer of the rifles. Intuition advised him – correctly – that these may not arrive, so he decided to despatch Agnew to London with a number of letters to convey the decision. The Ulster sea captain informed the officials that he was the superintendent engineer and had to travel to the capital.

One of the letters in Agnew's possession was destined for Elsa

Kanzki. He notified her that: "We have had a very rough passage and I have been anything but well", and that: "I shall send someone for the *Fanny's* papers as soon as possible".[5] That envelope also contained a personal letter from Captain Falck, and Fred did not want the authorities to gain a hint of the latter's location.

Fred now headed for Lundy Island, from where he felt they would be reasonably safe from the attention of British warships which were clearly on the look-out for them. After breakfast on 8th April in London, Agnew – who was told by Fred that he could not visit Belfast where he was too well-known – searched for Craig at his hotel and Carson at his home, but succeeded in just missing both of them. He then went to the London office of the Cunningham business where, by sheer chance, James Cunningham was visiting. The latter informed the sea captain that a small steamer was to due to leave Glasgow to attempt a rendezvous with the *Fanny* in the north of Scotland. The company was wired to cancel the sailing, but Cunningham told Agnew that he should travel to the Scottish city in person. Early next morning (9th April) Agnew arrived at the office just in time to ensure that the steamer did not sail, and then raced back to London to await instructions.

James Cunningham also informed Agnew that we "could not land the guns in Ulster and that I would have to go back to the ship and throw them overboard.". This was in accordance with the instruction, on 6th April, of General Richardson that "You are not under any circumstances to attempt to come into British waters".[6] Agnew remarked that, after all they had been through to date, such a recommendation would infuriate the gun-runner. At that very time Fred was coincidentally manifesting his ill-humour.

When they had departed Great Yarmouth, Fred headed past the Thames Estuary across to the French coast-line of the English Channel "so that no British man-of-war could stop us for inspection". He had also now changed the name of the *Bethia* to the *Doreen* (the name of his middle daughter). He was suffering from what he believed to be malaria, and his quinine was finished. He was extremely ill and unable to eat. Off Dunkirk he was approached by Falck – who appears to have still known him as John Washington Graham – who said that Fred was suffering from enteric fever and would die unless he received treatment ashore. Fred refused to contemplate leaving the vessel and told the Norwegian to continue. The latter's protestations caused Fred to call him into the cabin, where his illness and stress rose to the surface. He took out his .38 Colt automatic pistol, and informed Falck that, if he disobeyed the order to continue at sea, he would shoot him. Falck was clearly shaken, and complied. Fred noted that, following this episode, the two men became firm friends, but Falck stated – also referring to Agnew – that "I never sailed with two such men before in all my sea experience". Fred appended the observation that "I believe he never wanted to do so again".

Spender in Scotland

Around the time that Agnew was in London, another visitor arrived at the offices of James Cunningham asking to see Wilfrid Spender.[7] The latter assumed it was his Director of Ordnance, and did not relish the prospect of informing him that the delivery had been cancelled, and that he would have to dispose of the guns and the boat as he best saw fit. It was, however, Schneider with the pin-holed map identifying Loch Laxford as Fred's originally intended rendezvous. Schneider had done rather badly out of the original contract for packing the rifles and, as a result of his badly miscalculated quotation, had barely broken even. As Ulster no longer wanted the rifles, the German saw an opportunity to make a profit, and offered to purchase the rifles and the *Fanny* for £2500.[8] Spender felt that such an arrangement would solve many of the UUC's problems, as the authorities could do little if the guns and the vessel were the property of a German. Anxious to settle this deal as quickly as possible, Spender and Schneider headed north to Loch Laxford, blithely unaware of the gun-runner's new destination in the Bristol Channel.

Spender recalled that his companion looked totally out of place, dressed in patent leather boots and a bowler hat, but admitted that he also found it difficult to blend into the landscape. He found it a wearisome, embarrassing and disconcerting few days in the remote north of Scotland on a fruitless wait for the *Fanny*. On Easter Monday Craig was at the Midland Railway station to greet Carson who had come to discuss the gathering crisis.[9] Lilian Spender was also there to meet her husband, who had not left any contact details, but he did not arrive. She called at the Old Town Hall where Dawson Bates informed her that he had received a wire indicating that Spender would return the following day;[10] consequently he was to miss the meeting on Tuesday at Craigavon with a very agitated gun-runner.

Fred only learned about the financial transaction undertaken between Schneider and the arms committee a few weeks later when he was in Hamburg, and the German presented him with the documentation. The gun-runner at first thought Schneider had gone mad, but realised that "it was the Committee in Ulster who had lost their reason temporarily through sheer funk". When Schneider pressed Fred for settlement, Fred retorted – inaccurately – that the guns belonged to him, and no-one else had the right to sell them. The shipping agent pressed that the guns now belonged to him, so Fred pointed out that there was no specific clause about delivery, so he would have to go and collect them himself – knowing that the guns had been dispersed around the entire province. Fred said that, if Schneider preferred, he would give him the *Fanny*, but Schneider knew that it could not be sold at that time. On 31st March Fred had written from Danish waters to Spender and Craig urging them to treat the German like "a prince" or "a brother". He noted that Schneider "has got me out of innumerable difficulties and has been a loyal and true friend to Ulster". Consequently he probably felt it only honourable to respect the arrangement of which he disapproved so strongly and, on discussing it over with Spiro, paid Schneider £500 – which he later reclaimed from the Ulster coffers.

Lundy Island

In London on Good Friday Agnew met Richard Cowzer, who arrived from Belfast with a letter from James Craig, which stipulated that either he or Fred should repatriate the guns in Hamburg, and that the other should return home. A similar letter was presented to Agnew for delivery to Fred. It was indicated that he would receive further instructions at the North Western Hotel in Holyhead. The sea captain despatched a letter to his wife via Cowzer, and took the train to Wales where, on Easter Sunday, he met Captain Morrison, Lord Leitrim's skipper. Clearly the UUC was taking no chances, for Agnew was given another letter from Craig, reiterating the instructions he had received in London – but "not to let it fall into Crawford's hands".

At 11am that Sunday, in the charge of Captain William Luke,[11] the *SS Balmerino* of the Kelly Coal line, sailed into the Holyhead breakwater. Agnew and Morrison were collected, and the future decoy vessel headed down the Welsh coast, inside the bird sanctuary of Bardsey Island, en route for another: Lundy Island. Fred – himself a *rara avis* – was indulging in a substantial grouse. He had arrived, via gales and a heavy head sea, at the entrance to the Bristol Channel on Saturday afternoon. He noted that "We wanted to be left severely alone", but that the *Doreen* (as she now was) seemed to attract the flirtatious attention of every pilot vessel and trawler in the vicinity. Without appearing too reluctant or obviously evasive, they avoided all approaches; nor did he want to sail too close to Lundy itself, as the lighthouse was equipped with a powerful telescope.

Fortuitously, the adverse weather abated and Fred spent the rest of Saturday and all of Easter Sunday using the agreed signal to all passing steamers "by means of an empty fire bucket and hurricane lamp". It was, he complained, "lonely, dreary, disappointing work, hour after hour passing without any reply" and he was concerned that their erratic movements were beginning to attract undesirable attention. With a cargo of 260 tons of guns under his feet, Fred was beginning to ponder: "would they pick me up at all?"

The *Fanny*-cum-*Doreen* and the *Balmerino* finally fulfilled their tryst on the morning of Easter Monday (13th April), but the four maritime captains – Falck, Agnew, Luke and Morrison – were not to witness resurrection, but insurrection! Agnew had no alternative but to convey the instructions from Ulster to the chief gun-runner. Agnew later wrote that he did not have the nerve to give Craig's letter to the loyal servant and burned it, but he had to inform Fred that he could not land the cargo and faced taking it back to Hamburg for storage, or to cruise with it in the Baltic for three months. "I am sure there was never a wilder man", wrote the messenger.

Fred was outraged to be sent an anonymous communiqué, which he felt simply confirmed his opinion that some of the UUC did not have the stomach for the fight. Craig knew Fred too well and warned

Agnew that there was very little hope of Fred acceding to the instructions. The latter, in retrospect, was pleased that Craig respected his commitment, and he chose to believe that the future Prime Minister had not been party to the letter. There was, however, considerable nervousness in Ulster at that time with regard to prospective action by the military and naval might of Britain to quell Ulster resistance; the British Government was on a state of high alert and there was a strong possibility of the sea-borne cache being intercepted – and Craig was as prudent as any of his colleagues.

Fred was not so readily deterred; he hoped that Sam Kelly of the arms committee – who owned the *Balmerino* – might be induced to provide another vessel to which the cargo could be transferred. Fred was astute enough to know that the *Fanny* was readily recognisable as a foreign vessel and would be stopped and searched if it approached the Loughs of Ulster. What better cover than one of the Kelly boats which regularly plied the route between Belfast and Scotland?

Agnew gained Fred's eternal admiration by agreeing that he would not take the guns back to Germany, but would stay at sea with them until he heard from Belfast. Fred's instructions were that, if the Committee refused to go through with the delivery, he wanted the *Fanny* beached at high tide in Ballyholme Bay at Bangor, where he would arrange for "plenty of boys" to salvage what they could.

Agnew was instructed to rendezvous on the following Friday night (17th April) off Tuskar Light, seven miles offshore from Rosslare harbour. Luke took Fred and Morrison in the *Balmerino* via Caldey Roads to Tenby. Fred allowed his colleague to answer the interrogation by the coastguards, then they caught the Irish Mail train to Fishguard and then the boat train to Rosslare, arriving on the Irish coast at 5am. Amongst Fred's kitbag of possessions was the pistol which he had used to intimidate Falck, about which he had forgotten; his ill-humour was exacerbated at Rosslare when it was confiscated by the customs officer. From Waterford they took the train to Dublin, from where he telephoned Richard Cowzer to meet him in Belfast. He asked Cunningham's right-hand man to say nothing to anyone, except Sam Kelly, whom he hoped to persuade to loan the *Balmerino*. He believed that the latter could sail up Belfast Lough even if the waterway were punctuated with the entire British fleet: "They would never have suspected a local collier that had been in Belfast the same week discharging coal to be filled with rifles and ammunition in two or three days' time".

CRAIGAVON

Cowzer met Fred from Dublin at the Great Northern Railway station in Great Victoria Street and told him that he had a car ready to take him straight to Craigavon to attend an Emergency Committee of the UUC. Fred told Cowzer, very impolitely, that after the anonymous instructions he had received "I would have no truck with such a cowardly lot", admitting that he was suffering ill-health and shaken nerves "from want of food and sleep and anxiety". The traveller was only appeased when Cowzer pointed out that Carson was also waiting at Craigavon.

Craig, the host at Circular Road, attempted to greet Fred with a hand-shake but, to Fred's later personal shame, he was rebuffed; Fred said he would shake hands with none of them until "I know what they propose to do with *SS Fanny's* cargo". Fred later admitted that "I could have wept with remorse", as Craig had always demonstrated faith in him; after fifteen minutes' conversation the others joined them and Fred felt suitably compensated by Carson's emollient praise: "Well done, Crawford, I am proud of you".

The Emergency Committee asked "to hear what you have done, and what you wish done and intend to do". The impassioned smuggler addressed the guardians of Ulster Protestantism for an hour, essentially berating them for potential betrayal. He said that the men of Ulster had been promised the weapons to resist Home Rule if the time ever came: "Did that piece of paper which was sent to me tend to fulfil these promises? I say it did not, and you Gentlemen who sent it are breaking your promises to the whole of Ulster". He made it categorically clear that he would never return the guns and equated whatever decision they made for the salvation of the province with events at the siege of Derry: "Had Derry been taken, there would have been no Ulstermen today fighting for religious and civil freedom". Although it never occurred to him to say it in so many words, his attitude was that the guns may have been off Lundy, but he would never be one.

After a series of questions, Fred was asked what he wanted done. He explained that he wished to purchase another steamer to which to transfer the rifles. Whilst the Committee baulked at further expenditure, Fred stated that the chances were that a foreign vessel such as the *Fanny* would probably be intercepted and not least of the problems was that she had no papers. It was also quite likely that the Norwegian crew would mutiny in the face of threats from the British Navy. Many in the room were dubious about the practicality of transferring rifles in mid-ocean, the biggest doubter of them all – once again – being Sir George Richardson, who tended to make the disciple Thomas seem mildly quizzical. Eventually Carson placed his confidence in Fred's ability and said that he should be allowed to complete the job.

Samuel Kelly recommended a suitable coal steamer, which had once served his company. Whilst the price of £4500 might not have proved attractive to the Committee, there was a feeling that its scheduled arrival with a delivery of coal on the next day in Belfast was most providential. As "a regular well-known boat, no-one would ever suspect that she could have a cargo of guns on board". The *SS Clyde Valley* had begun life in July 1886 as the *Balniel*, built and launched in Belfast by the iron shipbuilding firm of McIlwaine & Lewis. The latter, Richard Lewis, was a grandfather of C.S. Lewis; his bearded countenance bore a striking resemblance to that of James Wright Crawford and, in common with the latter, Lewis showed an interest in the self-improvement of the working-classes and advocated abstention from alcohol. Fred would have approved of Richard Lewis's writings: "God's purposes, whether of justice or mercy, shall be carried out …" .

Fred and his colleagues then debated where the guns should be landed. Some of the Committee were keen on Donaghadee and Bangor, but Fred felt that these towns could be too easily isolated by the military authorities. He himself argued for Larne, which he had always favoured, but "It was eventually settled that I should run her up the Musgrave Channel [in Belfast]" on Friday 24th April. Fred then made it an absolute stipulation that he would accept no changes to the arrangements, except that they were signed personally by Carson.

There is no indication that Fred took the opportunity to visit his family on the other side of Belfast and, having been entertained to "a very sumptuous supper", he probably spent that night at Craigavon. The next day (Wednesday 15th April) he finalised arrangements with Craig, Cunningham, Kelly and the solicitor Alexander McDowell. Kelly arranged for a new crew for the anticipated *Clyde Valley* and that night Fred and Richard Cowzer travelled to Glasgow to purchase the collier. Fred acquired it under the shallow alias of Hugh Crawford and indicated that the sale was conducted even more rapidly than that of the *Fanny* in Bergen. Cowzer then returned to Belfast, and Fred took the night train to Llandudno, where it had been arranged that the *Clyde Valley* would send a boat ashore to collect him on Friday morning.

Day Trip to Great Yarmouth

He was to spend the whole of Friday in the Welsh coastal town, growing increasingly nervous at the non-appearance of the ship. Eventually, in the late evening, by which time the seas had turned choppy, and "my patience was giving way to serious apprehension", he spotted its lights and was collected from the beach by the ship's lifeboat. The *Clyde Valley* was captained by William Luke, who had evidently been recalled to Belfast from the *Balmerino* on the instructions of Kelly. On the previous night there had been a formal opening of Kelly's new offices. The owner had been presented with a silver casket by his employees and the focus had been diverted from the arrangements for the *Clyde Valley* which, in addition to the crew, had required coal and fresh water. The rather casual approach to these matters nearly resulted in disaster for the vessel on its final leg to the Ulster coast and delayed its sailing from Belfast to Llandudno. Fred noted with sarcasm: "I told him [Luke] of the pleasant ten or twelve hours I had spent looking for him".

Fred had also arranged with Kelly that the *Balmerino* should anchor at the Holyhead breakwater. They headed there, collected a fireman and other crew they needed to assist with the transfer of the guns from the *Fanny*, and then turned in the direction of Tuskar Light. They failed all night to find the Norwegian vessel and on Sunday morning Luke made an admission that stunned Fred. When they had left the

Balmerino on 13th April, it was to remain at anchor to be joined later by the *Fanny* to replenish the latter's bunkers. As they did so, a rather inquisitive pilot came on board, so Agnew raced away to be joined later by his partner in crime. It seems that Luke had misunderstood the original instructions from Fred, which required Agnew to be off Tuskar Light at the required time. Luke confused the matter even further that Sunday morning, when he could not find Agnew and the *Fanny*, by telling Fred that he may have told Agnew to meet him at Great Yarmouth.

Fred was astounded by this revelation and realised that he had no alternative but to go to the coastal town on the other side of Britain to see if Agnew were there. He gave Luke written instructions for all eventualities – that is, whether or not he traced the *Fanny* – to communicate with him from Fishguard by telegram at Great Yarmouth Post Office. If the rifles were transferred in his absence, Fred told Luke then to take the *Fanny* to Fehmarn (or Bergenstock) off the German coast, pay the necessary fines, recover the ship's papers and await Fred's eventual arrival.

Fred was dropped in Fishguard just after midday, waited for an evening train to London, which arrived at 4am on Monday 20th April. He took an early train to the Norfolk town, and spent a miserable morning realising that, after all his pontificating at Craigavon, his plans were rapidly disintegrating. After a number of fruitless ventures to the Post Office, 'J. W. Johnston' eventually received a telegram at 2pm from Goodwick (twinned with Fishguard). He went into an adjacent alleyway and, when he discovered that it was from Agnew – who told him to meet at the Holyhead breakwater at 5pm the next day – he said: "I felt like sinking to my knees in that lane and thanking God from the bottom of my heart". He travelled back to London and caught the night mail train to Holyhead. It was a long wait, but he appreciated the rest, and – although he had to wait a further two anxious hours – he eventually saw the *Clyde Valley* turn the headland.[12] Agnew then explained that he had been sailing between the Welsh and Irish coasts all the time, but that the instructions had been confused: "All I can say is that Luke gave us both a foretaste of Hell … I was glad to get a rest and a wash and shave after four days and nights without my clothes off".

LARNE

Fred was reunited with his guns for the first time in eight days. At about 8pm on Sunday 19th April the *Clyde Valley* had finally encountered the *Fanny*. Although it proved rather nerve-wracking for Captain Falck, the two vessels were tied together, and all the rifles were transferred to their new holds by 4am. As Fred was being collected from the beach at Holyhead a customs boat visited the *Clyde Valley* and asked why they had come into shore. They claimed that they were en route from Fishguard to Glasgow, but had to collect their superintendent engineer. Fortunately Agnew was believed, but it necessitated heading briefly in the direction of Glasgow.

They had three days to make the rendezvous in Ulster, so could afford to travel at a leisurely speed. On Wednesday afternoon they were actually passed by a large battleship which Churchill, First Lord of the Admiralty, had despatched to Lamlash in Scotland in order to intimidate Ulster! They also took the opportunity to sort out the rifles, which had been rather jumbled during the transfer, into different types; nearly half were placed in slings ready for discharge at their destination. During the journey Fred carried out a patchwork transformation of the *Clyde Valley*, which had first occurred to him in the train from Glasgow several days previously: "It struck me it would be a good idea if I called the *Clyde Valley* the *Mountjoy II*, as she was going to the relief of Ulster, just as truly as the old *Mountjoy* had relieved Derry. I decided to paint *Mountjoy II* on her bows and stern – I had as many aliases as most criminals had and the *SS Fanny* had three; why not the *Clyde Valley* one?" He disguised the ship's name with lamp black and oil, and then took three strips of canvas about six feet long and twelve inches broad, and painted the new name in white on the black canvas.

On Thursday they sailed round the Isle of Man and at noon on Friday 24th April they set course for the Copeland Islands, with their coal and drinking water in very short supply. One further problem was that, in the haste to find a crew for the *Clyde Valley* in Belfast, a Nationalist fireman had been hired by mistake.[13] There were fears that he could cause trouble and Fred eventually had to lock him in a cabin for his own safety.

At about 7pm off the Copelands, the *Milewater*, a tender belonging to George Clark's company, approached them carrying Richard Cowzer and Dawson Bates.[14] They shouted that they had new orders for Fred, who immediately retorted that he was not interested if they were not signed by Carson. Bates explained that Richardson had had to be told by Cunningham that unless they were autographed by the hand of Carson, who was in London, Fred would never accept them. Fred Hall had been despatched to obtain the signature.

The new directive was that, apart from small quantities destined for Belfast, Donaghadee and Bangor, the Committee had decided that the arms should be unloaded where Fred had originally recommended – Larne – because the authorities would find it most difficult to seal off completely. The fact that such detailed plans were made within a week speaks volumes for the organisational talents of the UVF hierarchy – in particular, Spender, whose wife wrote at the time: "Need I say that for the organisation itself, Wolf [her pet name for her husband] was mainly responsible, the scheme having been originally drawn up by him".

Spender, who was "especially enthusiastic about the tremendous potentiality of the motor car",[15] had also been responsible for the institution of the Motor Car Corps, placed under the command of F. H. Rogers of Derryvolgie Avenue. Spender issued regulations for about 500 cars – about half the number in Ulster at the time – arriving at Larne that night,[16] which specified that all vehicles should arrive punctually for 'a very secret and important duty'; there should only be two people per car; cars should drive carefully on the way to Larne and back, so as not to attract unwanted attention; and – with no apparent irony – no arms were to be carried that night! Perhaps the most surprising fact of the night was that Spender "had bicycled part of the way to Larne, and ridden the whole way back, getting a tow for some miles by a motor cycle". For his wife's birthday in early June, Spender bought his wife a rifle.[17]

Arrangements for the use of Larne harbour had been made with William Chaine, a member of the Board of Directors of the port, and

Commander of 2nd Battalion of the Antrim Ulster Volunteer Force.[18] The unloading went, in Spender's phrase, "like clockwork" and was effected by the early hours of Saturday 25th April. Two small quantities were loaded directly on board motor-ships named *Roma* and *Innismurray* for delivery to Belfast and Donaghadee. The rest, apart from 40 tons of Mausers destined to be dropped in Bangor, were discharged on to the Larne quayside for rapid distribution, in small quantities, around the province.

Although the UVF made it almost impossible for the Army or police to enter Larne, the lack of interference was facilitated by the diversionary arrival of *SS Balmerino* along the leaden blade of Belfast Lough into the Musgrave Channel, an action clearly designed to mislead the authorities.[19] The latter clearly believed that they had intercepted the rumoured arms' delivery when Samuel Kelly's collier sailed extremely slowly into Belfast harbour – carrying nothing but coal. The crew occupied the port officials further with obstructive tactics and it proved too late to move once the mistake was realised. It was probably no coincidence that when Spender led the inspection of the 36th Division by the Lagan at Malone on the morning of 8th May 1915, and attended the march-past later that day in the city centre, he was mounted on a horse called Balmerino.[20]

Spender concluded that: "It was certainly a weird night; the bundles … were passed from hand to hand to boat, motor lorry, pony cart or steamship of whatever other form of conveyance was selected". He recalled that: "One of the most wonderful sights that I have ever seen was the sudden lines of lights along the different roads leading to Larne Harbour when the various motor convoys began to arrive".

One ten-year-old boy – who was also taken to Belfast to see the parade on 8th May 1915 – who lived in the rectory at Kilwaughter, on the periphery of Larne, also witnessed the arrival of the vehicles: "all through the night on the road beside the rectory, we can hear the cars and we can see the trees constantly illumined by the headlamps". Later to become a noted author and poet, George Buchanan – a nephew of international journalist, Arthur Moore – was born into staunch Protestant stock; his father, "a man without ambition", sympathised with the UVF and held a service for the rebels, while his mother retained with pride the pen with which she had signed the Declaration.[21] Young George witnessed the *son et lumière* returning from the quayside as the rifles were secreted around the province – some of them being so well hidden that they were not discovered until searches by the British Army in 1969.[22] Count Gleichen was well-aware that many of them were destined to be hoarded by the leading businessmen and landowners of Ulster and he later recorded that, at Antrim Castle, "I made a private discovery of my own account ... I shall never forget the noble owner's face when I acquainted him with the result of my search [for tennis balls]!"[23] A handful of rifles found their way to Cabin Hill, the home of Lord Mayor McMordie who had died the previous month. Seven or eight years later, Craig and the members of his Cabinet, and Spender, who was Secretary to the Cabinet, were to sit beneath the roof-space where they had been stored, conducting the executive affairs of the Government of Northern Ireland.

Back at the brilliantly illuminated Larne harbour, Fred was recognised and embraced; amongst those who had made the effort to be there was Lord Leitrim, who had made a special journey from Donegal. Fred was elated to have fulfilled his mission. Somewhat indifferent to the needs of his neglected family, he reflected: "I cared nothing for the consequences now that I had accomplished my task. If I were imprisoned, I would have taken it as an honour. If I were shot at my post by the police or the military it would have been a glorious death – the same as being killed in action in battle. I knew that Ulster would see to my wife and family, and that was enough for me".

General Sir George Richardson, who had constantly doubted the likelihood of such an event, ordered the smuggler ashore. As ever, Fred ignored the wishes of his superior officer – which was a total contradiction of the requisites of UVF membership – and said that it was his duty to see the ship safely out of British waters. As it was rumoured that "the greyhounds of the British Fleet" were already steaming out of Lamlash, he knew that he had to depart promptly. After partially re-coaling and watering, he left for Bangor at about 5am.

Legend

As a consequence of half-a-dozen hours in Larne a self-deprecating starch manufacturer became an Ulster legend. Even in the years after the First World War, Fred never sought public gratitude and compensation – indeed, he actively avoided it: "I felt Ulster was saved and that was my reward". The political circumstances, however, had changed irrevocably. Asquith was never a politician to appreciate reality or irony – only four months later, when *The Times* newspaper published the first authentic report (the so-called Amiens Despatch) from the Western Front, the Prime Minister reacted irately to the unpalatable truth by stating that the public was entitled to the truth![24] The truth of Larne clearly stung in Downing Street; Asquith was both embarrassed and outraged. George Buchanan neatly encapsulated the political reality: "From this night the rebellion [passed] beyond the stage of play acting", and as one historian noted: "The success of the Larne gun-running had increased the possibility of conflict between the Government and the UVF during the summer of 1914".[25]

This was, of course, an eventuality which no-one wanted. As it transpired, the so-called mutiny at the Curragh had meant that the British Army was not in a position to impose a military settlement in Ulster, but 25,000 rifles scarcely established an irresistible force, and "the effective value of the gun-running, beyond the undoubtedly central issues of morale and publicity, is questionable".[26] To Ulstermen, nevertheless, the latter was crucial; one correspondent wrote to Fred in April 1915:[27]

> *Your feat of last year was not merely one of which we shall always be proud, but one that changed, at a critical time, the whole situation. It not only gave us arms. It gave us the prestige of an actual victory. I believe it impressed ... more than all ... the oratory and writing and demonstrating over Home Rule since that trouble began.*

Ultimately, the rifles imported at Larne by Fred Crawford were never fired in anger in Ulster, primarily because of the declaration of war on 4th August. It was an incalculable irony that thousands of Ulstermen learned their shooting skills with rifles that were imported from Germany, only to travel to France and Belgium in October 1915 to be slaughtered by the thousand at the hands of Germans. At the close of day on 1st July 1916, men who had proudly served the UVF, such as

James Davidson and Elliott Johnston and over 5000 others, no longer appreciated the irony.

Notes

1. D/1415/B/34, p.70. Much of this chapter is derived from this source, plus the condensed version: Fred H Crawford, *Guns for Ulster*, (Belfast, 1947). ATQ Stewart, *The Ulster Crisis*, (London, 1967). D/1415/B/36 (Agnew's account). D/1700/5/17/1/-.

2. D/1700/5/17/1/109, 17 April 1915.

3. *Belfast News Letter*, 27 March 1934.

4. D/1700/5/12/56, -/62 (end of 1952).

5. Early in the journey Fred had enclosed to Spiro a letter from Falck asking for his ship's papers. Fred added: "You could get some broker in Hamburg to take this matter up with the Danish authorities".

6. Stewart, p.187.

7. The full details of this episode can be found in D/1763/6 (Spender's own account). Stewart, pp.185-190. D/1415/B/34, pp.108-111.

8. In his later account, Fred stated that the rifles had been sold for £500 by the Committee, or by Spender acting on behalf of the Committee.

9. Carson stayed at Craigavon from 13 to 18 April and, on leaving, wrote: "Too many events to record" – an understatement! D/1415/D/1.

10. D/1633/2/19.

11. At this time, Captain Luke is described in the *Belfast & Ulster Street Directory* as 'a master mariner'. He lived at Upper Meadow Street, not too distant from Alexander Crawford & Son but, in the 1920s, he was to reside at 100 Castlereagh Street in East Belfast, only three doors from where his boss, by then Sir Samuel Kelly, had lived in the 1890s.

12. There is some additional information in a supplementary note written by Fred: D/1415/B/35. In this, Fred says that he did fall on his knees in the passageway in Great Yarmouth.

13. Agnew claimed the man was an engineer.

14. On 27 May 1960 Sir Wilfrid Spender wrote to Helen Crawford claiming that Bates had always been strongly opposed to the importation of arms, and "could not forgive your husband and me for getting Carson to overrule his advice": D/1700/5/11/41. Lilian Spender referred to Bates as a "tiresome person": D/1633/2/19.

15. Ian Maxwell, *The Life of Sir Wilfrid Spender 1876-1960*, (QUB Ph D thesis,

1991), p.47

16. D/1238/71.

17. D/1633/2/19.

18. Alf McCreary, *A Vintage Port: Larne and its People*, (Antrim, 2000), pp.52-54. Stewart, pp.197, 199.

19. General Macready, who had been sent to Belfast as military governor in late March 1914, admitted that the arrangements for Larne had been so well-kept that the troops and police were totally unprepared: General Sir Nevil Macready, *Annals of an Active Life*, (London, no date), Vol.I, 184.

20. D/1633/2/20.

21. GHP Buchanan, *Green Sea Coast*, (London, 1966), pp.36-37, 45-49.

22. Alvin Jackson, 'Unionist Myths 1912-1985', *Past & Present*, Vol.136 (August 1992), 174.

23. Major-General Lord Edward Gleichen, *A Guardsman's Memories: a book of recollections*, (Edinburgh/London, 1932), p.387.

24. Keith Haines, *The Looted Paradise: the life and times of Arthur Moore*, (Ballymaconaghy Publishing, Belfast, 2004), pp.146-151. For the Amiens Despatch, see Chapter 11.

25. Maxwell, p.74.

26. Jackson, pp.180-183. One other consequence of the events at Larne was that the Nationalist Volunteers "increased their enrolment prodigiously": Denis Gwynn, *The Life of John Redmond*, (London, 1932), p.307.

27. D/1700/5/17/1/107, 5 April 1915.

Images

A bright-eyed Fred Crawford in March 1931 (approaching his 70th birthday).

Fred Crawford's parents, James Wright and Margery (known as Madge) Crawford, photographed at Chlorine.

Cloreen, Fred Crawford's family home, built off the Malone Road behind where the Eglantine Inn now stands, and demolished when Queen's University acquired the land.

Fred Crawford in pilgrim guise (sitting, front right) on the
Mount of Olives in Jerusalem, May 1890.

Fred Crawford in his role as an engineer with the White Star Line, 1885-86.

Second Lieut Fred Crawford wearing the uniform of the Mid-Ulster Artillery, 1894.

This photograph probably shows at Fred at the camp of the Donegal Artillery, Letterkenny, in which he served as a Captain from 1897 to 1909.

Fred served in the Boer War with the Donegal Artillery from 1900 to 1901. He is seen here mounted on his horse Bobs (probably named in honour of Field Marshal Lord Roberts).

A photo of Fred in uniform taken in 1899, but signed for a relative on 28 July 1903.

Hamburg arms supplier, Bruno Spiro, who autographed the photograph for Fred - "Dedicated to one of the best" – on 1st January 1932.

Fred Crawford and Captain Andy Agnew on board the *Fanny*, 8th May 1914, on which they had both agreed during the previous month never to return the guns to Germany.

Captain Marthin Falck (front left) photographed on board the *Fanny* with his Norwegian crew.

Captain Marthin Falck, Fred Crawford and Captain Andy Agnew on board the *Fanny* in the Kiel Canal, 8th May 1914.

Captain Marthin Falck poses on board the *Fanny* with (probably) the Norwegian officers of his crew.

(Below) The *Fanny* which carried the Unionist guns from Denmark to their transfer on board the *Clyde Valley*.

Fred Crawford, Captain Andy Agnew, Bruno Spiro (rear), with Captain Marthin Falck and Helen Crawford, make the final journey on board the *Fanny*, down the Kiel Canal, 8 May 1914.

The silver casket, paid for by public subscription, presented to Fred Crawford "to commemorate signal services rendered by him to Ulster, culminating on the night of April 24th 1914". It is now in the care of the Ulster Museum.

The Garden of Consolation which Fred created
at Cloreen between 1924 and 1928.

Fred Crawford, listed as a District Inspector in the Royal Ulster Constabulary, once again in uniform in the early 1920s.

Even in the face of commercial failure in later years, Fred Crawford conveyed the air of the dapper businessman.

Fred and Helen Crawford at Cloreen in February 1948 with the silver casket and a copy of his recent book *Guns for Ulster*. He was presented to Lady Carson at the Ulster Hall on what was his final public appearance.

Fred Crawford's final journey to Belfast City Cemetery, November 1952, led by his two sons and a grandson, accompanied by his former employee, Ernest Knowles.

A Pink Pearl

Fred Crawford and Andy Agnew sailed out of Larne Harbour at 5am on Saturday 25th April, reaching Bangor about two-and-a-half hours later. Agnew tried to dissuade his partner from travelling, but Fred said that he felt it only fair that he should share the responsibility if the ship were intercepted. As the authorities, and their signalling equipment, were efficiently incapacitated by the Ulster Volunteer Force (UVF) in the Co. Down harbour, the remaining guns were unloaded without incident.[1] Whilst berthed, Fred's cousin, Crawford Brown,[2] asked him what he would like to eat. As Fred had not enjoyed fresh milk for about a month, Brown brought him half a pint, which he placed on the shelf in the cabin; when he went to drink it before they departed at 9am, Fred discovered that someone else had consumed it!

They finally completed loading their complement of coal and drinking water, which had been interrupted at Larne, and Fred finally released the Nationalist he had locked up for his own safety, paying him reasonable compensation for the latter's inconvenience. Before setting sail for Hamburg, the ship's firemen indicated that – even despite being offered double wages and a bonus – they were not prepared to travel further, so the UVF provided replacements. They then sailed promptly on hearing that a 30-ton cruiser was closing in from Lamlash. Fred commented to Agnew that there was a fair chance that they would be gracing a cell in Belfast on the following day, but that they would at least be enjoying "a good long much-needed rest cure".

The rub of the green, however, continued to radiate an Orange tinge. Agnew was ordered to mislead the cruiser by heading for the Clyde, and Fred removed the *Mountjoy II* name canvases, rubbing off the lamp black to resurrect the collier, *Clyde Valley*. Off the Copeland Islands they hit fog and, after a mile out of sight, they changed course for Fishguard. Over the next few hours Fortune most decidedly favoured Fred. When he had obtained UVF relief firemen in Bangor, the arrangement was that they would sail only as far as the Welsh destination. Fred had felt it would be unfair to ask them to travel as far as Hamburg, so he asked a UVF officer to contact Samuel Kelly "to send the firemen from the *Balmerino* which was still lying in Holyhead Harbour down to Fishguard to relieve the Volunteers and to take the ship from there to Hamburg".

Clearly neither Fred nor Agnew, nor any of the Volunteers in Bangor, was aware at that stage that the *Balmerino* had sailed into Belfast on the previous night. As luck would have it, as Fred tried to get some sleep that night, they emerged from the fog and he began to worry that there were too many imponderables in the plan: what if Kelly never received the message,[3] or if the *Balmerino* had already sailed from Holyhead ? (which had, of course, happened); he also feared that the released Nationalist fireman would talk, and that the latter's supporters would contact the authorities to notify them of the intended arrival in Fishguard.

At midnight Fred woke Agnew to change their direction to Rosslare. This meant that any prospective frantic attempts to communicate with Fred – that there would be no relief from the *Balmerino* at Fishguard – no longer mattered and it is strange that neither Fred nor Agnew ever referred to this potential disaster in his retrospective account. Fred knew that if there were no British man-of-war in the vicinity of the south-east Irish coast, he could land at Rosslare, and the *Clyde Valley* would be beyond British waters before it could be intercepted. He was disappointed at not being able to continue in the collier to Hamburg, but felt some obligation to report to Richardson so, passing Tuskar

Light one last time, he disembarked at Rosslare with one obstinate firemen who refused to travel further.

The South of Ireland

Soon after he descended from the breakwater wall between the harbour and railway station in Rosslare, the fugitive smuggler managed to purchase two tickets to Dublin and gave one to the firemen, telling him to mix in with the passengers just arriving on the ferry from Fishguard. Fred was then approached by a customs officer who quizzed him about his unorthodox arrival. Fred persuaded him that he had simply hitched a lift on a friend's collier, as he was wont to do. He added that he did not know the fireman, which was fundamentally the truth.

After he boarded the train, Fred was concerned to be approached by the coastguard. Fred rehearsed the explanation he had pre-arranged with Agnew that he had begged a lift on the collier *Balniel*, travelling from the north of Ireland to Swansea with a cargo of coal. The coastguard then spoke to two other men whom Fred knew, from the intuition he had gained over three years, were detectives. They then spoke to a District Inspector of the Royal Irish Constabulary, who penned Fred in his carriage. The Ulsterman began to grow both irritated and anxious by the questioning, but pointed out that the coastguard had looked through his bag – admittedly cursorily – and been satisfied. Fred boldly stated that he did not recognise the authority of the District Inspector to question him, and refused to co-operate further.

Fred was well aware, nevertheless, that he would have to wait in Waterford until 3pm for the connecting train to Dublin and that in that time authority could be obtained from Dublin to arrest him merely on suspicion. In his bag were his UVF HQ armlet, and a wad of incriminating documents. These included the personally-signed order from Carson to change the landing of the rifles from Belfast to Larne; receipts for large sums of money connected with the purchase of the rifles and correspondence that would reveal the whole plot. He was unconcerned about his own arrest – he believed that it was probably imminent in any case – but he did not want others implicated. With enormous reluctance, he shredded the papers and cut up the armlet, hiding them in the recess of the carriage window into which the frame dropped. He then disguised himself in the train's toilet and moved compartments. At Waterford he strode behind the fireman and warned him surreptitiously not to wait in the station; the uncomprehending glance of the man convinced him that his disguise was effective.

Assuming that he would be arrested at some stage, Fred had written a number of letters during the train journey to General Richardson and others explaining the situation, to help them take precautions against their own possible arrest. He posted these surreptitiously and went to a hotel to get some breakfast. Whilst there two more detectives entered the restaurant, and were inquisitive about whether he had arrived on the Fishguard boat. Fred adopted a southern brogue and an alias as a cattle and sheep dealer; his experience on his farm on Islandmagee gave him an air of authority on the subject and he bored the two men with pre-emptive questions of his own.

He decided to blur his trail by heading for Cork. On reaching Blarney he alighted and tried to stay for a few days at St. Ann's Hydro near the castle. Rather to his surprise, the manageress proved reluctant to allow him to enter, and he found a small cottage which offered bedrooms. He decided not to stop there as he could not obtain a room to himself, but the landlady offered Fred a meal; when he went to wash and shave "I immediately saw the reason of my rejection at St. Ann's Hydro. I looked a regular low-class tramp or criminal. I had a beard sprouting of 48 to 60 hours' growth; my face was dirty and my collar filthy. My eyes were red and bloodshot from want of sleep and I looked half-starved".

He then travelled into Cork, booked in at the Hotel Metropole and slept soundly for the first time in a week. The following morning (Monday 27th April) he astutely called on a customer of Alexander Crawford & Son "with a view to establishing an alibi there if necessary", then phoned James Cunningham in Belfast. He asked the latter to meet the fugitive that night at the Great Northern railway station in a covered car and to take him to Glencairn where he hoped to learn what orders he may receive from General Richardson.

Hamburg

The Cunningham family accommodated him and, as he added

gratefully, "could not do enough for me". Fred's wife and five children were transported across the city to see him for the first time in about a month. He recalled that he was "dead beat" and slept sixteen hours that night. On the following evening, after dark, he was taken to Chlorine to see his near 90-year-old mother, who "was more proud of what I had done than if I had been made a peer". That day (Tuesday) he had confided in a correspondent that: "I only wish I could take it easy, but ... I have reason to believe I shall be arrested and, as I must go to Hamburg, I am lying doggo here [Glencairn]".

On the Wednesday evening, Fred and Helen Crawford – travelling as Mr & Mrs Johnston – took the Heysham ferry to England, but Fred "had a bad time of fever" on the boat, so they stayed overnight at her brother's home near Grimsby. They then took the *SS Munich* from Harwich to the Hook of Holland, and arrived in Hamburg on Saturday afternoon. They were greeted enthusiastically at the station by Bruno Spiro, and rapturously by the latter's secretary, Elsa Kanzki. The couple were accommodated at the arms dealer's expense in the massive, modern Hotel Atlantic (opened in 1909) on Lake Alster.[4]

The German had been very apprehensive about the fate of Fred and the rifles. He had not received any of Fred's letters from Trelleborg during the voyage of the *Fanny* and, after his fruitless tour round the north of Scotland, Schneider had returned to spread the mistaken news that all was lost. No doubt to show Spiro that his original pessimism had been misplaced, en route to Hamburg Fred had written home asking for copies of the Ulster press to be posted to Elsa Kanzki's address; during that week, however, the news of the Larne landings had caused a sensation all over Europe.

The other conspirator waiting for Fred at Hamburg station was Captain Andrew Agnew. After leaving Fred at Rosslare on 26th April, he had sailed the *Clyde Valley* up the English Channel, mooring at Hamburg four days later. On 1st May he found Schneider and they paid off the Volunteer crew, who returned to Leith on a steamer that was leaving the German port that evening. On the following afternoon he met Spiro and the Crawfords at the station. Fred had sent a personal plea to the sea captain from Belfast and it is likely that the weary gun-runner asked if Agnew had had any success with the enquiry; sadly, there is no record of whether Agnew found the spare set of dentures which Fred believed he had inadvertently left on the *Clyde Valley*!

Fred was considerably disappointed, however, to make one discovery on the erstwhile collier. As a result of the international press coverage of the events in Ulster, the ship's notoriety had preceded it. The British consul in Hamburg became agitated when no papers were forthcoming and he could not discern who the real captain and owner were. He maintained a daily watch at the port, so it was difficult for Fred to get aboard. A watchman managed to indicate when it was clear and Fred was disappointed to discover two bundles of rifles and ammunition hidden under the deckboards – as the ship was likely to be searched he was obliged to ditch them in the harbour.

The real captain of the *Clyde Valley* was William Luke who at that time was on board the *Fanny* – renamed *Naomi* (Fred's eldest daughter) for its journey after transferring the rifles at sea – which was currently anchored in German waters off the island of Fehmarn.[5] It was still awaiting the return of its papers abandoned at Langeland. When Agnew visited it two miles offshore on 5th May it was pervaded by misery.

Captain Falck had received letters and newspapers from home, where it seems he had become "a very unpopular man for what he had done to a friendly power" – presumably Denmark. He claimed that Luke, the Mate and Engineer, had combined against him and he had locked himself in the cabin. When he emerged, he was carrying the log book and said that he was taking it to the consul, so Agnew permanently confiscated it.[6] The latter also complied with Fred's request to take photos of the ship, with *Fanny* painted on one bow, and *Naomi* on the other, before it was fully re-christened with its Norwegian name, ready to sail down the Kiel Canal. On 6th May Fred and his wife briefly visited the ship and later that day it seems that its papers were finally being returned.

Richard Cowzer had been sent to Hamburg at the end of April probably to act as paymaster on behalf of James Cunningham, as loose ends were being tied up. In the event, matters did not run smoothly and on 11th May Fred had to contact Belfast to say that Cowzer would need to stay longer. Luke was paid off and from Fehmarn Fred wrote to Samuel

Kelly asking him to pay the captain a £20 bonus. Later Fred was to admit that he could not have achieved anything single-handedly and accorded others fair praise. Nevertheless, Fred was to have his doubts about Luke. He said that the latter's mistake in telling Agnew that the rendezvous was at Great Yarmouth had come closest to scuppering the entire enterprise. Fred was to be severely nettled when a presentation was made by Sir Dawson Bates to Luke in 1927 for "his services to Ulster as commander of the *SS Fanny* and later the *SS Mountjoy*" and pointed out that Luke had never captained the *Fanny*, and had not been aboard his own ship when it was renamed the *Mountjoy*. Fred wrote to Agnew to say that the latter had been "deeply wronged by a committee who knew nothing about what you had done for Ulster"; the only blessing was that Luke had not been present to receive the award in person.[7]

Early on 7th May 1914, the *Fanny* prepared to sail for the Canal and came to rest early in the evening at Kiel Roads. With a degree of inevitability, its progress was not straightforward. They were fined eleven marks for not flying the ensign and, despite the fact that it rained without interruption, a customs officer walked their deck for fourteen hours. Eventually at noon on 8th May Fred, his wife and Bruno Spiro boarded for the eight-hour voyage to the Brünsbuttel gates and ultimately on to Hamburg.

The journey was not without incident. Fred requested that some photos be taken of his final voyage aboard the Norwegian vessel.[8] Clearly they were more celebrated than they might have expected or hoped, for Fred says that they were asked by every German steamer they passed if they had any guns on board! Bonhomie and good humour apart, there were nevertheless unmistakable signs of the impending fracture of Europe. Near Kiel Fred witnessed the German Fleet manoeuvring (often illegally in Danish waters), and practising with its heavy guns; he conceded that "it was a very fine sight". The Norwegian crew was paid off with a bonus once they sailed into Hamburg. Falck received double wages and "£50 for his worry and trouble". He evidently hoped to be made a gift of the *Fanny*, but Fred refused to be so generous.

Falck, the *Fanny* and the *Clyde Valley*

It is unclear whether Fred ever again met the elderly sea-captain who, unlikely as it may seem, possibly only ever knew Fred as John Washington Graham! Whilst the purchase of Falck's boat at Bergen had briefly resurrected his fortunes, the evidence suggests that he came to regret the day he ever met the dogged Ulsterman. He had endured the barrel of Fred's pistol in the English Channel; he had reluctantly tied the *Fanny* to the *Clyde Valley* in the Irish Sea; and by the time it was docked in Hamburg it was clearly the worse for wear, requiring considerable service, attention and repair. They proved unable to obtain the original mortgage papers, which made it difficult for Falck to reclaim his old ship.

There are indications that the Norwegian may have visited the offices of the Ulster Unionist Council (UUC) solicitor, Alexander McDowell, in Royal Avenue in March 1915. Later that month he made a proposal to move *Fanny* from Hamburg to a Scandinavian port if he could be given a monetary advance, but this plan did not materialise. He had received 750 marks in July 1914, and was posted a further £75 in January 1915, but it is evident that, after the First World War, Captain Ole Marthin Jensen Falck had fallen on very hard times.

On 18th September 1922 from Fevik near Arendal on the southern coast of Norway, he again contacted the solicitor to reveal that his finances were in a critical state, "as a consequence of the disastrous *Fanny* affair". He said that he had been brought to "the brink of ruin", having mortgaged his home and life policy. He was effectively destitute, with debts of over 30,000 kroner, and was on the point of losing his home in Fjaere where he had been born. He said that he was 75 years old and "consequently too old to go to sea again". He wanted Carson & McDowell to approach "the principals in the *Fanny* case and induce them to help me in saving my home which Messrs (sic) Graham at that time promised me to do if my position should become so bad". The solicitors contacted Fred and said that the sum equated to £1250, and asked what should be done.[9] Fred took the honourable course of action, which may have given some comfort to Falck's final two years.[10]

These later events reveal that the costs of Fred's gun-running escapade continued to mount long after 25th April 1914. On 7th July an account was submitted from Hamburg for expenses related to the *Clyde Valley* and *Fanny*, which included pilotage, harbour fees, penalties to the Danish Government for the release of the papers of the *Fanny*, Canal dues, and even a rat-catcher, which totalled £3360. This was in addition to payments of over 3500 marks in June and July 1914 for "services" to both vessels.

Despite a variety of efforts, it proved impossible to sell the two vessels before war broke out. In mid-July 1914 Schneider was asked to look after them and he even made an offer to purchase the Ulster collier. The shipping agent was a devious character and in those early days of May 1914 in Hamburg, although he had his suspicions about Schneider's motives, Fred had given the German the benefit of the doubt over his financial arrangement with the UUC. Twenty years later, however, Spiro was to reveal that later in 1914 he had had problems with Schneider, who may have had gambling debts and, at some stage in the intervening years, the shipping agent had committed suicide.[11]

At the end of July, with war looming, Fred wrote to Spiro suggesting that, with the boats in Hamburg, they could be placed in the latter's name; this meant that they could not be seized or sold as alien property. Fred said that the arms dealer could keep any profit in excess of £3000 for the *Clyde Valley* and over £2500 for the *Fanny*. He later recorded that the Norwegian ship was sold during the war and that he settled his claim in 1924 for 100,000 marks: "This, owing to the depreciation of the mark, was equal to only £250 instead of £5000, but it was the very best I could do. In fact, if Spiro had been dishonest … I could have done nothing. I placed the amount in the bank till the mark went up, but it went to pieces and all was lost". After the Armistice, Richard Cowzer purchased the *Clyde Valley*, reconditioned it and sold it on.[12] It was to return occasionally to Belfast carrying cargoes of coal before crossing the Atlantic. It was discovered in 1968 in Canada and was brought back home, but insufficient funds were raised to renovate it as a museum and it was sold for scrap.[13]

Fugitive

After docking the *Fanny* at midnight on 8th May, life became uncomfortable for Fred and Agnew in Hamburg. They were under the surveillance of about a dozen Scotland Yard detectives and the British consul made representations to the local authorities to encourage the two Ulstermen to leave before they were officially ordered out of the country. Although later correspondence with a London journalist showed that, following the gun-running episode, Asquith declared that "the Government has decided not to take criminal proceedings against the persons concerned in the recent incident",[14] Fred clearly believed that he was a wanted man.

Agnew returned to Belfast for a long overdue reunion with his family. Fred and Helen Crawford travelled via Cologne and Brussels to London. Major McCalmont, who had ridden into Balmoral with Fred in September 1913, and had been instrumental in mobilising the Ulster Volunteer Force at Larne, was also a Westminster MP. He invited Fred to the House of Commons – which, if Fred were a wanted man, was impudent to say the least – and in the lobby they encountered a Nationalist MP who pointed out McCalmont to a friend with the words: "There is one of the gun-runners". McCalmont commented that his opponent might have been even more sardonic if he had known who Fred was!

Fred attended another parliamentary debate a couple of days later when Bonar Law was advised by a Government minister and the Speaker to quieten the rebel spirit of Ulster. Bonar Law's tetchy response led to an adjournment of the House. There were many who were beginning to feel that the Conservative leader was not proving the most impressive of political figures. Two months later Michael McCarthy, a London-based Cork-born Protestant, wrote to Fred offering the opinion that the Unionists had never had "a weaker and more incompetent" parliamentary leader and described Bonar Law as "Ulster's worst enemy in Parliament".

Whilst Fred was in London he was invited to lunch with Carson, in company with Lord Londonderry and his son, Viscount Castlereagh. Fred said that he needed to return to Belfast as his business, which he had severely neglected over the previous three years, needed his attention. Carson was adamant that he should not do so, as "you will be arrested on arrival". Fred required some serious persuasion to stay away, but he did get Carson to make one promise: "If there is any fighting, you will see that I am there at the start".

Fred and his wife headed for Ostend where they were joined by Andy Agnew and his wife. The Crawfords made a brief visit to Namur and Dinant, which were soon to suffer under the German advance into France and Belgium. The two wives returned home and Agnew seems to have spent much of the next four weeks in the Belgian capital; his return to Belfast was delayed until the week after the Twelfth as a consequence of a technicality of maritime captaincy, which was eventually resolved by the resourceful Alexander McDowell.

Fred spent much of June and early July flitting between Brussels (from where he apprised his brother of recent events) and Hamburg, where his notoriety attracted a variety of unwelcome offers. Bruno Spiro paid a visit on Fred in Brussels and introduced him to an Admiral of the Royal Portugal Fleet and a Portuguese count who asked him if he would run a cargo of guns into their country in an attempt to restore the monarchy. Money was clearly no object to these plotters, but Fred politely explained, amongst the odd game of skittles, that he had no intention of making a career out of gun-running: "that all the risks I ran for Ulster were on patriotic grounds, and I would not accept money for what I had done if I were offered it".

Ulster and the Kaiser

Fred showed even less enthusiasm when asked by a member of Kiel Yacht Club to join him at the annual Regatta (held during the last week of June) in order to meet the Kaiser. At this time, the relationship between Ulstermen and the German Emperor was rather like trying to square the circle. As the war clouds began to darken northern Europe in those weeks, Fred spent many an hour discussing, in Spiro's Hamburg office, the escalating international tension, "amongst the dozens of different sorts of arms, and one old French *mitrailleuse* which had been captured in the Franco-German War of 1870-1871".

Referring to the German High Seas Fleet which he had recently witnessed, Fred pointed out that this only served to antagonise Britain; yet it was merely one facet of German imperial ambitions. Ulstermen could probably not satisfactorily explain the inherent polarity of their imperialist philosophy. Their membership of the Empire was integral to their stance and actions in the years before the First World War; it was a *sine qua non* of their identity. This was intensified in the period following Partition; as Fred expressed it: "the loss of Ulster would be the beginning of the end of the British Empire".[15] The aspiration of Germany to establish its own empire threatened what was viewed as Britain's rightful place in the world order – yet Ulstermen were clearly not averse to cultivating Teutonic assistance and admiration.

Edward Saunderson, the first Unionist leader, had dined with Kaiser Wilhelm II during Cowes Week in August 1894 to discuss Ireland and consequently claimed, three months later, when opening Knocknamuckley Orange Hall (near Portadown), that the Emperor "sympathised with the plucky stand taken by the Orangemen of Ulster". Five years later, the two men met at the Kiel Regatta, and in May 1902 they enjoyed a lengthy private conversation in the imperial palace in Berlin. Carson was to meet the Emperor at Bad Homburg in August 1913 although, when pressed on Ulster, he diplomatically changed the subject.[16]

Nevertheless, fidelity to Germany seems to have become something of a mantra with Ulster Unionists during the Home Rule crisis. At the end of 1910 the Rt. Hon. Thomas Andrews stated that, if Ulster were deserted by Britain, "I would rather be governed by Germany than by John Redmond and Company". Shortly afterwards, Craig made much the same comment. At Bangor on 29th April 1912, Fred added his confirmation that: "If we were put out of the Union … I would infinitely prefer to change my allegiance over to the Emperor of Germany". On the very eve of war he noted in correspondence with Spiro that: "We in Ulster would much prefer having the Kaiser over us to a Parliament in Dublin. We admire him in many ways". In the months following the War he noted that many people reminded him of these comments, but he responded that "I still hold the same opinion. The Emperor William looked well after his subjects …".[17]

Fred was asked a by a club member to attend the dinner at Kiel at the request of Kaiser Wilhelm; it was implied that the latter was interested in the use of private cars for the distribution of weapons. Fred expressed his reluctance, but agreed as long as there was no publicity. It would have been intriguing to discover how the arch-imperialist would have reacted to the personification of the ideology, but the meeting did not occur as the Regatta was abandoned on the news of the assassination of the Archduke in Sarajevo. Fred was sitting with Spiro in the Hamburg office on 29th June when they read the news; the arms dealer and the gun-runner, not without some irony, recognised that this was going to result in a very bloody conflict.

WAR

As the declaration of war on Serbia by Austria made the involvement of Germany in a European conflict inevitable, Fred was anxious to return to Belfast. He received permission from Carson on 7th July, called on Agnew in Brussels, and was in London on Friday 10th July. In Belfast that day there was a meeting of the Standing Committee of the UUC, in its guise of the Ulster Provisional Government, and McNeill noted in Craig's Visitors' Book that they were "at the threshold of the crisis". Fred arrived with impeccable timing at Larne on the Saturday to witness Carson reviewing 3000 local Volunteers.[18] A couple of days later Fred wrote to Agnew that: "Most of them were armed, and to see these arms out for an airing after your and my work was a sight for me".

On that Monday (13th July), as the Twelfth parade passed Cloreen, Fred shook hands with Carson and Wallace. His family shared the spectacle – with Naomi displaying her *'Hello Fanny'* banner – but, if they were delighted to see him, it was a short-lived pleasure for, apart from Stuart, who had to wait until the Campbell College term finished on 24th July in the presence of Gleichen, within two or three days the *paterfamilias* had packed them all off to Ramsey on the Isle of Man.

This was prompted by the sustained political impasse in Ulster; although within three weeks the British declaration of war on Germany was to postpone the Home Rule issue, no-one realised this at the time. Fred certainly had very little faith that the political process could resolve matters. In incidental comments to Whittington, in Cunningham's London office, Fred concluded that the Buckingham Palace Conference, which the King had called to allow all parties to air their opinions, and which Asquith regarded as a means of his own political salvation, "is bound to fail".[19] Fred added rather ominously that "We may, and probably will, have bloodshed, but we will win in the end". Evidently others were in similar mood, as Craig was asking Carson about the possibility of obtaining further weaponry, and Fred appears to have been incorrigible in his commitment to the cause. He was still under surveillance, and the Post Office was becoming "so inquisitive", that he contacted Miss Dove Browne (Ashfield House, 282 Ravenhill Road), intending to make her "a centre for some of my correspondence. I know I can trust you absolutely and that you will see that it reaches me as quickly as possible".[20]

Over the next fortnight Fred, in his capacity as Director of Ordnance of the UVF, adopting such aliases as W. H. Matheson, was making enquiries about, and obtaining quotations for, further arms and ammunition, including Maxims. Even as late as 30th July he was writing to Bruno Spiro asking for his comments on quotations received for arms which could be shipped via Hamburg, "as our people seem inclined to buy more" – this despite the fact that, earlier in the same letter, he had written with remarkable understatement: "I suppose now that the war has broken out, as you prophesied, it will be difficult to buy rifles in Hamburg"!

At this time Ulster was still anticipating having to run its own government and even Richardson had been emboldened; he discussed with the UUC and local businessmen an attack on the Customs & Revenue Department, to seize such items as valuation papers and Income Tax documents. As Director of Ordnance, Fred was consulted as to the best means to effect a raid, and to transport and store the papers: "I had all the tools collected including jemmies, crowbars, heavy hammers, etc for a forcible entrance into two or three offices simultaneously" – but it was all abandoned with the declaration of war and the call to form the Ulster Division which, as Fred pointed out sardonically, was "to help the Government that had a few months previously given an order for an Army to occupy Ulster and shoot down its loyal inhabitants".

In retrospect he claimed extravagantly that: "It will go down in History that what Ulster did in 1914 was the greatest act of unselfish, self-sacrificing patriotism that ever any people or Nation performed". On 7th August Carson, in a communication to City Hall to be read out by the Lord Mayor, had urged support for the war effort.[21] Ulster, however, did not rush into this venture without caution. On 19th August Fred informed Carson that he was constantly being asked what the UVF should do and that he always replied that they should "volunteer for service in Ulster without conditions, but not for abroad until you are satisfied with the safeguards that Home Rule will not be put upon us when our men have left the country", and he even suggested that the UUC should devise a "common action". At the end of the month Mrs Spender said she had just received a letter from Carson who was still considering urging a UVF contingent to volunteer for service "in spite of the fact that no guarantee has yet been given about Home Rule".[22]

From the Old Town Hall on 2nd September – in the wake of the Amiens Despatch published in *The Times* three days previously[23] – Colonel Hacket Pain, Chief of Staff of the UVF, issued a Special Order (which he personally commended) for Enlistment in the Imperial Forces, in response to the appeal by Lord Kitchener.[24] By this stage relationships had changed and the dramatic events partnered strange bed-fellows. Arch-threat to Ulster, John Redmond, offered the services of the Irish Nationalists (a fact which Lilian Spender admitted privately "makes me sick"),[25] whilst one of those who had done the most to empower Ulstermen – a German arms dealer – became an immediate and undiluted *persona non grata*.

Mementoes

Fred was to admit towards the close of that year that the events of the previous three or four months had made the gun-running a distant memory.[26] He had, however, created mementoes for others. At the review at Larne on 11th July he presented Carson with a pencil case, and he later dispensed others to selected individuals, including – probably with a degree of relish – Sir George Richardson. The pencil cases were fashioned from empty cartridge cases which he and Bruno Spiro collected from test firings on the ranges at Hamburg: "Spiro had sent them to Birmingham and [had them] mounted as a pencil with a silver bullet". In the week after he returned from involuntary exile, Fred paid a visit to the Great Victoria Street stationers and printers, William

Strain & Son, and asked them to design a label for the cigars which had shared his voyage on the *Fanny* and *Clyde Valley*. These were distributed in a specially commissioned silver case to those he felt would most value them or most deserved them. These included Field Marshal Roberts, Viscount Castlereagh, James Craig and his brother, Charles Craig, Dawson Bates and Sir Edward Carson (who was also the beneficiary of a rifle and bayonet). The gesture was much appreciated by all concerned, and at the end of 1935, Major Tristram of Darlington, who by then had moved to the south of France, notified Fred that: "I still keep the cigar you sent me from the *SS Fanny*".[27]

The most individual of all the mementoes, however, was not given to an Ulsterman or Briton. Shortly after the Twelfth, Fred had visited an Ulster pearl fishery and selected – "for its beautiful tint and lustre" – a pink Ulster pearl, which he took to the noted Royal Avenue jeweller, Sharman D. Neill, to have it mounted as a scarf pin. Like many Ulster businessmen, Neill was a staunch opponent of Home Rule and he was rewarded by becoming sole supplier of special UVF bronze cap badges.[28] His two sons, one of whom was a very close friend of James Davidson of Sirocco Works, were members of the UVF and, within a few weeks of their father's creation (20th July) they had both enlisted. As both his sons lay dead in battle against the Germans by 1st July 1916, one wonders whether Sharman Neill ever regretted creating the pearl scarf pin.

That July (1914) Carson had sent an autographed photograph to Spiro with, as Elsa Kanzki acknowledged, "some nice words written on the photo ... We are naturally quite proud of this photo and the spirit that gave it". A few days later Fred despatched his gift to Hamburg, asking Bruno Spiro to "wear it in remembrance of Ulster and one who tried to do his duty by God's help to save this fair Province from the devastating influence of Rome". Despite the problems of communication that the war on the European mainland must have caused, Spiro wrote via Rotterdam towards the end of August to express his appreciation of the scarf pin. He concluded by saying that: "I only wanted to submit you my thanks and regard, because against you personally I have nothing".

Fred reciprocated the sentiment, and on 2nd August had written to

Elsa Kanzki – admitting that the letter may not reach her – saying that he was quite willing to accommodate her if she found it necessary to leave Hamburg. He was, however, a little naïve when he added that "you will have a warm welcome in Ulster for what you have done for her". Sir Otto Jaffé – whose family had originated in Hamburg – had been twice elected Lord Mayor of Belfast; he was a member of the Unionist Party and his son served with the British Army. This did not stop him being declared a German spy and he left Belfast in 1916. Even Lilian Spender had no sympathy; Jaffé's wife, an American, paid a visit to her on 6th May 1915 which the hostess found embarrassing as she had recently signed a petition "pleading for the greater restriction of aliens".[29] Her husband proved equally ready to change his allegiance – only two days after the declaration of war, Spender wrote to Fred from Chatham, adding a postscript: "I fancy the Germans counted on the UVF proving an obstacle to England. Hope they will find out their mistake". It is quite probable that, had he not died in 1913, even Gustav Wolff would have been arrested as an undesirable alien.

Fred was only to meet Bruno Spiro once more, when he travelled to Berlin in 1924 to make the reparations' claim on the *Clyde Valley*. They met in the Adlon Hotel,[30] a stone's throw from the Brandenburg Gate, and talked of the War, inflation and the changing world. The two men maintained a sociable correspondence until the mid-1930s, when the elderly Ulsterman sought details of his gun-running activities from the arms dealer's files. On 26th May 1934 Spiro added the comment that he and his associate "remember all the times [as] if it had been yesterday. These were the times we will never forget. Same as our friendship, which will last forever if you don't mind, and I know you don't".[31]

Sadly, 'forever' proved an extremely short time. Spiro had continued to trade after the War; in 1928 he purchased arms for the Finnish Government and sold Japanese rifles, purchased from Czechoslovakia and Romania, to Albania! At some stage in the later 1930s the Nazis confiscated his business and, as a result of his Judaism, he was sent to a concentration camp where he committed suicide. Thus perished the German "whose name", Fred had written, "Ulster ought never to forget".

Notes

1. Most of these events are related by Fred in his account in D/1415/B/34.

2. He was presumably related to Fred through the latter's brother-in-law, Lawson Brown. The cousin lived at Mornington Park, Princetown Road, Bangor.

3. It is not clear whether Kelly ever received this message but, if he did, it cannot have calmed any nerves amongst the Ulster Unionist Council.

4. Most of the information for the rest of the chapter comes from D/1415/B/34, D/1415/B/36 (Agnew's account) and a large collection of Fred's correspondence: D/1700/5/17/1/-.

5. Fred usually referred to this island as Bergenstock, or alternatively Burgstaaken.

6. Fred later claimed that Agnew loaned the log books to someone and that they could never be traced: D/640/30/10, 8 January 1937.

7. D/1700/5/6/19. *The Northern Whig*, 2 June 1927. A presentation was made to Agnew a year later, but Fred was too unwell to attend: D/1700/5/4/89, 21 November 1928.

8. One well-known photo (see p.219), which features four men and a woman, has caused some confusion. It shows Fred, Agnew and Spiro standing at the rear; seated are Falck and a woman. David Hume, *For Ulster and her Freedom: the story of the April 1914 gunrunning*, (Ulster Society, Lurgan, 1989), p.23 states that the woman is Fritz Schneider! ATQ Stewart, *The Ulster Crisis*, (London, 1967), opposite p.116 does at least get the correct sex, but says that it was Elsa Kanzki. It was, in fact, Helen Crawford.

9. D/640/29/3, –/5, 18 & 25 September 1922.

10. Falck (born on 13 September 1847) was married, and had raised one son and three daughters. They were all born, and all died, in Fjaere (except the son who was born in Havana). They are buried in Fjaere close to Grimstad, about twelve miles south-west of Arendal. Captain Falck died on 13 February 1925; his widow, Anna Ovidia, survived him by 16 years. His three daughters do not seem to have married. I am indebted to John Crawford (Fred's grandson) and Inger Eik, and to Trine Bogenes of Fjaere, for all this information.

11. D/1700/5/6/22A, 28 April 1934.

12. Craig arranged with James Cunningham to pay £10,000 for the *Mountjoy*: D/1700/10, 20 December 1918.

13. D/640/29/1, 22 August 1922. Stewart, p.272.

14. D/1700/5/17/1/147, 6 March 1917.

15. D/640/11/2, p.51.

16. Alvin Jackson, Colonel Edward Saunderson: *Land and Loyalty in Victorian Ireland*, (Clarendon Press, Oxford, 1995), pp.133-135. Stewart, p.226.

17. D/1415/B/34, p.127. D/1700/5/13/23 – a cutting from the *Dublin Evening Telegraph*, 30 May 1918. D/1700/5/17/1/43, 30 July 1914. Denis Gwynn, *The Life of John Redmond*, (London, 1932), pp.205-206.

18. Ian Colvin, *The Life of Lord Carson*, (London, 1934), Vol.II, 402-403.

19. Written on 20 July 1914. The Conference broke up on 24 July without any breakthrough.

20. She is probably the 'Miss Browne' who attended Lilian Spender's tea-party with Helen and Naomi Crawford on 30 November 1914: D/1633/2/19.

21. D/1507/A/7/5.

22. D/1700/5/17/1/65A, 19 August 1914. D/1633/2/19, 31 August 1914. Carson was also personally receiving letters from men asking whether they should enlist before guarantees were given: D/1507/A/7/6, 8 August 1914.

23. For the Amiens Despatch, see the next chapter.

24. D/1700/5/17/1/73, 2 September 1914.

25. D/1633/2/19, 5 August 1914.

26. D/1700/5/17/1/41D, pre-November 1914.

27. D/1700/5/5/102, 29 December 1935. Tristram was commiserating on the death of Carson earlier that year.

28. D/1238/96, 21 March 1914 (UVF Order no.26)

29. D/1633/2/20.

30. The luxurious Adlon Hotel, opened in 1907, is still there – reconstructed after the Allied bombing during the Second World War.

31. Stewart, p.243. D/1700/5/6/22A-c, 28 April, 14 May and 26 May 1934. Spiro had a daughter, Gerda-Elena, who was engaged at Easter 1935: D/1700/5/6/29.

The Silver Casket

The First World War compiled its own dossier of strange and inexplicable coincidences.[1] Bruno Spiro sat down at the end of August to thank Fred for the pearl scarf pin; he added that, with regard to the War, "I suppose you will only read what the English reporters write about it".[2] What he cannot have known is that, as he posted the letter, international journalist, Arthur Moore, late of Campbell College, was gathering information which would result in the publication of the first, and possibly the only, authentic virtually-uncensored report from the Western Front during the First World War.

The Amiens Despatch

By that stage, the British Expeditionary Force (BEF) was in retreat from Mons and Le Cateau, but Kitchener had learned his lesson from the Boer War – that journalists were not always tractable – and he refused to allow reporters near the front lines. Only anodyne notes from official military sources were published in the press during August 1914, which asserted that the BEF was putting up gallant resistance to the German advance. As Arthur Moore, who had just arrived in France from Albania, met many of the retreating soldiers by the roadside, he learned that the reports in the British press to that point were nothing more than "children's prattle" and "eyewash".

He wrote his report in a hotel in Amiens, despatched it across the Channel and when the so-called Amiens Despatch was printed by *The*

Times, in one of its occasional wartime Sunday special editions, on 30th August it caused a total furore in the rest of the press, amongst the public and in Parliament. Asquith, who made the angry and ironic assertion that the public was entitled to the truth, would probably have descended into apoplexy if he had known that the despatch had been written by an Ulsterman! The fact that Moore's name was never given in *The Times* meant that no-one was aware of his authorship, not even *The Northern Whig* when it copied the statement in the rest of the British press by which *The Times* defended its report as being "from the pen of an experienced and trustworthy correspondent, who had seen fighting in many parts of the world".[3]

The Times had, in fact, not expected to be allowed to print so much of Moore's original report, but the Press Censor had read it and actively reinstated some of the paper's own deletions before giving his *imprimatur*. *The Times* vigorously and successfully defended its publication of the Amiens Despatch and very shortly afterwards the Press Censor, admitting that he had not handled the matter well, resigned from his post.

F. E. Smith, later Lord Birkenhead, had been a staunch supporter of Ulster's stand against Home Rule; he had been a guest at Craigavon, had spoken at many venues across Ulster and had ridden at the Balmoral review in September 1913. Despite this, after the War Fred described him as "our bitterest opponent in the Cabinet"[4] – although it was his 'betrayal' by coming to terms with Michael Collins that particularly alienated Ulstermen. As Smith stood on the steps at Craigavon in 1913 and 1914, he cannot have guessed that a pupil educated only a mile down the road would shortly prove the cause of his embarrassment and resignation – for Smith was the Press Censor!

Smith, who clearly recognised the significance of what he described as "this most able and interesting message", concluded his editing with a personal plea to *The Times* "to use the parts of the article which I have passed to enforce the lesson – reinforcements and reinforcements at once". Moore later reflected that "none of my subsequent war service was half as useful as this article (written with FE's help) in my civilian days", and noted that it prompted an influx of recruitment in its wake. It was probably no coincidence that the UVF's Special Order for Enlistment in the Imperial Forces was issued three days later.

In that same week Fred, in his capacity with the Royal Army Service Corps (RASC), was asked to visit Derry on 7th September to address three battalions of the City of Derry UVF Regiment in order to raise recruits. He was asked "to rub in a bit of patriotism – tell them what you have done for the Ulster cause, and explain the conditions of service to the men". Fred told them that Carson had sent a message: "Tell them I expect as much from Derry as Derry has ever given before".[5]

Totally incognisant of the storm that his despatch had caused in the United Kingdom, over the next few days Moore, in the company of the correspondent from *The Daily Mail*, Joseph Jeffries, continued to tour the front lines. Eventually they were arrested by the military authorities and, in accordance with Kitchener's instructions, could have been shot as spies. They were, however, put on board a frustratingly slow train to Tours and ordered never to return to the area.

Fred was to record[6] that on 18th November 1921 he encountered Joseph Jeffries, still employed by *The Daily Mail* – in the Old Town Hall. "He was trying to convince four Ulstermen" – which included two MPs, the Editor of *The Northern Whig*, and Northern Ireland Minister of Labour, John Miller Andrews – "that we in Ulster should come under a Dominion Government in Dublin as a federal state". Fred was asked to "give this beggar some ginger and straight talking to".

Fred engaged in a lengthy conversation with Jeffries, presenting his opinions on political developments over the previous decade, and told the reporter that "thousands of Ulstermen lying buried in France, Flanders and elsewhere all over the world had paid the highest price possible to keep the Empire free from enemies, and there were thousands more who were prepared to die for Ulster and their homes". Jeffries later visited the offices of *The Northern Whig* and was apprised of the man "who had given him an awful time of it", and who had effectively thrown him out of the Old Town Hall.

A few months later Jeffries may have reflected that this treatment was more agreeable than that he received over five hours in early July 1922 in Dublin.[7] He was kidnapped near the Gresham Hotel whilst observing fighting during the civil war, and was interrogated as a British spy. He was released, but he may have regarded it as unique that he had been grilled by both the British Army and Irish paramilitaries, and threatened on both occasions with being shot as a spy!

OC, RASC

Fred had been notified as early as 8th November 1911 by the RASC at Ebrington Barracks in Derry that, in the event of mobilisation, he would be appointed Officer Commanding, RASC, Belfast Defences – based at Victoria Barracks in North Queen Street, only ten minutes walk from Alexander Crawford & Son. On 31st July 1914 he received a telegram telling him to report for duty at once, and on the same day he notified a correspondent in London that "I have been appointed to an important command in Belfast … doing duty with full Army rank and pay". On 5th August he contacted his outfitters, W. W. White of Woolwich, asking them to send him a second-hand Sam Brown belt, as his old one had gone AWOL. Admitting that "I thought my soldiering days were over", he signed himself proudly: "Frederick Hugh Crawford, Major, OC, RASC, Belfast Defences".[8]

The previous four years had been particularly arduous and stressful for the businessman, who was appointed to his military command on the eve of his 53rd birthday. In addition to the daily domestic and business demands, he had travelled a great deal and, up to the outbreak of the War, had been continuously on the move for about four months. Over the next four years he adopted an even more punishing schedule and it is scarcely surprising that he was confined to bed for at least a couple of extended periods.

Around March 1915 he wrote to his brother saying that he had been in hospital for a fortnight. He had been working "practically day and night since the War broke out", visiting his office in Wilson Street from about 8.30 to 9am and then walking down to Victoria Barracks until midnight. In the early days it was often 2am before he returned to Cloreen.[9]

He received £360 per annum for his RASC work, and he conceded that "my salary comes in very conveniently and has saved the situation once when a depositor wanted to be paid off". He also endeavoured to raise a loan from the nursery, as business was effectively at a standstill. By May 1917 Fred was obliged to call in a favour or two and Craig arranged (from London) "for a limited amount of wheat to be purchased for manufacturing purposes". Craig replied to Fred's note of gratitude: "I am very delighted to know that another Irish industry is not to be closed down"[10] – but he may not have been aware of the commercial realities of the business. The bank had been pestering the owner and a couple of years earlier his estate agents had sold the Mill Street property to the Corporation for £4250. They struggled to achieve that figure, and thought it a good one in the circumstances, but Fred had hoped for £5000. He still owed creditors £9250.

His duties at Victoria Barracks – in which capacity he was promoted to (Temporary) Lieutenant-Colonel – placed him in charge of "supply and transport in Belfast". He told his brother that "I now have nearly 10,000 men to feed and look after their comforts". There were probably many hours spent on fastidious and elaborate paperwork which might have been better spent with his family. Early in 1915 he submitted a very detailed analysis of the workload of himself and his clerks to his HQ – Irish Command at Parkgate in Dublin. Lt-Col. Arthur Collard thanked him for these, but felt disinclined to evaluate Fred's facts and figures. He was ready to accept at face value that Fred employed his staff to the best advantage and "had safeguarded the interests of the public in every direction". He said that Fred's efforts were "fully appreciated" in Dublin and that it was conceded that he was doing "excellent work".[11]

He was informed that on Monday 8th February he should meet General Landon who was undertaking an inspection of transport, but that he would also inspect "your Depot offices and arrangements during his stay in Belfast". The outcome is not recorded, but it was probably favourable, as was a review of his Barracks on 19th October 1916: Lt-Col. Armstrong reported that it was "in a very satisfactory and efficient condition, and that great credit is due to the OC and his Executive officers for Supply, Transport and Barrack services respectively. In my opinion they are all above average in zeal and ability".[12]

The Somme

Between February and March 1916 the RASC arranged for Fred to visit the front lines at the Somme.[13] He left for London on 18th February via Dublin. He met his elder son, Stuart, and on his 20th wedding anniversary (20th February) he called on Carson, but the latter was ill, and asked him to call on his return to the capital. By chance he met Col. Bob Wallace – who had also recently been quite ill – and they travelled together via Boulogne and Amiens to Divisional HQ at Acheux.[14] Here they met a number of erstwhile UVF colleagues, now in the 36th (Ulster) Division at Mailly-Maillet (close to Thiepval). Spender arranged for Fred to spend a day in the trenches at Auchonvillers "where the communication trench starts". This position was only about 200 metres from the German front lines and they were all plagued by snow and freezing weather.

Fred gained a good impression of the challenges and dangers faced by those engaged at the Front. He probably never realised it at the time, but he probably passed the very spot where, seven weeks previously on 8th January, Second Lieutenant Robin MacDermott had become the first officer of the 36th Division to be killed in action. MacDermott – who had served with his two brothers in the East Belfast Volunteers of the UVF, and had drilled and trained at Ormiston – had been in charge of a working party in a trench and was killed by an exploding shell.[15] He was the middle son of Rev. Dr John MacDermott, minister of Belmont Presbyterian Church, and a fellow Governor at Campbell College, where he had sent his three sons. The youngest, Clarke – who was appointed Minister of Security at Stormont in 1940 and Lord Chief Justice of Northern Ireland in 1951 – recalled his twenty-second birthday in 1918: "At several moments of acute fear I had thought it would also be my last".

Dr MacDermott, a recent Moderator of the General Assembly, may well have adopted a degree of Calvinist fatalism about his son's death. Although the Ulster Division had not travelled to France until October 1915 – and the Somme was to prove its first serious engagement – the British roll-call of death had mounted horrifically; in March 1915 Lilian Spender had commented on the dreadful casualty lists. Clergymen had not quailed or railed in the face of arming the UVF and, according to one source, MacDermott claimed to be happy with his rifle, "but I would like another hundred cartridges".[16] Ulster's clergymen appear to have been perfectly comfortable with the enlistment of their sons. Another Presbyterian, Rev. Dr William Wright, who was a member of the Standing Committee of the Ulster Unionist Council (UUC), and UVF chaplain at Newtownards, wrote to Carson to say: "I shall give them my blessing and let them go".[17]

Of all those who lost sons, Ranfurly was perhaps the most phlegmatic. His only son was in the Coldstream Guards, and had been killed on 1st February 1915. The Earl acknowledged Fred's condolences over the loss and admitted that "we are all in the gravest distress", but added that "if we had a dozen sons we would have wished them all to go to the Front for their country's honour".[18] It was all rather redolent of Siegfried Sassoon's line in his satirical poem, *To Any Dead Officer*, "… the War won't end for at least two years; But we've got stacks of men …". In a letter to Carson at the end of 1916, Fred endorsed the principle that putting large numbers of men into the field was the solution to victory.[19] If he seems rather casual with other men's lives, particularly as this was in the wake of the carnage on the Somme, it should be borne in mind that he had come very close to losing his elder son on 21st October 1916; the latter had been shot through the body and right lung and was incapacitated for several months.[20]

Fred Crawford was to maintain an ambivalent attitude towards the German nation. As we have seen, he was due to meet the Kaiser, whom he admired, only weeks before the outbreak of war, yet his hostility to German actions was genuine and he, as much as any other Ulsterman, felt that the War was justified. The events of 1916 can only have served to intensify his alienation, but his uncertain loyalty was expressed in the early 1920s in a reference to Elsa Kanzki, when he conceded that she was "a splendid type of a capable woman. The only thing I have against her now is that she is a German, and this feeling has arisen since the War".[21] Shortly after the outbreak of the Second World War, however, Stuart – again on active service – wrote to his father saying that he could find very little sympathy for a nation which had conspired to start a second war and chastised him: "You say they are a wonderful people, and so they are in ways – the chief being their stupidity ...".[22]

The earlier antagonism to all things 'Hun' was encapsulated in a letter to *The Northern Whig* at the end of September 1916, from Fred's own bookkeeper and manager at the Wilson Street Works, Ernest Knowles,[23] who chastised the City Council for the insult of continuing to display the street name-plaque for Berlin Street. He wrote that: "The minister of a church on the Shankill Road told me today that a short time ago he had received from a soldier a letter (written in the trenches) stating ... that if he and a few of his pals came home on leave they would very soon remove 'Berlin' from the sign ...". It is strange that there was no mention of Moltke Street (always pronounced 'Moltek' by locals), which bore the name of the 1914 German Chief of the General Staff, who was an enthusiastic exponent of the War. There was, however, as much logic in this contempt as in refusing to read the war poetry of Siegfried Sassoon, because he bore the name of a legendary Teutonic hero.

Campbell College

One pupil of Campbell College, who was later killed in action at the end of 1917, described the Germans extravagantly as "the greatest foe civilisation has ever known", and another preferred an early echo of William Armour's opinion that 'Hun Kultur' was "lacking in moral fibre, vicious in triumph and spiteful in defeat". Perhaps the most balanced and judicious view of the conflict was expressed by George Buchanan, who had witnessed the UVF cars at Kilwaughter. He had been taken to see the march-past of the 36th Division through Belfast on 8th May 1915, and heard that *dulce et decorum est pro patria mori*. However, he later commented on the victims of the Somme, at which ten per cent of all Campbellian deaths occurred in the War: "So end, for the most part, those kindly, obstinate, easily-deceived neighbours of ours. The houses are full or mourning, and thousands of women walk in black dresses".[24]

It should be borne in mind that Fred's attachment to Campbell College as a Governor was not a casual or incidental role. He regarded the school very much as a microcosm of the Ulster which he cherished: it educated the province's businessmen and professionals; the Officer Training Corps offered the means to train its defenders; and its Headmaster proclaimed the ideology of 'muscular Christianity' by which Fred set so much store. He would have applauded the sentiments of the principal at the 1917 Speech Day, that the War "has brought home to the boys ... the great principles we try to inculcate – principles of patriotism, self-sacrifice and devotion to duty. Thus the war ... is having an incalculable influence for good on the characters and lives of those who will in a few years be called to play their part as citizens in shaping the destinies of the Empire". The Chief Guest, Sir Robert Kennedy, echoed this aspiration: "the dominant characteristic of Campbell was her unwavering loyalty to the House of Windsor and the indissoluble link to the Empire".[25]

Fred effectively occupied his post on the Board of Governors for over half a century, and he put both his sons through its doors. He paid regular visits in the 1920s and 1930s to talk to the pupils. Shortly after Fred's death, Professor J. Ernest Davey, who that year was appointed Moderator of the General Assembly, wrote to Cloreen to express his condolences, and recalled meeting Fred with interest as a schoolboy and later as a fellow Governor.[26] The longest-serving Headmaster, Lt-Col. William Duff Gibbon DSO wrote to him on his (Gibbon's) retirement in 1943 to express his gratitude, and to recount that the school owed Fred a great deal.[27]

Fred was one of the leading lights in the erection of the school's War Memorial to 594 serving pupils, of whom nearly a quarter perished. His familiarity with Field Marshal Sir Henry Wilson enabled him to invite the widely-respected General to inaugurate the memorial in July 1922. Both men were staunch imperialists; they both expressed their contempt for non-Ulster politicians, especially those in the Cabinet: "They are a miserable crowd ... They will ruin England and the Empire", noted Wilson in his diary. They both particularly despised Lloyd George and Churchill for talking with Michael Collins in 1921. Unfortunately Fred did not get his wish to see Wilson at Campbell as, only a few days prior to the occasion, Wilson was assassinated on his London doorstep by the IRA (22nd June 1922). Fred had accompanied Wilson only a fortnight previously on a visit to Mount Stewart (the Londonderrys' residence), and he wrote Carson that: "Since the loss of my mother some years ago, I have not felt the death of anyone so much as his".[28] Fred probably accorded with the sentiments of one member of the school staff, who wrote to Craig the following day with extravagant anguish: "Ulster is poorer; the British nation is poorer; the world is poorer, and there is no language to express the feelings of this Imperial province … we are dumb".[29]

THE SILVER CASKET

Although attentiveness to the War Memorial demonstrated Fred's ready appreciation of the dedication and sacrifice of others, it proved much harder for him to accept the appreciation of others for his own efforts.

As he returned from the Somme district, crossing the Channel on 26th February, accompanied by a destroyer because of the fear of prowling submarines,[30] as requested he made the Carson household his first port of call – only to find him out. Over the next few days he visited his son twice at Woolwich and lunched with such notables as Lilian Spender, Frank Hall, the Duchess of Abercorn and Lord Ranfurly.

On 28th February he called to see Lady Carson, who produced "a beautiful silver casket specially designed and made for me in commemoration of the landing of the arms and ammunition in the *SS Mountjoy*", paid for from voluntary subscriptions in Ulster. Fred collected it as he departed London on 2nd March and took it home to Belfast via Dublin. His journey took him, appropriately, via Holyhead where he had waited for the *Clyde Valley* at the breakwater two years previously. On his return he wrote to the Carsons to "express how much I value it, representing as it does the affection and appreciation of my fellow Ulster countrymen for the service, through God's help, I was instrumental in rendering to the cause of freedom, civil and religious". He added that it had been intimated that there would be a personal letter from Carson's own hand to place in it, which he would value even more highly.

The Crawford Testimonial subscription – which appears to have totalled £1386–8s – had been raised by the start of 1915. The casket cost in the region of £50 or £60 and the rest was to be presented in the form of a cheque to Fred. When this was hinted to the intended recipient he later noted that he had given the messenger "such a bad time of it that I thought it would not be mentioned again". Lady Carson had also stated that there would be a cheque to accompany the casket, but – although he refrained from being abrasive with her – he made it categorically clear that he would never accept such a gift: "in fact, it nearly turned me from accepting the casket". As late as May 1917, even Carson himself braved the potential flak to urge Fred to accept the money "as a token of our high regard for you". The gun-runner was mortified and replied that he could not do so: "As a favour, I ask that this matter never again be mentioned to me … This is the first time, and I hope it will be the last time, I have had to refuse a request from you".[31]

As early as January 1915 Dawson Bates made the eminently reasonable suggestion that "the money should perhaps instead be settled on Mrs Crawford and the Crawford children". There is no doubt that both the Crawford family and the business could have benefited at that time from such a donation and in retrospect Fred's refusal may appear crassly obstinate. His reasoning, however, was not pride or indifference to financial reality; it was because he refused to be singled out for reward. All the others involved had played an integral part in the venture and he could not have achieved the landing without their contribution; he believed it would be unjust to accept the entire collection: "the beautiful casket seems in fairness to belong to them as well as to me". Ultimately the money was given to UVF charitable causes.[32]

As he had passed through Dublin with the casket in his luggage, he attempted – unsuccessfully – to call in on his friend, Captain John Bowen-Colthurst, at Portobello Barracks.[33] It is possible that he had known the professional soldier since the days of the Boer War, but he had become more familiar with him since Bowen-Colthurst was based at Downpatrick under Col. Bob Wallace around 1910. Fred and Helen Crawford were invited to his wedding in April 1910 in Co. Clare to the youngest daughter of Lord Dunboyne, but were unable to attend because they could not find anyone to look after the children! Fred arranged to meet his acquaintance at Downpatrick on several occasions before the outbreak of war. He described the soldier as "a very nice fellow" who, after some wild years in India, had become a great reader of the Bible. Fred found in him a kindred spirit, and in 1911 confided that "I always feel a better man after being with you. A Christian in the Army has to be so out-and-out, it is like a regiment always fighting and facing the enemy".

Three years later, however, Bowen-Colthurst had become increasingly unstable. Early in 1914 he found himself unable to accept the authority of his commanding officer. He was a man of great personal courage, but lacked sound judgement. He was probably shell-shocked after Mons and was one of those in retreat from Le Cateau whom Arthur Moore might have encountered; however, he disobeyed orders, turned back to face the Germans, and had to be relieved of command. A Medical Board found him to be suffering from nervous exhaustion and when Fred searched for him on 3rd March in Dublin he was between two further assessments, so may have been confined.

Virtually two years to the day after Fred landed the rifles (26th April 1916), during the Easter Rising, Bowen-Colthurst took a number of innocent civilian prisoners from Portobello Barracks and shot them dead in cold blood. He was tried and found insane. He wrote to Fred in February 1918 from the south of England to say that he had been released and asked to be remembered to all of Fred's family. He added that he hoped that they would meet again some day, but there is no evidence that Fred ever replied, or that he had been in touch with Bowen-Colthurst since his arrest.[34]

Demob

It is not surprising that Fred also suffered from stress caused by overwork, as a consequence of his duties, responsibilities and other pressures upon him during the War. On 18th June 1918 he suffered from influenza, complicated by a mild attack of broncho-pneumonia. He was sent to hospital on 15th July 1918, and his heart was diagnosed as "slightly irregular", and he was recommended for transfer to Gilford Convalescent Hospital (Co. Down) at a Medical Board for Disabled Officers. A month later, although easily fatigued by severe exertion, he was instructed to return to duty at Victoria Barracks.[35]

On 22nd April 1919 the OC RASC, Belfast Defences, was sent orders from the War Office that he would be relieved of duty on 1st May and would revert to the Retired List;[36] in June he returned to the recurrent and enduring problems posed by Alexander Crawford & Son. The War Office, however, had not finished their dealings with him. It sent a communication to his former HQ at Parkgate on 16th October 1920 to notify them that Lt-Col. Crawford "did not pass through a dispersal station, and consequently Army Form Z3 was not completed in respect of this officer". Whatever the reason for this may have been, they calculated that up to 31st August 1920 he had been overpaid by £1106 9s 6d. Taking into account tax payable and an unissued gratuity, the War Office claimed that he owed them £612 15s 8d.

The retired Lieut-Colonel seemed disinclined to co-operate with their pursuit, so they wrote to him on 3rd January 1921 asking what steps he intended to take "to regularise your position". On 21st March 1921 the War Office wrote to him directly at Wilson Street and ordered him to attend GHQ in Dublin "to arrive at a settlement". They pointed out that, because of an error he had been overpaid, which had resulted in considerable correspondence; if he did not visit Parkgate they threatened "further drastic disciplinary action". He replied that it was not convenient for him to visit Dublin and did not see that it would "serve any good purpose". On 2nd April he deigned to meet an official, but stated that he was no longer subject to military law, and refused to accept their instructions, but said that he was prepared to help finalise the matter by correspondence.

GHQ asked what they could do with "this blighter"; another officer described him as "a slippery person". It was hinted that they could resort to a Court-Martial for absence, but accepted that they were "unlikely to get a conviction". Fred made the perfectly valid point to them that, with the best will in the world, he could not repay any money because of the depressed state of his company affairs.

On 22nd February 1921 Fred said that he had made an enquiry at an earlier date and had been told that he had not been officially demobilised; he also noticed that his name was still on the Active List until at least June 1920. He believed that, as RASC officers were in short supply, this implied that he could still be called up at short notice, even for continental duty. He pointed out that to fulfil any such obligation, and as he was still being paid, he had had to refuse "several very important business undertakings". He claimed that during this period he had been offered tempting and very remunerative work in Ireland but, as he was still in receipt of a War Office salary, he had had to reject it: "Under these circumstances I consider I owe the War Office nothing, either legally or morally, even were I in a position to pay what you say I owe".

Silence beyond this gauntlet would suggest that the War Office decided that any further pursuit would engage the law of diminishing returns, and they surrendered. In all honesty there seems to have been a degree of bluff by the arch-plotter; there is evidence that he was offered other work around June 1920 – and that he did turn it down – but not for the reasons he gave to the War Office.

The document was headed 'Secret Service'.[37]

Notes

1. There is none more touching than the tale of two Irish brothers from Dublin and America, born in the same house, but who had never known that the other existed, and who met by sheer chance in a French estaminet in 1916: James W Taylor, *The 1st Royal Irish Rifles in the Great War*, (Four Courts Press, Dublin, 2002), p.69.

2. D/1700/5/17/1/68, 27 August 1914.

3. *The Northern Whig*, 1 September 1914. For the full story of the Amiens Despatch, see Keith Haines, *The Looted Paradise: the life and times of Arthur Moore*, (Ballymaconaghy Publishing, Belfast, 2004), pp.146-156; and *Neither Rogues nor Fools: a history of Campbell College and Campbellians*, (Belfast, 1993), pp.99-104.

4. D/640/11/2, p.67.

5. D/1700/5/17/1/57, –/74, –/76. *The Northern Whig*, 8 September 1914.

6. D/640/11/2, pp.57-63.

7. *New York Times*, 5 July 1922.

8. D/1700/10. D/1700/5/17/1/53, –/92.

9. D/1700/5/17/1/41D-E (undated, but written c.August-October 1914 and March 1915).

10. D/1700/5/17/1/149-150, 27 & 30 May 1917.

11. D/1700/5/17/1/97, 7 February 1915.

12. D/1700/5/13/23.

13. The record of his visit is found in D/1700/5/17/1/127.

14. At that time, Captain C D Chase, who had founded the Officer Training Corps at Campbell College (see Chapter 4), was in charge of one of the four companies of 16th (Pioneer) Battalion of 36th Division engaged on building a railway from Candas to Acheux, to facilitate the assault at the Somme: S N White, *The Terrors: 16th (Pioneer) Battalion Royal Irish Rifles*, (Somme Association, Belfast, 1996), pp.68-85.

15. He was a member of 'A' Coy, 8th Battalion Royal Irish Rifles (East Belfast Volunteers), and is buried in Auchonvillers Military Cemetery.

16. Ian Colvin, *The Life of Lord Carson*, (London, 1934), Vol.II, 375.

17. D/1507/A/9/5, 17 November 1914. Five of Wright's six sons were at Campbell; the one who was not was killed in action. Of 126 pupils from Campbell who were killed, 30% were the sons of Irish clergymen. Additionally, the one member of staff who was killed was the son of a former Dean of Cork.

18. D/1700/5/17/1/96, 5 February 1915. Spender's cousin had also been killed on 22 December 1914.

19. D/1700/5/13/20, 10 December 1916 from Victoria Barracks.

20. D/1700/5/17/1/137, 22 December 1916. Stuart Crawford had passed through Sandhurst and joined the Royal Field Artillery in May 1916.

21. D/1415/B/34, p.118.

22. D/1700/10, 24 October 1939.

23. *The Northern Whig*, 30 September 1916. Fred implies in D/1700/8 in a letter to Craig, 19 July 1923, that Knowles started at Alexander Crawford & Son in 1907. His list of wedding gifts from 1896 indicates, however, that the connection was at least ten years longer.

24. GHP Buchanan, *Green Sea Coast*, (London, 1966), pp.49, 60.

25. *The Campbellian*, Vol.IV no.3 (July 1917), pp.80-81.

26. D/1700/5/12/99, 1 January 1953 – although Davey was a pupil between 1903 and 1909, before Fred's heyday. Davey lost his younger brother, also a Campbellian, in the War.

27. D/1700/5/8/6, 26 July 1943.

28. D/1700/5/6/14, 23 June 1922.

29. CAB 6/89. The War Memorial was inaugurated on 7 April 1923 by General Sir Alexander Godley. Fred acted as Chairman of the Governors for the occasion (which was attended also by Helen and Doreen Crawford), which Fred described as "short and very impressive": D/640/11/2, pp.102-103.

30. Such fears not unfounded; two days later the P&O liner *Maple* was mined off Dover.

31. This episode can be found in D/1700/5/17/1/126, –/128A, –/148-149. D/1507/A/11/2, –/11/4, –/14/15-16, –/23/16, –/26/49.

32. Similarly, the residue of the London account used to pay for the rifles – £493 5s 11d – was given to UVF charitable funds. Fred noted: "The transaction is the closing event of the first phase of the Ulster question": D/1700/5/17/1/138, –/140, –/142.

33. Fred did travel occasionally to Dublin in the course of his wartime duties: D/1700/5/17/1/135, 13 December 1916: "I was up in Dublin and the Curragh this week".

34. James W Taylor, *The 2nd Royal Irish Rifles in the Great War*, (Four Courts Press, Dublin, 2005), pp.35, 43, 46, 203-204. D/1700/10/1/769-770, –/847, –/895, –/922, –/935-936, –/960. D/1700/5/13/21, 21 February 1918. D/1700/5/17/1/127, 3 March 1916. John Bowen-Colthurst died in Canada in December 1965. James Taylor of Wexford is currently preparing a biography of him.

35. From his service record – The National Archive: WO/339/23234.

36. D/1700/5/13/23.

37. D/640/2/1.

Ulster's Watchdog

The transformation of post-War Ulster could be witnessed one Sunday early in February 1919 on the quadrangle at the front of Campbell College – although Fred probably did not witness it.

Captain Corrie Denew Chase, who had founded the Officer Training Corps at the school in 1909, and had joined the 16th (Pioneer) Battalion of 36th (Ulster) Division, assembled there for Church parade as he always had done before the War. He had served the Division well, helping to construct a twenty-mile small-gauge feeder railway in the location of Fred's 1916 visit to the Somme; he had also displayed courage, being awarded the Military Cross. In the company of Chase's father, Fred had in 1890 visited the Mount of Olives, the place where Christ had predicted his personal humiliation. Chase returned to Campbell College in the early weeks of 1919, and suffered his own humiliation.

It was witnessed and recorded by one of the pupils, Henry Cronne, a future Professor Medieval History: "[Chase] created something of a sensation on his first Sunday by turning out in pre-War formal full rig: long frock-coat, sponge-bag trousers, starched high collar and cuffs, white spats and top hat. But fashion had changed radically, and the poor little man must have been horribly embarrassed".[1]

For all his attachment to Old Testament lore – and having described himself as feeling like Noah when building the Ark – Fred could not interpret the omens. God had created Man from dust and clay and had sent a flood to purify and transform his creation; Ulstermen had recently fought through the flood and sodden clay of Flanders, but could not, or would not, recognise the metamorphosis. The old world order had been irretrievably re-fashioned, but Ulstermen – like many others – were reluctant to accept it. In late 1921, in a letter which he composed to Carson – but never posted – about the betrayal of Ulster by the British Government, Fred described the circumstances as "the collapse of the Great British Empire, of which we are all so proud and now so much ashamed of".[2]

Ulstermen chose to believe that they had defeated their pre-War foes. Their resistance in the guise of the Ulster Volunteer Force (UVF) had witnessed a natural transition into the 36th Division, the men of which, as Fred articulated it, "gave their lives cheerfully not for Ulster, but the Empire". Early in 1917, Fred passed on to James Cunningham and James Craig a cheque for £493 15 11d, the balance in the account raised to pay for the importation of rifles, or what Craig referred to as "the shipping concern". As Fred expressed it, "this transaction is the closing event of the first phase of the Ulster question".[3]

The second phase was to prove more insoluble. In the post-War world, Ireland hosted two irreconcilable enemies; in Sinn Fein, Ulster faced a more implacable opponent. Both political creeds felt legitimised by the recent conflict. The Nationalists believed that John Redmond's support for the War – and the sacrifice of his brother – consolidated their claim to the full Home Rule enacted before the War. On the other hand, as Fred was to berate the journalist, Joseph Jeffries, Ulster believed it had sacrificed itself for the Empire and was entitled to govern its own affairs, free from the clutches of an alien power.

Fred's simple philosophy was perhaps most concisely framed at the conclusion of *Guns for Ulster*: "We in Ulster ask no favours, seek no enemies, only that we may continue to enjoy the civil and religious liberties of the United Kingdom, for which we have struggled for so many years and for so many generations". As Fred was probably too frail to edit the original version which he had penned, it is probable that this ending was composed by another hand. More expansively in his own version, he explained that Ulster had sacrificed itself for a

Government which, only a few months previously had threatened to send in its Army to shoot down uncompromising Ulstermen:[4]

> This act of the Ulster Unionists shows more than anything else could have done the true love and loyalty for the British Empire and Constitution that inspired them to be ready to fight to the death against any interference with their citizenship and liberties. They have never agitated for the rest of Ireland to be put under Ulster; then why should the rest of Ireland want Ulster to be put under them?

The post-War era proved discomposing politically and ideologically for those in the north of Ireland; they were, in effect, attempting to re-define their identity. In those critical years of the Home Rule crisis, Ulstermen resented being labelled rebels; as Fred wrote: "In what sense are we rebels? ... We are not against, but ultra loyal to, our Government ... We armed ourselves and were prepared to fight, not against the laws of the Empire, but against the illegal act of those representing or misrepresenting the British people". Nevertheless he was, during the War – although quite probably not present at the debates in 1915 – to remain a Governor of a school which specifically and consciously defined itself as "essentially an Irish institution".[5]

During the First World War, political identity could be blurred, but the situation changed within a very short space of time. As we have seen in an earlier chapter, Fred wrote to his brother barely a year after the Treaty of Versailles to reject his Irish persona: "I am an Ulsterman, a very different breed".[6] Yet at that time he would have been very hardpressed to define the archetypal Ulsterman. Men such as Fred Crawford knew where their loyalties lay – most specifically with the Empire – but they were unable to trust the heart of the Empire, the British Government, which they characterised as attempting to sell their citizenship and birthright via Home Rule.[7] They simply did not trust those shaping post-War Ireland. Fred described Hamar Greenwood, the last Chief Secretary for Ireland, as "the most brazen-faced liar the House of Commons has ever possessed"; and Lloyd George and others in the Cabinet, such as F. E. Smith, were immediately stigmatised when they were prepared to shake hands with Michael Collins: "The terms of the peace that was signed by the British Cabinet and Irish Roman Catholic murderers and assassins is the most humiliating document that any great nation ever produced".[8]

It was, nonetheless, disingenuous of Fred to profess surprise at the course of events. At Christmas 1916, the Campbell College school magazine reproduced from a local newspaper a poem entitled *Men of Ulster*, encapsulating the sacrificial nature of the War. It concluded with the couplet: "And whenever the fight is hottest, and the sorest task is set, Ulster will strike for England – and England will not forget". If Fred ever read the poem he might well have disabused the author of such romanticism, for fifteen years earlier, on campaign in South Africa, Fred had predicted: "What fools we British are. Nothing seems to teach us anything. Men who have done good service ... are now treated with less courtesy than those who are known to be rebels at heart. Ireland will be repeated as sure as I write this. Gladstone's policy has not died with him".[9]

SIX OR NINE COUNTIES

Ultimately Fred proved correct, but at least, when the Government of Ireland Act reached the Statute Book towards the very end of 1920, Northern Ireland had acquired its own separate government. Sentiments and opinions, however, then became ossified and polarised; there was no place for neutrality, and religion began to define one's political camp – a situation which has tended to prevail to the present day.[10] Even Fred, whose family had employed and forged sociable relationships with local Catholics, spoke rather warily and pejoratively of "Protestant Sinn Feiners" amongst the ranks of the Royal Irish Constabulary (RIC).[11]

Northern Ireland was now bordered by a legitimised neighbour, which it regarded uncompromisingly as a threat. Fred felt confirmed in this alienation by early information he received from the Republic; one correspondent told him of attempted bomb threats and intimidation as British troops finally left Athlone in February 1922: "This is freedom as [it] is known in the Free State". Fred's elder son, Stuart, had married in Ballina, Co. Mayo, in 1921, and later that year Fred had heard from his son's father-in-law, John Garvey. The latter conceded that, whilst the religious atmosphere tended to be virulent in the North, "with us there has been a very tolerant spirit evidenced at all times"; however, he admitted that silence was the best means "of security and safety" for Protestant residents.[12]

Garvey added that "I am anxious to see a peace much as I regret any severance from the Union. I would have preferred to see the Union cemented rather than dismembered but the Union is now a thing of the past". This more realistic approach derived at least partially from the abandonment of southern Unionists by those in the north, a process which – rather surprisingly – Fred actively exhorted. Much of the insecurity in Northern Ireland stemmed, for a number of years at least, from the fact that the Ulster which Fred and his Unionist colleagues acknowledged did not coincide with the historic Ulster.

Up to the outbreak of the First World War the Unionist definition of Ulster appears to have comprised all nine counties of the province. Even as late as July 1914 an amendment to the legislation on Home Rule allowed for the permanent exclusion of all of Ulster; and when the guns which were landed at Larne were distributed, quantities were sent to Cavan, Monaghan and Donegal. Fred later asserted that those who were engaged in these remoter areas were "the real heroes of the story".[13]

During 1916, however, the issue was re-negotiated and the option to opt out of Home Rule was reduced to the current six counties. There was an admission amongst many that they were wilfully abandoning southern Unionism and Ronald McNeill confirmed that this caused the Ulster Unionist Council (UUC) much angst and heart-searching: "It was the saddest hour the UUC ever spent".[14] 'Wolf' Spender had more of the lion in him than did others; he always opposed the reduced six-county exclusion, adding that "It seems to me a poor cowardly policy very unlike the days of Larne".[15]

The gun-runner himself adopted a more pragmatic approach to the issue. Even in the midst of his gun-running activities the problem exercised his concern. At that stage he feared that if individual counties were given a choice, some would opt to secede and to take Home Rule. In a letter to Carson from Hamburg in March 1914 he had warned that this would leave the Protestants of Cavan, Donegal, Fermanagh and Monaghan "in a position to say that we had deserted them".[16] Ultimately, that is exactly what happened.

At a UUC meeting on 10th March 1920 Carson and Craig favoured the six-county option, and in the following month Fred penned a pamphlet entitled 'Why I Voted for the Six Counties', which he distributed to each member of the UUC.[17] In this he rehearsed the motivation for the Solemn League & Covenant and justified the six-county approach as vital to the survival of the Empire: "A solid Protestant Ulster will be a prop in Ireland to the Empire without which the whole naval strength of England would be jeopardised. The Empire should count for something". He added that his main objective in signing the Covenant was to maintain a Protestant Ulster and that "If I had voted for the nine counties [some of which contained a large percentage of Catholics], I would have been going against both the spirit and the letter of the Covenant".

His most unconvincing section of the pamphlet compared the nine county Ulster to a lifeboat trying to save too many people – it would sink. He averred that a six county Ulster would be better placed to assist its amputated brethren. Fred chose to believe that Unionists in the three severed counties would not wish "to drag down the six counties ... I cannot believe that the Protestants in the three counties are willing to swamp 820,370 Protestants merely for the satisfaction of knowing they are all going down to disaster in the same boat".

Although any sense of guilt was anaesthetised by the fact that many of the Ulster aristocracy and political hierarchy claimed that the pamphlet had clarified matters for them, this, frankly, was not Fred Crawford's finest hour; the undiluted obduracy exhibited at Craigavon during the gun-running venture had, for once, evaporated in political realism. It left men such as John Garvey very much exposed, but by the late 1920s southern Unionists had come to accept the realities, severed their ties with northern Unionism, and moved to protect their own interests.[18]

Late in 1921 Fred revisited the issue in an effort to consolidate the Protestant hold on Ulster. He suggested to Craig a further revision of the boundary of Northern Ireland, giving up – 'surrendering' would be an inappropriate term! – the Catholic parts of Armagh and Fermanagh for the Protestant centres of Cavan, Monaghan and East Donegal. This he claimed, not without reason, would strengthen Ulster's position enormously"; "Ulster will back it to man", he assured the Prime Minister.[19]

Watchdog

There were occasions when Fred acknowledged that his opinion was not always valued: "… but I was not in a position to offer an opinion, as it was a matter for experts",[20] he wrote about the Irish frontier. There were times also when he realised it was injudicious; he wrote to Spender on 9th June 1924 with his personal observations on security around the border, adding that it was probably preferable that, although the then Cabinet Secretary could pass on the advice to Craig, he did not notify Wickham, Inspector General of the Royal Ulster Constabulary, of the correspondence.[21] As we have seen, at the end of 1921 he penned a lengthy letter to Carson about Ulster's relationship with England following the treaty with the 'Rebels', but concluded that "I had not the heart to worry him when I knew he must be feeling this awful betrayal even more than I"[22] and decided not to post it. Such presumption and ready interjection earned Fred, from Spender, the epithet of 'Ulster's Watchdog'.[23]

As a consequence of the events of April 1914, both Carson and Craig always gave time to Fred's views and humoured his opinions – and, in fact, exhibited unbounded affection for him – but there are hints that even they wearied of the constant bombardment of communications. There was a flurry of missives to London during May and June 1920. Fred was clearly anxious to convey his opinions to his Leader in private, and urged Craig: "When you are over with the Chief, try and arrange that you and I can get him by himself for half an hour. There are so many coming and going that I seldom see him for more than a handshake". With both politicians at that time heavily employed in London, Craig ultimately had to respond diplomatically: "I write at once to assure you that the matters to which you refer are daily engaging the earnest consideration of Sir Edward and myself. I will write when I think it would be advisable for you to come and see us. You will recognise that during the strenuous days in connection with the new Bill, Sir Edward is really overworked".[24]

Fred was not tempted in 1921 by the exhortation of a delegation that he stand for the North or West Belfast constituencies in the Ulster Parliament;[25] he was too busy with the development of the Ulster Special Constabulary. It was a prudent refusal, as he was always too blunt to manifest the necessary machiavellianism required by a parliamentarian. There was an occasional instance when Fred unnerved even his two most powerful political associates. On 11th June 1919, in the days leading up to the Treaty of Versailles, he contacted Craig at the Ministry of Pensions in London with a proposal. The original letter has not survived amongst the Crawford correspondence, but the implication of Craig's response is that Fred felt that it might be worth making political overtures to the Kaiser![26] Craig disabused Fred of the idea, pointing out that it was probably a contravention of the Defence of the Realm Act, and made it unequivocally clear that "under no circumstances should either Sir Edward Carson or myself be implicated – we should know nothing whatever about it".

Conspiracy

Fred appears to have found it difficult to break the habit of intrigue and conspiracy. If a memoir which Fred penned at Cloreen on 6th June 1920 is to be believed, in April he had been approached to visit Dublin "on a particular secret job", which was effectively an attempt to penetrate Sinn Fein and capture Michael Collins. Additionally, although the relevant documents have gone missing, it seems that a similar plot was hatched to kidnap Arthur Griffith.[27]

Fred travelled to Dublin and London to discuss the plots, but he made it clear that they were "up against the cleverest and most unscrupulous men in Europe; the German spy system was not in it with the Sinn Fein system. It [success] must come from within". To some degree this was an understatement; in a very short space of time Collins "consistently demonstrated acumen, flair, inventiveness, efficiency and imagination"[28] in constructing an intelligence system from scratch, which was more than a match for its British counterpart. Fred might never have admitted it, but he would have approved of the Big Fellow's single-mindedness and it is doubtful that either of them was ever burdened by regrets.

Fred certainly displayed some interest when the project was first mooted, as payment was considered; as was his custom, Fred stated that he would not accept a salary – only expenses – for doing what he regarded as his duty, but specified (as he was to do with regard to service in the Ulster Special Constabulary) that, in the event of his death, his wife and family should receive compensation of £20,000, or £1000 per annum.

Whether as a result of wisdom or intuition, ultimately Fred turned down 'the secret job', and never got to test the confidential tip revealed by an acquaintance who became heavily involved in affairs in Dublin that: "If you write with urine on the inside of the envelope there is no risk whatever of discovery".[29] It was a very wise decision by the failing starch-manufacturer. He offered the opinion that the best chance was for an unknown agent to penetrate Sinn Fein's American organisation, gain its trust and confidence, and return to Dublin. This, however, would probably take six months and by that stage the Republican movement was sufficiently well-attuned to smell a rat, even across the Atlantic.

Fred acknowledged that he, personally, stood little chance of penetrating the IRA screen; espionage was a young man's activity and, at almost sixty, he was far too old; also, "being a Northerner and a Protestant, I should be spotted at once and immediately shot". When he discussed the project at Cloreen in early June 1920 he argued perceptively that "I would be simply throwing my life away or else running the risk, if not of being shot, of being marked down for shooting when seen, and would be a fugitive all my life, and would have accomplished nothing".

There were few incentives, except for those impelled by the mere scent of danger. Fred was encouraged by neither the political nor the security realities. He pointed out in 1920 that Bonar Law had uttered brave words in the House of Commons against Sinn Fein, which had been immediately followed by the Government's release of eighty of the most dangerous men in Ireland. The IRA under Collins's leadership effectively neutralised the RIC – a reality which Fred sensed first-hand when he visited the Inspector-General at Dublin Castle in late August 1920.[30]

Thomas James Smith had arrived earlier in 1920 from Belfast, where he had been the Commissioner of the Belfast Police – despite having once unwittingly accompanied a delivery of Unionist rifles into Belfast before the War! In the Irish capital he appears to have become rapidly disillusioned and demoralised by the success of the IRA and within only a few months came to feel that the RIC was on the point of implosion. Dublin Castle quickly came to the conclusion that he was not equal to the responsibilities and that, rather as had happened to his predecessor, his nerve was buckling.[31] Fred visited Smith on 25th August 1920, a few days after the callous and public murder in Lisburn of Detective Inspector Swanzy, in an effort to exhort the support of Smith – whom he described as "a great friend of mine" – for the issue of "automatic pistols to certain of the loyal citizens of Ulster so they could defend themselves and friends when threatened by the Rebel assassins".

Probably inadvertently, he rather damned Smith's capability in concluding his memorandum by noting: "I also told him I could get all I wanted from another quarter if he could not get it done". Even Fred detected signs that Smith felt that he was fighting a losing battle. The visitor chastised Smith for the fact that he (Fred) had been able to get into the Castle without being checked or searched and that Smith's private address had been readily given to him; he indicated that, had he been so inclined, he could have readily shot the chief police officer.

With regard to his own importunity, Fred asked for Smith's discretion, particularly with regard to names, as he regarded Dublin Castle – with total justification – as "rotten and full of spies". He categorised James MacMahon, the Permanent Under-Secretary, as "one of the worst" because of his links with Sinn Fein and the Catholic Church. MacMahon was, around this time, specifically cleared of disloyalty, but there were other dubious characters. Collins's chief spy at Dublin Castle was, in fact, the Head Constable.

Fred indicated to those trying to engage his services that he did not fear death, indeed he "preferred this sort of death to dying in my bed", but he knew that he had virtually no chance of apprehending Collins, who ridiculed the British authorities daily by wandering freely around Dublin. It proved a barbarous, tribal and unforgiving struggle, and Fred was prudent not to become embroiled. Fred could never comprehend the callous, primarily English, indifference to the fate of the septuagenarian Cork lady, Mrs Lindsay, who had been kidnapped in March 1921 and later murdered by the IRA because she had warned the authorities of an intended ambush. The commanding officer of the British forces, General Sir Nevil Macready, refused to exchange her for five condemned Nationalist Volunteers; he regarded Collins's men as "soldiers … who systematically ignored every condition of warfare recognised amongst civilised nations",[32] although this rather ignored the so-called Amritsar Massacre only a few months previously. Mrs Lindsay's murder was barely mentioned in the British Press and when Fred was correcting the misapprehensions of the journalist Joseph Jeffries, in late 1921, he said that "Public opinion in England has lost all sense of right, fair play, truth and justice". In the context of the brutality, blood-letting and casual death experienced in those years, Jeffries could count himself very fortunate to have survived his brief captivity.

It was Macready's judgement that it was the fact that the British could not adequately suppress the IRA that led Lloyd George to call a truce in mid-1921, and formulate a treaty. In correspondence the following year Fred described Macready as "the true and trusted friend of Sinn Fein" and the "arch-enemy" of Ulster.[33] Fred despised such inability to deal with Sinn Fein "murderers and assassins", but it was not for the want of method. 'Hoppy' seems an innocuous sobriquet for another of Fred's military friends but, in retrospect, this soldier was to make Captain John Bowen-Colthurst seem quite sociable.

Captain Hardy

It is not entirely clear how Fred came to know Captain Jocelyn Lee Hardy of the Connaught Rangers, but he was one of those with whom Fred discussed the plot to kidnap Arthur Griffith.[34] He had spent much of the First World War escaping from German prisoner-of-war camps and eventually lost a leg on the front lines in March 1918 – his consequent limp earning him the nickname of 'Hoppy'. In providing an accommodation reference for Hardy in June 1920, Fred revealed that "I know Captain Hardy and his uncles who are wealthy men, and amongst our most respected citizens here [in Belfast]".[35] The family earned its living from the manufacture of cambric handkerchiefs; and in later life Jocelyn Hardy became an author and novelist. If such a brief biography presented the soldier with an air of service, decency and respectability, the reality was that he proved to be the kind of man who would have no hesitation in disabusing anyone of his mistake. Of all the intelligence officers in Dublin, Michael Foy reveals that "it was 'F' Company's legendary Captain Jocelyn Hardy whom the Dublin Volunteers hated and feared most".

When he arrived in Dublin in May 1920, Hardy wrote to Fred that "My job at Headquarters [Parkgate] is quite a cushy one – just an office job". There is no reason to suspect that Fred thought otherwise – but it was very far from the truth. In a letter to Fred on 6th August 1920 (written whilst he was visiting Belfast), he indicated in a postscript that "I am going round to see McLean" – who was probably Captain Donald McLean, an interrogation officer at Mountjoy Gaol, who was on the IRA's assassination list. Hardy's revelation to Fred about the alternative use of urine suggests that, at that stage, Hardy was already versed in methods of espionage and intelligence.

Hardy proved extremely versatile during practical interrogation, much of which verged on sadism, if not actually crossing the line. He used brutality including disfigurement, glowing pokers close to the eyes, loaded and unloaded pistols to the head and, when his long-term partner in interrogation was – like Bowen-Colthurst – charged with the murder of prisoners, Hardy was not averse to witness intimidation and perjury. In August 1920, during the early days of the resurrection of the Ulster Volunteer Force (UVF) under Spender, Hardy notified Fred that "I can let you know all the inside information possessed by the Police and Military as to Sinn Feiners in the Six Counties", adding rather nonchalantly: "Of course, I would be promptly arrested if I was caught, but I fight for the right".

Mistaken Identity

The resentment and fear caused by officers such as Hardy resulted in Collins organising an operation "to eliminate many enemy intelligence agents in one massive swoop" in Dublin, which became known as Bloody Sunday. On 21st November 1921 fifteen British officers were murdered – one of whom was Hardy's contact, McLean – and four were wounded. As tends to happen with intelligence gathering, not all the information was correct and even Collins was later to concede that at least one innocent individual had been shot as a result of mistaken identity, caused simply by the man having a similar name to a secret service agent on the list.

Such an eventuality tended to confirm the wisdom of Fred's decision not to become involved that summer in the hunt for Collins. One British Army officer who was exceptionally fortunate to survive Bloody Sunday was a Major Crawford who ran the motor repair depot of the Royal Army Service Corps in Dublin. The similarity of name and career with Fred's recent military past made both men very vulnerable; not only that, Major John Scott Crawford was also a former pupil of Campbell College! In the presence of Crawford's wife, his Dublin flat was raided on the fateful date by four armed IRA men, who eventually accepted (after scrutinising his papers) that he was not the man they were seeking; they did, however, order the RASC major to leave the country within 24 hours. He duly, and wisely, complied and went on to work in the War Office and, on the outbreak of the Second World War, to organise the production of tanks for the man who had sent the British Fleet to intercept Fred's gun-running enterprise – Winston Churchill![36]

It may be that, because the meeting on 6th June 1920 to discuss Fred's possible involvement in the Collins plot, had been held at Cloreen, the proximity of his family helped Fred to confirm his decision. Ultimately it seems to have been a business decision – he wrote that he had heavy stocks and a large overdraft, "and if I left my business I am afraid it would collapse", as he was the only person who understood the precise manufacturing process.[37] Apart from what he regarded as unwarranted risks, he decided that he would be better employed in helping to get "the UVF mobilised".

Notes

1. Keith Haines, *Neither Rogues nor Fools, a History of Campbell College and Campbellians*, (Belfast, 1993), p.153.

2. D/1700/5/6/5, 13 December 1921. See also D/640/7/1. In his diary of the years 1920-1922, Fred argued that "The British Government has done its level best to compel Ulstermen to become Rebels and join with the Rebel part of Ireland": D/640/11/2, p.32.

3. D/1700/5/17/1/142-143, –/159A+B. The money was donated to the UVF Patriotic Fund.

4. Final paragraph of D/1415/B/34.

5. D/1415/B/34, p.24. To Fred, 'Rebels' (always with a capital letter) meant Sinn Fein. Haines, p.149.

6. D/1700/6/1/11, 31 July 1920.

7. Fred wrote that "No Government has a right to sell the citizenship of their subjects to a people avowedly their hereditary enemies": D/1415/B/34, p.128.

8. D/640/11/2, pp.57, 70.

9. D/1700/3/2, 4 March 1901.

10. Claire Mitchell, *Religion, Identity and Politics in Northern Ireland*, (Aldershot, 2006), pp.2, 63, 133. See also Paul Bew et al, *Passion and Prejudice: Nationalist-Unionist Conflict in Ulster in the 1930s and the founding of The Irish Association*, (Institute of Irish Studies/Queen's University Belfast, 1993), and Brian Walker, *Dancing to History's Tune: history, myth and politics in Ireland*, (Institute of Irish Studies/Queen's University Belfast, 1993), especially pp.110-127.

11. D/640/9/1, p.54, which is probably extracted from D/640/11/2. By the term 'Protestant Sinn Feiners' Fred meant Protestants who exhibited nationalist tendencies or sympathies.

12. D/1700/5/4/62, –/68.

13. D/1700/5/6/23B, 29 October 1934.

14. Ronald McNeill, *Ulster's Stand for Union*, (London, 1922), pp.248-249.

15. Ian Maxwell, *The Life of Sir Wilfrid Spender 1876-1960*, (QUB Ph D thesis, 1991), p.95.

16. D/1700/5/17/1/11, 3 March 1914.

17. D/640/16/2. D/1507/A/33/43. D/1700/5/16/4.

18. L W McBride, *The Greening of Dublin Castle: the transformation of bureaucratic and juridical personnel in Ireland 1892-1922*, (Washington DC, 1991), p.290.

19. D/640/7/14, 7 November 1921.

20. D/640/11/2, p.63.
21. D/640/10/6.
22. D/1700/5/6/5, 13 December 1921.
23. A postscript in D/640/10/4.
24. D/640/7/9, 24 May 1920, and –/11, 4 June 1920.
25. D/640/11/2, p.38
26. D/640/7/3, 16 June 1919.
27. This information is contained in D/640/2/1, headed 'Secret Service'. The plot against Griffith is covered in D/640/8/1-2, but the papers are no longer in the PRONI file. See also Michael Farrell, *Arming the Protestants: the formation of the Ulster Special Constabulary and the Royal Ulster Constabulary 1920-1927*, (Belfast, 1983), p.18.
28. Michael T Foy, *Michael Collins's Intelligence War: the struggle between the British and the IRA 1919-1921*, (Sutton Publishing, Stroud, 2008), pp.43-44.
29. D/640/13/12, 6 August 1920. The correspondent was Capt Hardy (see below).
30. For this visit, see a memorandum written by Fred appended to D/640/2/1.
31. I am grateful to Michael Foy's recent volume for some of the following material.
32. Sir Arthur Hezlet, *The B Specials: a history of the Ulster Special Constabulary*, (London, 1972), p.90.
33. D/1700/5/6/10, 29 May 1922, and –/12, 5 June 1922.
34. Farrell, p.18.
35. Much of this is derived from Foy, and various letters of 1920 in D/640/13/-. One of Hardy's uncles, Saville Hardy, had been a pupil at Methodist College in the 1870s.
36. Autobiography of Maj-Gen J S Crawford, pp.26-33, 44-45 in the Churchill Archive Centre, Churchill College, Cambridge. Crawford had been in charge of the Shell factory in Dublin, which the IRA had made several efforts to destroy. He believed this was the reason for his being targeted, but the gunmen appear to have been searching for someone else. The current author has received information to suggest that another former Campbell College pupil, Thomas McCrae, was also threatened at this time as a British intelligence officer in Dublin, but has been unable to corroborate this.
37. D/640/2/1.

I Trust in God and my Automatic

∞

Fred was to describe the period 1920 to 1922 as "these terrible years of assassination and lawlessness".[1] The search for a political accommodation between Nationalism and Unionism in the post-War era was never going to be malleable, but it was confounded by the sudden domination of the Irish political scene by Sinn Fein.

From early 1919 the IRA became masters at making the country ungovernable, primarily outside Ulster, through its corrosion of the ability of the Royal Irish Constabulary (RIC) to effect law and order. Thomas James Smith's appointment in March 1920 as Inspector-General in Dublin failed to resolve the emasculation of the police force and the arrival of the so-called Black and Tans[2] two months later only served to reinforce the reality that the British Government was incapable of producing a political solution. The impervious obstinacy of northern Unionism to Dublin rule meant that the struggle would inevitably reach the north. By mid-1920 the situation had became increasingly destabilised; latent tensions were heightened at flashpoints such as the shipyards and intensified over the Twelfth.

The locality of Alexander Crawford & Son proved a microcosm of the deteriorating circumstances in Belfast. During the night of 20th July 1920, the Works were broken into, "and some stuff destroyed by what I consider must have been mischievous boys". The following day rattled any pretence of bourgeois normality. As he left Campbell College Speech Day at lunch-time, Fred learned that there had been further trouble three miles distant at Queen's Island; and he recorded that, as he trimmed a lawn later in the day, "I heard a machine-gun playing for quite a while". By 10pm he deemed it prudent to check security at Wilson Street. He intervened in the area to stop a drunken loyalist youth enflaming the situation by antagonising the police and, as he walked up towards Clonard monastery off the Falls Road about midnight, Fred was informed that several people had been shot. He returned to what must have been a rather concerned wife about 2am.

The Works were invaded again a couple of nights later, so Fred arranged for two men to act as an overnight guard until he could attach barbed wire around the perimeter. On another occasion all the panes in the Works and the office were smashed. Early in September Fred noted in his diary of events that "We have been the only firm who have kept their works open in the district". The shooting of a policeman and a civilian in Wilson Street demonstrated the personal danger that everyone faced.

The Home Rule struggle had filtered assumptions into readily identifiable, narrow political channels. Fred was as guilty as any of his contemporaries in this stereotyping, and in his lengthy diary of over 100 typed pages, which covers these unsettled years, he always employed the term 'Catholic' when referring to a Nationalist. Fred was wary of the local Catholic community and readily admitted that he felt that he "would not trust one of them". Nevertheless his own personal relationship with many of them – which would sometimes have stretched back two or three decades, when the company had hired many of the local populace – was surprisingly affable and generous and reveals that individual relationships often defied rigid categorisation. Even in those adversarial times such matters were never purely black or white or, rather, Orange or Green.

Fred pointed out that several "friendly Catholics" warned him that he had been marked down for assassination and two Catholic women were most appreciative that he responded to their plea to help them save some threatened valuable furniture. Fred was also friendly with Barney, the Catholic postman who delivered his company's mail. In June 1922

Barney expressed uneasiness about entering the district as a Protestant postman had recently been shot in a Catholic area. Fred admitted that reprisals were all too likely and agreed that his post should be delivered to a neighbouring company, where he would collect it.

The most revealing relationship with local Catholics, however, was with two brothers – Joe and Owen Kearney – who had nailed a threatening notice to the Works' gate on 23rd July 1920. A certain amount of trouble had occurred in the street that afternoon, but at 6.15pm – by which time most of his work-force had gone home – the taller brother (Owen) returned to apologise. As he did so, "the brother crept up behind him and … hurled half a brick at my head not six feet from where I was standing". It struck the wall close to the starch manufacturer's head, broke into a number of pieces, and dented a door. With Fred having been distracted, Owen Kearney "struck me a blow on each ear", and then both men fled.

Fred found the assault exceptionally painful and was sufficiently enraged to draw his pistol, "but [I] am thankful I did not fire as I was very angry". The entire story is difficult to piece together, as some of the original pages from the diary are missing, but Fred forbade onlookers to take revenge on the brothers. The attack caused him some deafness, and a few days later Fred was obliged to visit the Eye, Ear & Throat Hospital in Clifton Street, where Dr William Killen syringed his right ear, and revealed that the drum had been broken and perforated by the blow. Fred was probably thankful that at this time he had sent his family down the coast to Newcastle.

Fred was astonished when he was visited on 9th August by Joe Kearney, who took his turn to apologise. Fred was reluctant to be forgiving, but felt obliged to accept the apology: "I felt he was not responsible for his actions when he had taken some drink". He also knew that his Nationalist assailant had been wounded in the head in France during the First World War and had been awarded a medal for bravery.[3] He informed the shorter brother "I would have run you in long ago, only that you joined up like a man and did your bit at the Front, whilst other skulkers stayed away". This, he revealed, was the only reason he had resisted police pressure to prosecute Kearney. The factory owner noted that the man was grateful, "held out his hand, lifted his cap, and went out when I took his hand".

Fred refused to contemplate any retaliation against the Kearney brothers, as he had promised his protection, but he did warn them that there were many who were ready to kill them for what they had done and advised them, for their own safety, to stay away from the area. Even six weeks later, Ernest Knowles (Fred's manager) informed his boss that he had overheard a number of local youths bemoaning the fact that they could not deal with the two men because of their promise to "the 'oul' Colonel".

Unsettled Years

The aftermath of the very public murder of Swanzy led to widespread rioting and destruction in Lisburn, which Fred visited and described as reminiscent of "a bombarded town in France". In July he had already dispensed a couple of revolvers and cartridges to two men who had been intimidated near his Works and he recorded soon after that: "Nearly every day people are coming to me for rifles and ammunition. I have none of the former to hand out, but am glad to say I have plenty of rifle ammunition, but very little revolver [ammunition]".

Fred received seven or eight warnings from the police, local clergy or concerned locals that he was a marked man and likely to be shot. John FitzHugh Gelston, appointed Belfast City Commissioner of Police in June 1922, was later at a loss to explain the former gun-runner's miraculous survival.[4] Even amongst friends and acquaintances it was rumoured that he wore a steel vest for protection, but he showed one enquirer that his only armour was his shirt. Fred revealed that: "I always go thro' these bad districts with my automatic in my pocket, and they all know I am a deadshot ... I trust in God and my automatic, but without God the automatic will not save me". This resort to small arms for personal protection was not uncommon amongst the political, professional and commercial classes in Belfast and, when Lt-Col. William Duff Gibbon arrived in the city from Dulwich in the summer of 1922 for his interview for the headmastership of Campbell College, he cannot have been reassured when a number of the Board of Governors overtly placed their hand-guns on the table!

It had been the murder of Swanzy which had encouraged Fred to visit Smith in Dublin to attempt to obtain authorisation for the distribution of arms for the purpose of self-defence. In the circumstances he felt that Unionists had been rather cavalier and imprudent in handing over many Ulster Volunteer Force (UVF) rifles during the War. "Now these rifles are not available", he explained, adding, with no apparent sense of irony, that whilst these were being handed in, "the Rebels were getting them from Germany in submarines".

The reality was that there were probably still far too many in private hands, which could result in vigilante activity. Even Fred himself became concerned about the amount of armaments he had stowed away in the Wilson Street premises. With the help of Ernest Knowles and two other men – Robert Johnston and John Thompson – he placed many rifles into cold storage, "where they will probably stay for years, and where it is practically impossible for any search party to get them". What probably made him most vulnerable to detection was the presence of half-a-million UVF cartridges in the Works. Fred admitted that "If the military do search and find this, I shall be detained". He risked a lengthy spell in prison and did note – this time with deliberate irony – that "I do not fancy the Victoria Barracks guard room. I much prefer the gaol". He manifested greater concern about this military residue, which was uninsurable, than for the Works, for which he could claim compensation! He adopted a pre-War ruse and concealed these cartridges in bags of starch. All that was retained on the premises, each in a bag of starch, was four revolvers with ten rounds each, easily accessible in case "the Works were rushed".

The demobilisation of the UVF had been General Sir George Richardson's final order at the time of his resignation in April 1919, but a year later – for the safety and security of Ulster – Fred recommended its re-formation to Carson "on the old lines under leaders who have been thro' the War and have held commissions as officers". Carson received a large number of letters between April and July 1920[5] about the deteriorating political circumstances from members of the Ulster Ex-Servicemen's Association, with which Fred had close links, by which they pledged themselves "to assist His Majesty's Government by all means in our power to restore law and order in Ulster", and indicated that they had 3000 trained ex-service personnel "ready to obey any order upon which the Government may decide".

Both Craig and Carson were persuaded, and Carson used the occasion of the Twelfth (1920) to echo his pre-War tirades, warning the British Government that, if it did not take action against the threats, Ulster would do so through the re-organisation of the UVF – adding his usual caveat that such words were not bluff.[6] The principal means of re-arming the UVF was the store of rifles kept at Tamar Street in East Belfast. At the time he contacted Carson about using the UVF, Fred contacted Craig to recommend that an authorised guard of 50 UVF men should be placed on the vulnerable depot, then defended by a contingent of twenty soldiers – a request which he reiterated in early June,[7] recommending the use of men who had served in 36th (Ulster) Division.

The central months of 1920 witnessed increasing apprehension amongst the northern populace and the routine of daily life became increasingly disrupted. In the early days of September, just after her return from London, Lilian Spender commented on encountering "barricades and barbed wire entanglements in some of the streets, and … [stumbling] over a machine-gun sitting on the pavement outside one of the principal shops guarded by tin-hatted soldiers with fixed bayonets".[8] There was a 10.30pm curfew in place which was lifted on 20th September, which both she and Fred – and others – felt was far too soon.

In July 1920 Wilfrid Spender, who was then based at the Ministry of Pensions in London, visited Belfast for a Unionist meeting and, against his better judgement, was exhorted to take charge of the re-institution of the UVF as a body to defend Ulster. Despite his wife's approbation of and faith in the development, it inspired only trepidation and nervousness amongst some members of the Government and General Macready, who had accepted command of the British Army in Ireland a few months earlier.

It was Lilian Spender who unwittingly touched on official concerns about the UVF, which was regenerated on 26th July: "It is a pity the Government won't recognise the UVF", she wrote in her diary, "and allow the responsible ones among them to be armed. Order would soon be restored then". The difficulty was, as the principal gun-runner acknowledged before and after the War, identifying those who could exhibit a sense of responsibility in handling arms. As Fred expressed it: "These young hooligans on both sides, when they get united, will do anything", and all of the leading Unionists recognised that any ill-discipline in their ranks would invite national and international opprobrium. A year later in October 1921, in a letter to Craig, Fred again articulated his fears: "It is better to have the old UVF pulled together with its traditions and discipline, than have irresponsible individuals enlisting a lot of scallywags who will only be a menace and a danger to our cause".

It proved to be a recurrent anxiety throughout these turbulent years. As early as 14th May 1920 he had added a postscript to a letter to Carson: "If our people get out of hand and kill some Roman Catholics, there will be a massacre of Protestant men and women in the South and West". In April 1921 Fred admitted that, if the members of the authorised Special Constabulary were sufficiently antagonised, he "experienced considerable difficulty in keeping some of them from getting out of hand". Six months later he expressed continuing concerns in person to Craig: "what I feared more than the enemy was our own breaking out, who were so exasperated it was almost impossible to keep them in hand". Early in 1922, in correspondence to the Ulster Prime Minister, having made enquiries into a bomb outrage off York Road in Belfast, Fred made it clear that he resented "any hooligans" giving Unionism a bad name.[9]

One of the principal concerns of all parties, both before and after the establishment of the Government of Northern Ireland, was the creation of vigilante units and private forces – although one of those most evidently engaged in such activities was Fred himself. One of the problems in 1921 was that, although a distinct Northern Ireland was created, the latter did not gain full control over law and order matters until 22nd November 1921, and the sentiment prevailed that interim British politicians and civil servants simply lacked any real appreciation of the uncertainties of, and the dangers to, life in the north of the island.

Only a month earlier Fred had expressed this sentiment to Craig in person, saying that Ulstermen:

> have the feeling that the Ulster Parliament is useless and powerless and that the old leaders have forsaken them. I also pointed out that there were a number of societies springing up with rash and irresponsible leaders, and that their ranks were being filled up with some good men, but mostly composed of those who are either on the make or out for loot.

Many of these organisations tended to be transient and irrelevant. One such body was the Ulster Imperial Guard, which was formed in August 1921 from the membership of the Ulster Ex-Servicemen's Association, and which attended the service on Armistice Sunday that year. A fortnight later its representatives were invited to attend a meeting to discuss the nature of the 'C' Specials, a unit of the Special Constabulary, but none of them appeared. Those involved appear to have been absorbed into the latter unit,[10] along with the bulk of the reconstituted UVF.

The Ulster Brotherhood

For all his warnings to Craig about "a number of societies springing up with rash and irresponsible leaders", Fred evidently did not consider it to be a contradiction to form his own unit, which he named the Ulster Brotherhood. It was first mooted around March 1921, and he convened its first meeting in the Old Town Hall on 14th May, noting that: "This is really a continuation of a society I founded in 1893 ... called Young Ulster" – although the more immediate inspiration had been the murder of Detective Inspector Swanzy. As has already been seen, Fred had approached both Gelston and Smith in Dublin about allowing armed incognito civilians to mix with crowds in the hope of using "their weapons to shoot assassins".

This did not gain approval but, by early 1921, a number of policemen had been shot in Belfast, and Fred claimed that he was approached by "H, of the office of the Chief of Police, and asked if he could get up such a force of two hundred ... armed with Webley revolvers, .38 calibre". Both Gelston and his superior, Charles Wickham (Divisional Commissioner for the RIC in Ulster), appear to have favoured this approach to undercover policing, which they referred to, in an anodyne manner – as did Fred – as 'a Detective Reserve'. On 25th April 1921 Fred forwarded his plan to Sir Ernest Clark, Under-Secretary for Ulster, explaining that he believed that "the arming of picked citizens would practically stop further trouble", and justifying the selection by describing the men as "a lot of thoroughly reliable citizens in plain clothes".

Fred was asked to discuss the matter further with the Chief of Police in Ireland, General Tudor, who visited Belfast in May to inspect the police. Tudor was not unsympathetic, but confirmed – as Fred must have suspected – that Dublin Castle would be very hesitant. Fred broached the issue again with Clark on 6th June, but it was evident that the capital was not making any hasty decisions. Fred was undeterred and by 14th June the Brotherhood had held five meetings, and "already the members are called Crawford's Toughs or Tigers".[11] He had probably hoped that approval for his undercover group would be given in time for the Royal opening of the Northern Ireland Parliament on 22nd June 1921; the fact that it was not did not, however, appear to deter him. In the account of the visit he compiled on 4th July, he noted that he had 20 'B' Specials on duty, and "I also issued seven or eight revolvers to some men upon whom I could absolutely rely". The latter must have been members of the Brotherhood. Fred notified Gelston of what he had done, in case any of these men were arrested for carrying unauthorised weapons. He said he would go to gaol in their place, if necessary, but Fred claimed that the policeman laughed and said it was unlikely "as he knew the good work I and my men were doing".[12]

The second meeting of the Ulster Brotherhood was held on 21st May (1921); only those who had sworn the oath were thereafter invited, as Fred stipulated that he only wanted men of approved suitability, as "the work that we might be called upon to do being of such a nature that absolute silence was important". Fred believed that the character of the group bestowed upon it the cloak of respectability, probity and pious aspiration. The oath, the symbolism and the historical tenor of the Brotherhood were very much those of the medieval military Orders or of the Freemasons, pervaded by secrecy of the most extreme and intimidating kind. Members were required not to reveal any instruction they received, or the identity of any fellow member, "more especially the Head" (i.e. Fred himself).[13] Even were a member to resign, or be dismissed from the organisation, or "if the Brotherhood has ceased to exist", the oath must be maintained on penalty of "being shot through my treacherous and unworthy heart ... or punished in such other way the Brethren may think fit".

The singular – and rather contradictory – object of this association echoed the hardening politico-religious character of post-War Ulster: "to uphold the Protestant Religion, to retain an open Bible, and to establish full freedom religiously and politically for all, and to destroy and wipe out from Ulster by every means in my power the foul Sinn Fein conspiracy of murder, assassination and outrage, which at present is so rampant throughout all the rest of Ireland". Whilst, to some extent, Fred was merely reciprocating the intentions which he believed that Nationalists held towards himself, and the movement echoed the fears that were prevalent in Ulster at the time, it is fair to question whether Gelston, Wickham, Clark and Tudor would have felt that such an extravagant and introverted protocol best articulated the serious purpose.

Fred made certain demands for organising and running this 'Detective Reserve'. His attitude against Dublin had solidified and he stated that none of the names of his men should be revealed to the Castle; indeed, he said that the very existence of the body should "be kept absolutely secret". There should also be proper weapons training. He would operate it as a voluntary group and none of the men – himself included – would be paid other than standard RIC expenses, but all the volunteers were to be compensated for injury or death in the course of duty (for himself, this was to be £20,000). He requested an account designated 'Detective Reserve' in case of emergencies and in order to "carry on the work properly I will require a motor bike of the best and most reliable make and a large sidecar. It is less conspicuous than a motor car". Above all he was to be given a free hand over policy and dealing with his men, and he would accept orders only from the Head of the Police in Ulster, or a superior, and would be accountable only to the latter. He also demanded, in order for his work to be effective, that "All intelligence received by the Police be communicated fully and freely to me".

It would seem that Fred and his fellow conspirators were themselves a source of intelligence-gathering. On 11th April 1921, before the establishment of the Ulster Brotherhood, Fred handed a letter to Sir Ernest Clark, complaining of the apathy of the military and police authorities; he concluded: "I have often given them information, but they are invariably late, and always ask for proof, which as a rule cannot be given".[14] Whether Fred received information from Captain Hardy, or gathered it himself by whatever agencies he could muster, the indications are that it was being collected as early as August 1920, as his notes refer to an episode on the day of Swanzy's murder.[15]

Some of the material is listed simply as "considered worthy of investigation" and involves overheard conversations, hearsay and conjecture. One boarding house on the Antrim Road, which featured in the lists, enjoyed a large turnover in guests, although this could scarcely be regarded as unusual; they included two men "who appear to have no occupation, but go out at 11am and return at all times". Men in Castle Market in Belfast were observed making signs "by placing their hands on their lapels", and entering the door of a public house "at the back of Leahy Kelly's place in Cornmarket". A tailor's shop in Manor Street was selected for careful attention because its door was "painted green, yellow and white". There were recommendations that property be searched or grounds and gardens be dug up.

The observations attempted to identify and diagnose Sinn Fein activity and he passed on information about those with 'Rebel' sympathies who had infiltrated businesses such as the Post Office, Harland & Wolff and even Victoria Barracks. He pointed out that many RIC officers exhibited republican tendencies, targeting such as Glenravel Street Barracks where three-quarters of the complement was Catholic, and "the District Inspector is alleged to have strong Sinn Fein sympathies". When on patrol, Fred challenged a number of RIC officers whom he felt had deliberately prevented the search of suspects' property, or had allowed them to flee.

His lists pointed suspicion at a teacher who lived in an expensive area of the upper Antrim Road, whose home was visited by motors "at all hours of the night. He takes revolvers out round his chums in leather handbags". Again, irony eluded the notorious gun-runner who had approached the authorities to permit him to dispense private arms: he reported one Sinn Fein individual on the Milewater Road who was claimed to have "hundreds of revolvers, and boasts to his neighbours that he can get as many as he wants"!

On occasions the recorded information could be erroneous and, consequently, quite possibly injurious to the individual concerned. On 21st April 1921 there was intelligence noted about "S. W. Boyd JP, 1 Ardenlee Avenue [Belfast]; in this house four Sinn Feiners lodged, and the house was full of arms some time ago". The occupant of this property, Claremont House (which was demolished in 2007), was Samuel Boyd, a distiller. He had five sons, some of whom served in the First World War. The youngest, a pupil at Campbell College, served in the Royal Irish Rifles, and was shot through the head on 23rd November 1917 during the tank Battle of Cambrai.[16] Clearly the intelligence was wrong, and may well have related to the new owner of the property in 1921, who appears to have been a Catholic spirit merchant.

Although it operated occasional patrols and sought out intelligence, the Brotherhood was never officially authorised, and appears to have faded away about the close of 1921.[17] This was probably a consequence of the fact that Craig and the Ulster Cabinet (based initially at Cabin Hill) had acquired direct control over policing matters. As we have seen, in the post-War period Fred came at best to have little confidence in, and at worst to distrust, the English management of Ulster affairs.

This was one of the reasons why Wickham was not a popular choice as Inspector-General of the newly-formed Royal Ulster Constabulary (RUC) in September 1922. He had been Divisional Commissioner of the RIC since 1920, but a poster was circulated castigating his new appointment, saying that he had made errors during the previous two years, that under his leadership "there is practically no protection for law-abiding citizens". He had, it was claimed, never shown his face at the scene of an outrage and had given positions to "incompetent English officers who are giving all the fancy jobs to Englishmen while Ulstermen are unable to obtain employment". "These facts", the leaflet concluded, "prove he is utterly incompetent, and unfit to have charge of Ulster's little force".[18] Although a copy of the poster can be found in the Crawford archives, it is difficult to determine whether Fred had any role in its composition. On the whole, the latter seems to have enjoyed a reasonable and sociable working relationship with Wickham, who stayed in the post until 1945.

The Ulster Special Constabulary

Ulstermen, uncertain of the role and loyalty of the RIC, began to place greater faith in the Ulster Special Constabulary (USC), established in late 1920. This body received the approval of leading Unionists, including Spender who commanded the recently-restored UVF. On 20th October 1920, from the Old Town Hall, Spender circulated a explanatory letter to the Belfast regiments.[19] He outlined that Carson and others wanted to assist "the Government in restoring and maintaining order in the province", and that the new body would contribute substantially to this end. It consisted of three units: the 'A' Specials, would be a paid unit operating armed in the Six Counties. Spender added that this would effectively be an arm of the RIC, and the men would serve "under RIC officers and sergeants of all religious creeds". The 'B' force would be volunteers, who turned out on an occasional nightly basis, unpaid, but would be armed when on duty. The 'C' Specials were a general reserve force, which ultimately absorbed the UVF. The arms for the latter two units would be held at local police barracks.

Fred endorsed the concept of the USC and in December 1920 explained its purpose to a meeting of his own Malone & Balmoral Unionist Club.[20] Spender had said that its success was dependent upon the USC operating "conscientiously and impartially under discipline and with restraint towards those who disagree with us" – and Fred effectively reiterated this philosophy, claiming that they "only wanted justice for the whole of Ulster, whether Catholic or Protestant"; they wanted all communities to carry out the law "and if they did that, and practised it, they would hold out the right hand of fellowship to every Catholic who helped maintain the law". The one dissenting, or reluctant, Protestant voice was that of Orange Order and on 16th December

Fred wrote to his close friend, Col. Bob Wallace, to say that the Order "was letting down the Chief [Carson] by a non-committal attitude".[21]

On 6th December 1920 Fred was notified that he had been appointed as the District Commandant in the City of Belfast 'A' and 'F' Districts (Musgrave Street and Donegall Pass) in the 'B' Specials, with the largest contingent (800 men) under his command.[22] Patrols commenced at the end of January 1921 and the duties for constables involved accompanying the RIC from 8pm to 2am once every ten days. The position of Commandant, however, must have resulted in Fred having to neglect his family; he himself recorded that "the work was very onerous. I am out every night visiting barracks and patrols at different hours".

There were inevitably teething problems, and even enduring hostility, between the RIC and the Specials. This was predictable when the latter were viewed as a Protestant or Loyalist body, which was openly distrustful of the older force. Even Fred expressed serious reservations about the loyalty and impartiality of the Police and, on at least one occasion, intervened to point out to Gelston in person a sergeant and a constable whom he believed were deliberately preventing the arrest of criminal elements. Fred suggested, without moderation, that "they both ought to be court-martialled, and I will gladly be a witness to this serious breach of discipline on the part of these two RIC men".[23] Such tensions were never resolved, at least until the formation of the distinct northern force – the RUC.

Fred once had to deal with an incident on his domestic doorstep, when a 'B' Special constable sustained a serious leg wound from a gunman[24] in the nursery at the rear of his property at about 2.30am, near the junction of Chlorine Gardens and Stranmillis Road. Having dealt with the situation in dressing gown and slippers, even Fred knew it was tempting his family's patience to respond in detail to a phone call from the Donegall Pass Barracks when the *Belfast News Letter* called at 4am to ask for details of the incident: "my language to [the reporter] was not quite parliamentary".

Reprisals

By October 1921 there was concern that Sinn Fein had started to establish paramilitary training camps in Ulster, but this paled into insignificance compared with the outrage caused in late November and early December by the treaty between the British Government and the representatives of Sinn Fein. Lilian Spender threw her newspaper into the grate when she read that Lloyd George had shaken hands with Michael Collins, and she added that "W[olf] went off to work plunged in gloom and full of apprehension". By mid-December she had decided that "it's extraordinarily hard to capture the spirit of Christmas this year".[25]

Fred, as we have seen, described developments as a "criminal betrayal of Ulster by the Imperial Parliament" and "the most humiliating document that any great nation ever produced". His unposted letter in December to Carson concluded: "There are still many thousands determined to pay the supreme sacrifice to save their hearths, homes and religion from those who will show no mercy to them or theirs once they get the power to inflict their vengeance upon them".[26]

The anxiety and rancour that such actions of the British Government promoted in Northern Ireland, and the intensification of Sinn Fein activity inside the northern province in early 1922, led to Field Marshal Sir Henry Wilson suggesting the expansion of the USC, and a short-term Military Adviser, Major-General Solly-Flood, was appointed. Inevitably, Fred felt impelled to proffer his opinions to the newcomer, who responded diplomatically, thanking Fred "for your suggestions with regard to the organisation and functions of the Constabulary of Belfast. They are in the form of constructive rather than destructive criticism, and therefore are most helpful. We are working hard at this complex question", he reassured the District Commandant.

Solly-Flood's final sentence may well have baffled the ardent imperialist, who believed that there was a much simpler remedy for Ulster's frustrations. There were few subtleties in Fred's world, which was bounded by the divinely-ordained Empire. He could not comprehend why anyone would wish to live outside its certainties, let alone challenge it. The world had, however, grown more hostile and impermanent. Adopting a singular illustration: John Barkley, who was to be a pupil at Campbell College in the mid-1920s, and much later Professor of Church History and Principal of Presbyterian College, was the son of a clergyman. He found his early world, well beyond the claustrophobia of Belfast, changed from one in Co. Donegal in which "theological differences had not destroyed social relationships", to a new world after the War in Aughnacloy on the border where sectarianism and communal division were common-place, and one fell asleep "to the rattle of gunfire between the IRA and the 'B' Specials", and experienced "the fear of arson and assassination".[27]

Fred believed that the only way to deal with a Rebel campaign was to pursue reprisals. He admitted that such a policy "seems drastic, but to my mind it is the only way that will stop these cold-blooded murders ... I consider they are justifiable and right in the eyes of God and Man". Whilst Fred does not appear to have pursued such a practice personally, calculated reciprocation did occur and Hezlet's assertion that it was never employed by the USC is probably disingenuous.[28]

Nevertheless, Fred conceded by early 1923 that, for what ever reason, the political scene was much calmer. On the first full weekend of April that year he was fully occupied by varied responsibilities. The Earl of Derby, Minister for War, arrived to inspect the RUC and USC and Wickham asked Fred to accompany Derby to the Newtownards RUC depot on the Saturday morning. Fred, however, had to decline as a consequence of his prior obligation to inaugurate the Campbell College War Memorial with General Sir Alexander Godley.

Fred did attend the lunch at Stormont Castle at the invitation of the Prime Minister, in company with Wickham, Gelston and others. Craig embarrassed him by introducing him to Derby as "the finest man in Ulster", and referring to his gun-running escapade. After lunch he accompanied the Minister and Wickham to inspect nearly 3,000 USC men at Lisburn. Afterwards at the home (Conway House) of Sir Milne Barbour,[29] the largest linen thread manufacturer in the world, Fred again conversed with Derby, who expressed himself impressed with the turn-out of the Specials.

On the following afternoon (Sunday 8th April 1923), after a drum-head Church parade, the Minister for War inspected 6000 Specials in Ormeau Park. Fred marched 600 of his 'B' Specials of 'A' and 'F' districts from his headquarters at Donegall Pass, along Botanic Avenue and University Street on to the park. His meticulous attention to detail is evident in his account of this short march and his pride was reflected in the fact that he claimed that: "My Battalion was the strongest of the B [Special]s, and on the whole the largest men. They looked very well everyone said".

Marked

The early 1920s proved problematical and dangerous for Fred personally and as a businessman. In the first half of June 1921 he stated that "Belfast was in a blaze". He witnessed many businesses burned out in the vicinity of his Wilson Street Works, and felt it prudent to spend all night on the company premises on the eve of the Twelfth. At the close of 1921 and into early 1922 he spent many a night wandering his premises with a pistol in hand, fully expecting that "the Works will go next". In mid-1922 his private memoir echoed the previous year: "Things are pretty hot all about Belfast just now", and in May he witnessed more destruction as he fixed the barbed wire entanglements at Alexander Crawford & Son, because no one else would brave the danger. He wrote to Craig: "If this goes on at the present rate, it will utterly ruin the city".[30] Whilst a number of commentators have been hasty in accusing the starch manufacturer of having no interest in his family firm, he always continued to defend it, even though he admitted that he would probably be more secure financially if he claimed compensation for its destruction.

There were a number of occasions when Fred's life was placed in danger. Towards midnight on 7th July 1921 he was returning in a taxi with three other officers from Glenravel Street Barracks. They had just reached the junction of North Queen Street and Clifton Street (close to Victoria Barracks) when they were approached by three men; the latter departed quickly when faced with the sergeant's gun, but Fred had a hand on his own automatic and he was "satisfied these three men would have held us up for some purpose" if they had not seen the policeman's revolver. As noted in an earlier chapter, Fred's younger son overheard threats to his father's life in Berry Street on 7th January 1922.

As probably the most notorious Protestant figure in Belfast, it was inevitable that Fred would be marked out for unwelcome attention and he does seem to have been very fortunate to survive a planned attack on 22nd June 1922. It was the day on which Craig moved from Cabin Hill to his new office and home at Stormont Castle, which had been attacked three days previously because Sinn Fein believed that he was moving on that date. It was also the very same day on which Field Marshal Wilson was assassinated on his own London doorstep and, although no commentator mentions the fact, it was exactly one year since the opening of the Northern Ireland Parliament. It seems quite probable that the IRA was intent on celebrating the first anniversary in memorable style.

A builder named James Kidd – whose own son had been shot only a few days earlier – who was working in the Millfield area had been warned by one of his well-disposed Catholic employees that Sinn Fein were targeting the factory owner, intending to shoot him as he left the back door of his Works. Fred wrote that: "I must say that I can't help feeling very grateful to this unknown Roman Catholic friend, and appreciate his kindness". There was also a simultaneous attempt to destroy his factory by means of incendiary bombs and paraffin. A Detective Inspector Lewis at Donegall Pass and Gelston both endeavoured, without success, to persuade Fred to accept protection. He was inclined to believe that his family – "They would get compensation or a pension, perhaps both" – and that Ulster would benefit from his death. He also demonstrated his faith in divine will: "Don't worry, I won't go before my time", he assured his police colleagues.

CBE

A year previously, on the morning of the inauguration of the Northern Ireland Parliament (22nd June 1921), Fred had taken his wife and youngest daughter, Bethia, to see the arrival of the King and Queen: "We were as close to Their Majesties as etiquette would permit".[31] He was invited to the reception at City Hall and then walked the short distance to the Ulster Hall to receive the award of the CBE. He had taken literally the words 'private and confidential' on the envelope by which he had been notified and had not even told his wife of the presentation!

Even on this dignified occasion he could not entirely escape his roguish past. Lady Craig said that she felt that there was no-one more deserving of an honour and Rosalind, Duchess of Abercorn, concurred, adding that the decoration was "not half good enough". Ruby, Lady Carson, was even more enthusiastic and, as Fred went up to shake hands with both Their Majesties, she called out loudly: "Here is the gun-runner". Fred added in his memoir that the official reason for the award was past service "for the Unionist cause and the Six Counties, War work and the part taken in raising the 'B' Specials", but he was enough of a realist to conclude that "all my friends know it was for what Lady Carson called out in the Hall: gun-running. When His Majesty finds out the real reason, he will likely have a fit of nerves".

Upon the formation of the Government of Northern Ireland, Fred was probably not the only importunate acquaintance of Carson, but few were probably more solicitous of the latter "to hold the reins of leadership till the new Government is steady on its feet", and he urged the Dubliner "to start us on this venture as First Prime Minister of the First Ulster Parliament for at least six or eight months".[32] His 'Political Leader', however – "[the] one man that I have implicitly trusted and whose advice I have always taken without question" – lacked the energy or will for such a demanding workload, and the post fell to Craig.

Whilst the Parliament met in Belfast City Hall during the earliest months, the Cabinet Secretariat was based handily to Fred's regular haunt of Campbell College, at its neighbour Cabin Hill. Spender had hoped that the effective absorption of the UVF into the USC would enable him to return to England. The new Prime Minister, however, according to Lilian Spender, "begged him to stay on till March, saying it was the greatest comfort to 'Fredward' [presumably a portmanteau abbreviation for both Fred and Carson] … so, of course, we stay".[33] Her husband became Secretary to the Cabinet, and eventually Head of the Northern Ireland Civil Service.

To ensure that Ulster's imperial credentials were not forgotten, Fred visited Cabin Hill quite regularly. Whilst he could command ready entrance to its portals – ironically on the site of the erstwhile home of two of the most influential United Irishmen, Sam McTier and William Drennan – others, despite the presence of police and barbed wire, also found access a little too easy. One of Cabin Hill's near neighbours, the eccentric and prolific artist, J. W. Carey, penetrated its defences and was arrested when found decimating offending dandelions on its lawns[34] in early 1922. Nine years later Carey painted the unloading of one of Sir Samuel Kelly's coal boats, but sadly there is no indication as to whether or not it might have been the *SS Balmerino*, which was to prove the most enduring of the Kelly steamers.[35]

The Craig family had moved out of their celebrated and historic home on Circular Road in Belmont during the First World War and never returned. Craigavon was loaned as a hospital for recuperating soldiers, and after the War it was sold to become a sanatorium for ex-servicemen. When the tenancy at Cabin Hill expired in June 1922, Craig transferred – as Prime Minister – to Stormont Castle, as we have seen, on the day Fred Crawford was supposed to be shot.

By the end of 1922 Fred felt that the actions of Craig and his Cabinet colleagues were beginning to have a positive impact, and he admitted that "things have been comparatively quiet … with the result that now we are practically free from political crime" – at least in the north. Life in the Free State, however, had become much more violent and destructive, which occasioned Fred one personal headache. A distant relative, Rev James Hamilton, had died and had bequeathed Fred a number of family heirlooms, which included a painting, crested damask and snuff boxes. Fred was notified by Hamilton's Dublin solicitor on 7th November 1922 that the items were confirmed as his inheritance.

Fred was apprehensive about having them sent by rail from Dublin but, on being reassured by the transportation company and the manager at Belfast station, he decided to take the risk. Packing problems meant that it couldn't be delivered on the promised date – Friday 15th December – but on the following Wednesday he was telephoned and asked to meet the train at the Great Northern Station at 5.45pm: "All the articles were perfectly in order". It was a very close call: "Before I had the goods at my house, the next train had started from Dublin, and on the Dublin side of Dundalk it was held up and the whole train, with all its contents, was burnt to a cinder"!

Notes

1. D/1415/B/34, p.124. Much of the following chapter is taken from this source, D/640/11/2, and Sir Arthur Hezlet, *The B Specials: a history of the Ulster Special Constabulary*, (London, 1972).

2. Black & Tans was the name given to British recruits brought to Ireland to augment the declining numbers in the Royal Irish Constabulary. The nickname, purloined from a well-known pack of Co Galway foxhounds, resulted from the nature and colour of their uniform (military khaki and dark police green).

3. Sergeant Joe Kearney of the Royal Irish Rifles was awarded the DCM: Cyril Falls, *The History of 36th (Ulster) Division*, (Belfast, 1922), p.324.

4. Fred's brother in Australia wrote to him in July 1922: "I have been continually dreading to hear that you have been assassinated …": D/1700/6/1/14.

5. D/1507/A/35/1-55.

6. D/640/7/7, 14 May 1920. *Belfast News Letter*, 13 July 1920. Timothy Bowman, *Carson's Army: the Ulster Volunteer Force 1910-1922*, (Manchester University Press, 2007), p.48. Ian Maxwell, *The Life of Sir Wilfrid Spender 1876-1960*, (QUB Ph D thesis, 1991), p.119. The Presbyterian Home Ruler, Rev J B Armour of Ballymoney, had criticised Carson from as early as September 1919 "for threatening the Government and trying to bring back the feeling which eventuated the gun-running": D/1792/A3/10/18.

7. D/640/7/8, –/10, 17 May and 2 June 1920.

8. D/1633/2/23.

9. D/640/7/7, 14 May 1920. D/640/11/2, p.53. D/640/12/5, 25 April 1921. D/1700/5/6/6, 20 February 1922. Fred seems to have been reluctant to call the new government in Dublin the Free State; he nearly always refers to it blandly as 'the South and West'.

10. D/640/9/1. Bowman, p.197. Michael Farrell, *Arming the Protestants: the formation of the Ulster Special Constabulary and the Royal Ulster Constabulary 1920-1927*, (Belfast, 1983), pp.143, 168.

11. For this, see Fred's account: D/640/12/1, plus –/3-5. D/640/4/1. D/640/15/1-2.

12. D/640/16/2.

13. His second-in-command was Hugh Wright.

14. D/640/13/3.

15. Much of the intelligence material is to be found in D/64013/1, –/2 and –/6, plus D/640/6/1-24.

16. See Tom Hartley, *Written in Stone: the History of Belfast City Cemetery*, (Brehon Press, Belfast, 2006), pp.53, 248. C V Boyd's name is inscribed on the family tomb in the cemetery.

17. Farrell, p.56.
18. D/640/3/1.
19. D/1700/5/16/5.
20. D/1700/5/16/6 – a cutting from *The Northern Whig*, 8 December 1920.
21. D/1700/5/6/9.
22. D/640/5/1. D/1700/5/16/7.
23. D/640/6/1.
24. Details of this incident are found in D/640/11/2, pp.94-96.
25. D/1633/2/25, December 1921.
26. D/640/7/1, 13 December 1921.
27. John M Barkley, *Blackmouth & Dissenter*, (Dundonald, 1991), pp.20-21.
28. Hezlet, pp.37, 64.
29. In 1908 Barbour's sister had married Thomas Andrews, who in 1912 drowned on the *Titanic*, the ship he helped to design.
30. D/1700/5/6/10, 29 May 1922.
31. Much of the occasion is outlined in D/640/16/2, written on 4 July 1921.
32. D/640/7/12, –/13, 1 January and 2 May 1921.
33. D/1633/2/23, 11 November 1920.
34. St John Ervine, *Craigavon: Ulsterman*, (London, 1940), p.402. Honor Rudnitzky, *The Careys, (Belfast, 1978)*, pp.5-6, 24. For all his eccentric habits and absent-mindedness, Carey defeated the 'invincible' world chess champion, Capablanca, during a simultaneous chess challenge in Belfast in the same year.
35. It was built in Ailsa for John Kelly in 1898, and was eventually scrapped (as the Ballybeg) in 1957: Ian Wilson, *John Kelly Ltd: an history*, (Belfast, c.1980), pp.6, 31.

The Garden of Consolation

∞

To someone of Fred's disposition, who had inherited some of his father's lack of confidence in his personal future, and who wrote to Carson in December 1921, at the age of sixty, that "I feel I have lived too long",[1] it would have been astonishing to learn that he still had one-third of his life ahead of him. These were, nevertheless, increasingly fragile years, and he was eventually subject to what medieval philosophers described as *accidentia senectutis* – the accidents of old age.

For all the satisfaction that Protestant Ulstermen may have experienced at the creation of a Government of Northern Ireland, economically it could not have happened at a less propitious time. The impact of the Treaty of Versailles, and the downturn in the global economy by the early 1920s, were the dampen the apparent vibrancy of the province's pre-War economy and for all the prolix palimpsest of a biographer's apologia,[2] and the enduring admiration and gratitude of friends such as Fred Crawford, the new Prime Minister never successfully tackled the economic and fiscal problems that beset Northern Ireland in the inter-War period.

The impending injustices and circumscription of opportunities were flagged up to Fred well before the establishment of a discrete Northern Ireland government; even the professional classes were affected. Thomas Davidson, a surgeon acquaintance, sought Fred's intervention in June 1919. He complained to Fred that, after suspending his medical practice in Clifton Street for five years to serve in the War, "it is really disheartening" that he was unable to obtain any medical post in the city, whilst those "who have not sacrificed anything by their absence as I have done" have ensured that their "practices have increased enormously during our service".[3]

Fred will also have been made well-aware of the financial misery during this period as a consequence of his work with the Ex-Servicemen's Association. The working classes were, in fact, agitating for change within weeks of the end of the War. For all the enormous wealth generated – in Belfast in particular – in the pre-War era by world-ranking industries, the benefits were experienced by few. In the past the labouring man had endured a broadly penurious life-style, and the effort and sacrifice made in the War engendered a new perspective; he showed himself vigorous in the pursuit of a fairer share of the industrial and commercial spoils.

In letters to his eldest son during 1919, Rev J. B. Armour of Ballymoney recorded that strikes were undermining the economy; the attitude of the working classes was causing embarrassment to Ulster politicians, but Armour – never an admirer of the pre-War Unionist leadership – crowed: "Sir Edward Carson has been knocked into a cocked hat. Neither he nor one of his followers who got in dare open their mouths over the strike". Armour himself was not hopeful for the new world order; he said that the Labour community appeared to regard Belfast as "the new Jerusalem ... Everyone seems to be out on strike for forty to forty-four hours a week. How that would ultimately work is not clear".[4] As we have seen, even Fred was concerned that "a great number of our men are fed up with fighting and want a rest and to enjoy the result of high wages and better times".[5] The mass sacrifice of manpower at the hands of a detached officer class had alienated many: "The Ulster contingents are very bitter", Armour concluded, "against their officers, who were incapable, cruel and cowardly".

Whilst some employers, such as Fred, were – as we have seen in the instance of his generous treatment of William McKee in 1916 – acceptably paternalist towards their workers, most were viewed as exploitative. Press obituaries tended to be overly fulsome and ingratiating towards the barons of Ulster industry, such as Viscount Pirrie of Harland & Wolff, whilst recent commentators have tended to highlight "the toil and tyranny of the job".[6] The decimation of the labour force on the Western Front no doubt created a better negotiating position in the post-War world, but by the early 1920s employment became hard to find. As world trade suffered retrenchment, companies collapsed – and one of these was Alexander Crawford & Son.

The Closure of Alexander Crawford & Son

Fred rationalised the failure of Ulster industry in these years as the product of the British adherence to a Free Trade policy (introduced in 1906). In mid-1924 he stated that if Britain persisted in this approach, Ulster would have to become like Canada: "truly Imperial, but fiscally independent". By 1932 he noted to an acquaintance in the Far East that the British Government had finally seen the error of its ways, and had adopted a more protectionist stance but, by this stage, the world's economic ills had multiplied because of "mass production and machinery that is labour saving", which had resulted in over-production and stockpiling, which in turn led to unemployment.[7]

This had been too late for Northern Ireland; the Free State had taken advantage of its separate status to impose tariffs on goods manufactured in the north, and it freely admitted that this was designed to encourage northern manufacturers to build factories in the Free State and provide employment, which would erode the industrial base of Northern Ireland. "Against this", Fred conceded, "bravery and pluck can avail nothing, any more than can a fixed bayonet prevail against a poison gas raid".

Fred attributed at least some of the collapse of his starch business to the Free Trade policy. As he wrote to Craig in July 1923: "The bottom fell out of my business (established more than one hundred years ago) so suddenly and completely owing to foreign competition, that I was powerless to meet the crisis".[8] It was at time that he notified his brother, Alexander, that "If things do not improve, I must shut up shop and send the youngest [child] to business".[9] Fred was, nevertheless, well aware that this was the culmination of a long process of commercial decline in the family starch business; Alexander Crawford & Son was never in a position to resist the post-War economic downturn. He revealed to Craig that: "during the War the Government stopped me for six months and put my customers in a hole, and the firm also in the same position. Now foreign starch was being dumped on us from Hungary, Switzerland and Japan at a price that I paid for my raw material, and the slump in the cotton trade had simply made the bottom fall out of my business".[10]

Occasional company correspondence shows that it still enjoyed some orders from around the United Kingdom in 1921 and 1922. It sold Amylaceous Food at 12s 6d for a 14lb box, including carriage, but clients began to notify Fred that his prices were expensive, and that they could now obtain it much more cheaply from abroad. By mid-1922 the Crawford manufacturing process was uneconomical.[11] There appear to have been some efforts to convert it into a limited liability company, but it had effectively closed by 1925. That year saw its final entry in the *Belfast & Ulster Street Directory*, and in the following year the property at 18 Wilson Street was listed as a vacant site.

Fred was grateful to Sam Cunningham for all the latter's endeavours to salvage his economic distress – he obtained a loan on mortgage at 4.5% – and the starch manufacturer added that he felt that the Bank had behaved honourably. Nevertheless he confirmed to his brother that "the only property I can call my own is the field in front of the house".

In 1927 he told Spender that there was no prospect at that time of disposing of his property in the city centre, "and in the meantime it costs me about £140 per annum for rent, insurance and repairs ... which is a bit rough on the family". Two years later he revealed to Sir Dawson Bates that he was still encumbered with this burden and, at the end of 1936, the situation remained unresolved, as he lamented to Charles Craig: "I have a lot of property, but all that is let is mortgaged: one acre and a rood in the centre of town in the Smithfield district on which stands my old Works, and which I had to close down after the War ... This ground cannot be let, and I have to pay a heavy ground rent and keep the building in repair". He bewailed to the Prime Minister's brother the fact that he effectively had nothing to bequeath to his wife and regarded the manuscript of his gun-running adventures as "my only asset".[12]

In his jeremiad to his brother in mid-1923 he admitted that he found it depressing and distressing to have to tell his wife and children that "I can't give them more money for things, even looked upon as necessary", and agreed that it was not pleasant for a man of sixty-two years of age "with a wife and four children depending on him for home, food and raiment". He said to Alexander that he had even tried to obtain an agency or an alternative business post but that, if he had not found alternative employment by next May [1924], "I may not be living in Belfast at all. If I had to 'sweep the streets', I do not want to do it in my home town … For the sake of the children I would go to Timbuctoo or anywhere else I could earn an honest penny". The trade depression made it impossible to find alternative work in commerce, and he conceded that "I am in real trouble … I want work and pay for it. I want no charity".

Alternative Employment

In the Old Testament imagery that so appealed to Fred, he probably acknowledged that, from a commercial perspective, the writing had been on the wall since the end of the War. In May 1919 he contacted Craig at Westminster hinting at the possibility of an appointment. Craig responded cautiously and without commitment:[13] "I will keep your name prominently before me and, when the appointment is announced of the new Director of Ways and Communications for Ireland, I will see what the future may hold".

It is difficult to know whether Craig treated the request seriously and, even if he did, whether his word carried sufficient weight at that time. Four years later, however, Fred's diary of events reveals that on St. George's Day (23rd April 1923) he decided to slay the dragon of uncertainty: "I have come to the end of my tether … I had no alternative but to try and get a job".[14] He noted that the British Government was to appoint five Commissioners – including one in Northern Ireland – to supervise the construction of homes for ex-servicemen. He reflected that he was on several relevant committees,[15] and visited Craig at Stormont Castle to argue his case; the Prime Minister "received me, as he always does, as an old and trusted friend".

Fred explained his commercial predicament frankly and indicated that he was well-qualified to act as a Commissioner, but Craig disappointed him by pointing out that the post "will be honorary and unpaid". Fred underlined his urgency by saying that he would undertake any role, anywhere, "so long as it was strait [sic] and honourable. I would do it for my children's sake, even should I be sent to Timbuctoo". He added that "I should like the governorship of a prison", but Craig felt that his long-time friend would find that uncongenial. The occupant of Stormont Castle said that he felt unable and unwilling to send Fred from Belfast and indicated that he would cogitate upon the matter for a fortnight, promising not to disappoint his Unionist associate. Fred recalled that "I then bade him goodbye with a lighter heart than I have had for two years … All I can do now is to wait and ask God to give Sir James the power (I know he has the heart) to get me a position".

He was summoned on 18th July to visit Dawson Bates, the Minister of Home Affairs, who notified him that Craig was finding him a post. The despondent and impecunious starch manufacturer wrote the next day from Cloreen: "I cannot thank you enough for the time, thought and trouble you have taken in overcoming the serious difficulty of age in my case … by it, I am placed under a deep debt of gratitude to you". He said that he was particularly grateful that he could complete the education of his three younger children – the youngest being mid-way through his Campbell College career at that stage. He concluded: "I should feel much happier if I were in a position to give to Ulster instead of taking from her, but this is not to be, at least for the present".

Craig responded two days later from his residence at Streatley-upon-Thames, near Reading, hoping that Fred would find the post – which was not yet defined – congenial, hinting that it was effectively compensation for his efforts in 1914: "The whole Government is agreed that had it not been for you, none of us in Ulster would be in the position in which we find ourselves today and, so long as we live, none of your name will be allowed to suffer". The atmosphere in Cloreen was sufficiently emotional for Fred to regard this sentiment more highly than the actual appointment and he revealed that "I have placed [the letter] in the safe with my other valuable documents and, with them, it will be handed down to my children".[16]

Repaying the Debt

Fred was notified in late August 1923 that he would be expected to take up his position in the Ministry of Home Affairs on 1st September. Even at that advanced stage, it seems that the duties were not yet clarified and the suspicion is that his erstwhile Unionist colleagues were endeavouring to create a post that had some purpose and was not merely a sinecure, at which Fred would undoubtedly take offence. As late as February 1929 Fred said that "I ought to be giving to Ulster and not taking from her".

When the Prince of Wales officially opened the Stormont parliament building, with all the grandiose indifference he could muster, on 16th November 1932, Fred and Helen Crawford appear to have received prestigious seats (B1 and B2) for the ceremony.[17] He undoubtedly felt privileged to be provided with an office there. John Oliver, a noted Permanent Secretary, joined the Northern Ireland Civil service in 1937 and later recorded that "the new [1921] Government felt obliged to reward some of its more ardent supporters with jobs and made a few pretty blatant appointments. When I entered, I was amazed to find Colonel Fred Crawford of gun-running fame in 1914 still shamelessly occupying a chair, unnoticed and undisturbed".[18]

He was still in residence when they coated Stormont's Portland limestone façade with a mixture of tar and cow dung during the Second World War, in an attempt to deceive the Luftwaffe. The process seems to have worked inasmuch as when German planes headed out of Belfast at the end of their second raid on 4th-5th May 1941, they dropped a handful of bombs on Campbell College (then General Hospital No.24) probably mistaking it for the parliament building. An incidental parliamentary question at Stormont in 1951 revealed that Fred's post as Stores Inspector for the Ministry of Home Affairs finally ceased on 29th February 1944, when Fred was 82 years old! There was one near-coincidence in the entrance hall of Stormont of which the erstwhile gun-runner may never have been aware: the central chandelier, boasting the Reichsadler (or Imperial eagle), had originally been a gift to Edward VII from the man Fred very nearly met at Kiel in 1914 – Kaiser Wilhelm II.

Despite occupying his post for two decades there are few published details of Fred's work. Correspondence from late 1923 asserts that one of the departments in the Ministry was being reorganised, "dealing with police maintenance, stores and equipment"; two positions were made available, one filled from the War Office in London and one which required Royal Army Service Corps experience.[19] Sometime around 1930 Fred told Lady Ranfurly that "My present post in the Northern Ireland Government requires me to visit every police station in Ulster about once a year".

Even by that stage he had had to struggle to retain the job, as in August 1927, having passed his 65th birthday, an Establishment Officer at the Ministry wrote to him to state that his employment would not continue beyond the last day of that year. Fred was clearly shocked by the decision, and decamped for short time to Mrs Shaw of Arcadia House in Whitehead, "to keep me out of the dumps". At the end of August, Spender (who was technically responsible for the Civil Service establishment) sent his gun-running acquaintance a palliative letter saying that he was disappointed by the shock Fred would have suffered, but promised to discuss it with the two relevant knights of the realm – Craig and Bates – when they returned to Northern Ireland.

Fred responded immediately to thank Spender for his courtesy, admitting that the revelation had caused him anxiety: "When I am depending on an income to keep going, it is a bit of a shock to see it end in a few months". He harboured no resentment: "I am thankful for the generous treatment I have received for the last three or four years, and it is the fortune of war and the result of age. I will have to look for something else". Within a short period, his Unionist acquaintances with longer memories – such as Spender, Craig, Bates and Andrews – rallied to his support and ensured the continued renewal or extension of his job. In late 1927 they appear to have justified his position by bolstering it with responsibility for the disposal of the Ulster Volunteer Force (UVF) arsenal.[20]

In February 1929 John Miller Andrews encapsulated the prevailing attitude from the Ministry of Labour in Ormeau Avenue, thanking Fred for his letter of appreciation: "It is really to Bates that you are indebted as he has upheld your position all along; not that it really needed defending because, in my opinion, the debt which Ulster owes you can never be fully repaid. All that we can do is to show that we do not forget what you did".

In reality much of the work must have constituted a sinecure, although Fred would have approached it with all due diligence and attention to detail.[21] It did not, however resolve his financial difficulties, which remained in a parlous condition until his death in late 1952. When he finally departed his Stormont office in early 1944, he was given a gratuity of £356 – which was effectively one year's housekeeping given to Helen Crawford – and several years after Fred's death Spender apologised to the latter that her husband could not be given "a reasonable pension … for his not very long service with the Government after it was formed" – which suggests that he probably received an official pension only to the age of sixty-five.[22]

LIFEBELTS

There were occasional financial lifebelts thrown to Cloreen. For all his multifarious pre-occupations, Fred always took a close interest in the Crawford family history and kept in touch with distant relatives. In 1923 one of these left him £200 and Fred noted that: "I shall apply this money to finish my boy's education. He is called after the old ladies' only brother, Adair. I know it would please them if they knew their money was being put to this purpose".[23]

Ten years later Fred benefited from a bequest from his family doctor, friend and close neighbour, Sir William Whitla (who died in December 1933). As Methodists, both men became heavily engaged in the post-War temperance and local lay Missions movements. The celebrated and very wealthy medical man had been as committed a Unionist as Fred, urging his co-denominationalists in March 1912 in the Ulster Hall to unite "as one man in the deliberate conviction that Home Rule means disaster and ruin to our native land, and irreparable injury to our Church and to the civil and religious liberty which we and our fathers have enjoyed under the impartial freedom of the British flag".[24] He inevitably signed the Solemn League & Covenant six months later. Whitla's will left Fred the not-insubstantial sum of £1000 "as a token of my appreciation of what he has heroically done for Ulster and the British Empire".[25]

As heir to a once-successful company, and a Victorian *paterfamilias*, Fred was embarrassed to be beholden to anyone; he admitted to at least two of his benefactors that he would far rather have been able to dispose of his commercial property in Belfast than be the recipient of the generosity of others. Around 1927 he sold a substantial holding of shares to clear some of his indebtedness to the Bank. At that time, the Crawfords considered letting Cloreen as a furnished property – "we could live in a quiet way in a cottage", he suggested to Sir Charles Blackmore (then Secretary to the Cabinet) – and once his post was finally extinguished in 1944, Helen Crawford admitted to a correspondent that they were "in a bad jam", and were contemplating turning Cloreen into flats.[26]

Although the precise chronology of events is not clear, it may be that the ignominy of the latter possibility was obviated by the arrival of a cheque for £3000, which Fred used to pay off an overdraft with the Northern Bank. During the early stages of the Second World War, many of the unserviceable rifles of the original Ulster Volunteer Force were disposed of as scrap, but following the débâcle of Dunkirk, some of the rifles were sold (at £2 12s 6d each) to the Ministry of Supply for almost £34,000 – with the cheque made out personally to Sir Dawson Bates. Fred himself appears to have sold a further quantity in mid-1942 for £8743, although he admitted that, as a consequence of advancing glaucoma, he could never check the invoices satisfactorily, "my eyesight then being defective".

The ageing former gun-runner recorded in June 1945 that he was asked to visit the office of Bates: "There were a few other people present, but I could not see who they were". The recently retired Minister of Home Affairs gave him a piece of paper which he later discovered was a cheque for £3000, part of the proceeds of the sale of the rifles which Fred had originally brought into Ulster. Fred, who by this time, was increasingly frail, did not argue, but admitted to being bemused as to how Bates came to handle all this money personally. "It was never intended by Lord Craigavon that this should be", he added.[27]

The Garden of Consolation

Apart from the award of the CBE, there were other occasional highlights for Fred in the post-War years. In October 1923 he was a guest at a dinner in the Ulster Hall given by the Marquess of Londonderry in honour of the Carsons. It was typical of Fred's self-deprecation that, despite his considerable affection for his Leader, he was content to be seated at the far end of a table, furthest from the high table. On 24th July 1925 – eleven years to the day since, at Campbell College, he had smiled quietly to himself about his treasonable activities in the presence of one of the Crown's senior military officials – he and Helen Crawford were invited to a Buckingham Palace Garden Party.[28]

In addition to an invitation to the opening of Stormont in 1932, he was a guest at Belfast City Hall on 28th July 1937 for the Coronation Visit of George VI and Queen Elizabeth. In March 1935, his family again took second place, when he postponed a visit to his daughter, Doreen, and grand-daughter, Angela, when he was appointed honorary secretary of a committee created to supervise the decoration of the city for the visit of the Duke of Gloucester on 11th May 1935.[29]

There was inevitably an increasing catalogue of nadirs: the frustration and frailty of old age and ill-health; the incompatibility of the elderly with a changing world; the departure of all his children to various parts of the globe; and the increasing roll of deceased associates, friends and relatives. For all that he might have been expected to feel some relief at the shelving of all commercial responsibilities, he admitted to Lady Ranfurly about 1930 that "I felt very sore about it … To help divert my thoughts I made a rock garden which took me four years [1924-1928]. It was useful in helping me to forget my worries, that I called it the Garden of Consolation".[30]

Even in this pastime, time conspired against him. He noted to a relative in Dublin in mid-1932 that the garden was starting to become weedy; he did have occasional help, "but I have not much time and generally am too tired when I get home to do garden work". Additionally he had sustained a shoulder injury two years earlier and appeared to continue to suffer from its effects.[31]

Even with twenty years still to live, he wrote to an acquaintance in the Free Malay States at the beginning of 1932: "As I get older and nearer the time that we must all face and hand in our passport, and when looking round at all the gloom and trouble in the world and the darker clouds on the horizon, I thank God I have been trained up as a Christian to believe that, above all this, we have a heavenly Father who loves us and will take us to Himself at last". Living to the age of ninety-one, Fred witnessed the passing of an increasing number of friends and relatives, and in late 1933 he wrote to his very distant relation, Col. Sharman-Crawford, that "now that Willie Young and Lord Ranfurly have passed away … you and I are the only two left of the 'Old Brigade'".[32]

His bleakest year in the mid-1930s was 1935. Helen Crawford appears to have been sent away for a period to assist recovery from problems with her spine and correspondence with a relative admits to the couple's declining circle of relations to visit.[33] In November of that year his brother died in Australia, preceded by the man he most admired – Lord Carson. In early May he had been notified that the former Unionist leader had become very frail and Fred determined to make a final journey to the Dubliner. In early June Lady Carson wrote from her home in Minster, Kent, to say that she and her son would be very pleased to see Fred, but intimated that her husband may be neither well enough nor alert enough to recognise or talk with his old friend. That night, 18th June 1935, Fred communicated with Colvin, who was compiling Carson's biography, to say: "I have had one of the greatest pleasures in life today. I have seen my old Chief, and he knew me quite well".[34]

Carson died on 22nd October and Fred was delighted that his widow specifically requested that Fred be one of the pall-bearers at her husband's funeral. In company with the Marquess of Londonderry, Sir Dawson Bates, Wilfrid Spender, Lord Craigavon, Sir Crawford McCullagh (the Lord Mayor of Belfast) and others, he accompanied the coffin from the Belfast quayside, past the site of their former days of conspiracy – the Old Town Hall – to its unique resting-place in St. Anne's Cathedral.[35] Likewise upon Craigavon's death just over five years later (24th November 1940), Fred attended the service at Belmont Presbyterian Church and sent him on his voyage to eternity with such appropriate lines from the hymnal as: "You tranquil lie, your knightly virtue proved, Your memory hallowed in the land you love",[36] before another unique and honoured burial at the wing of the Stormont parliament building.

Fred also survived his eldest grandson, Ivan, son of the marriage of Stuart to Sheelagh Garvey. Fred harboured the aspiration that his grandson would be educated at Campbell College but, as the boy's parents hoped that their son would adopt a military career, he was sent to Wellington College early in 1935. Fred rigged out a boat for Ivan in 1936 and paid for, or at least contributed £10 towards, his grandson's uniform when he enlisted in the RAFVR in 1940 (aged 18).[37] He was awarded the DFC three years later, but was killed, aged 26, in a flying accident in 1948.

Memorial

Although this occurred in peace-time, it lacked nothing of the tragedy of other young men killed in action during the Second World War. These included many former pupils of Campbell College – a large proportion of whom joined the RAF – such as Head Prefect George Jackson and the school's most outstanding athlete, Basil Tweedie. Both these young men left the school in the summer of 1940 and by 1943 both of them lay dead in foreign fields, aged 19 and 21.

It was presumably this potential loss of young lives – despite the fact that he had conceded in 1921 that he had been too old to serve in the First World War – which encouraged Fred, in late 1938, to offer himself "to stop a bullet, which I could do as well as a young man" for the anticipated forthcoming conflict. He felt that at his age – then 77 – "My time for usefulness to my country is nil" and he suggested to Craig that he was still reasonably fit, although "It cannot be very long before 'I slip my cable', and doing so for the Empire as an Ulsterman is better than a feather bed departure". Craig's response was tactful: "you have already more than done your bit". Not dissuaded, Fred had also pestered Spender with the idea. The latter replied, diplomatically, that young men could learn from the old soldier's example: "I would only ask that they should not be forgetful of the fine example which you yourself have set throughout your life".[38]

It was to be a retired Spender who wrote from England to Helen Crawford as late as May 1960: "I am convinced that the history of Ulster would have been different if Col. Crawford had not been born, and that we should have never got that wonderful tribute from Churchill after the Second World War". W. A. Magill, Assistant

Secretary at the Ministry of Home Affairs went so far as to say (as early as 1937): "Would there be an Ulster at all, only for Fred Crawford?"[39]

It is a disputatious question, to which there will be many interpretations, but the reality is that Northern Ireland – or Ulster, as Fred almost invariably called it – has retained little that is linked to the Crawford name. Indeed, Belfast – and more particularly East Belfast – has been cavalier with its historical industrial heritage: Sirocco Works, the Belfast Ropework Company, and – apart from the Drawing Room at Harland & Wolff where, by chance, Fred was employed – the shipyards have all been demolished, just as surely as the site of Alexander Crawford & Son. Chlorine, Cloreen, the Belfast Nursery and the Garden of Consolation have all been submerged by a voracious university campus.

There are no direct descendants of Fred Crawford resident in Northern Ireland, or Ireland as a whole. Discounting the substantial Crawford archive which has been deposited in Belfast, there is virtually nothing left which can be closely associated with Fred, apart from – and perhaps most appropriately – the silver casket which was presented to him by his appreciative Unionist colleagues to commemorate the Larne episode of April 1914.

As he became increasingly frail, Fred was rarely seen in public in his final years. In 1946 he appeared at the AGM of the Ulster Unionist Council, where he "received a heart-warming welcome". He was given sustained applause at his final public appearance on Friday 20th February 1948 at a lunch in the Ulster Hall, when he presented a number of items – including two UVF batons, a round of home-made ammunition, the silver casket and a copy of his recently published *Guns for Ulster* – to Lady Carson and her son.[40]

Frederick Hugh Crawford had occasionally intimated over the years that he would welcome death. He believed that all his actions would be measured against God's favour and approval and he most probably readily anticipated and embraced his final journey on 5th November 1952. Associated with the landing of 25,000 rifles which had restored Unionist morale and resilience, he had become engrained in the mythology of the short history of Northern Ireland. Indirectly, he may also be linked to the renown of the 36th (Ulster) Division. The latter was the only Division to battle through almost insuperable odds to achieve its first-day objectives on 1st July 1916. In addition to the fact that the engagement took place on the anniversary of the Battle of the Boyne, many soldiers attributed this achievement to the military training they had received in the UVF.

KNOWN UNTO GOD

If one were to select a pantheon of Northern Ireland legends, Fred Crawford's name would surely find a pedestal, but he would have most certainly shunned such a worldly memorial. He would have preferred a different kind of legend – that is, a simple inscription. Substituting the indefinite for the definite article, he would have been content to find Kipling's epigraph on his gravestone: "A soldier of a great war, Known unto God".

He may have inherited a politically conscious and active gene from his ancestors amongst the United Irishmen, even if his aspirations had a different focus; yet the more recent Crawford generation had exhibited few signs of the political activism which absorbed Fred. It may be that, as one contemporary biographer observed of an 18th century Persian Shah: "the sword takes its merit from the natural strength of its temper, not from the mine from which the iron was taken".

Viscount Brookeborough, Prime Minister at the time of Fred's death, possibly best encapsulated the spirit of Ulster's watchdog: "His loyalist contemporaries hold him in high regard for his inflexible resolution and his passionate devotion to Ulster's cause. To the younger generation of Unionists he has bequeathed a fine example of political sagacity and personal integrity. Ulster's debt to him is incalculable".[41] Fred disliked being beholden to anyone, and would have refuted the notion that Ulster owed him any obligation.

Brookeborough had prefaced the above comment: "Among those who battled for Ulster through years of stern and vigorous campaigning, none showed greater resourcefulness and courage than Fred Crawford". Fred would have attributed the source of these qualities elsewhere, for he filtered all that he achieved through his religious faith and the grace of God. His philosophy was probably best defined in a postscript in a letter to his brother at the height of his personal difficulties: "I will fight against trouble till the end and never lie down to it. God has helped me thro' before, and he will again".[42]

Fred's life spanned ten decades of fluctuating, fractious and fractured political, professional and personal experience. He would have felt much satisfaction if it were said that, whether in petition, thanksgiving or praise, only God ever brought Fred Crawford to his knees.

Notes

1. D/1700/5/6/5, 13 December 1921.

2. St John Ervine, *Craigavon: Ulsterman*, (London, 1949)

3. D/640/17/3, 20 June 1919.

4. D/1792/A3/10/2-4, –/16, January & February 1919. For Armour's opposition to Carsonism: W S Armour, *Armour of Ballymoney*, (London, 1934), pp.247-269, esp. p.248: "Mr Armour respected the abilities of Sir Edward, but strongly disapproved both of his principles and policy, and was their most outspoken and persistent opponent on the Protestant side".

5. D/640/11/2, p.30.

6. David Hammond, *Steelchest, Nail in the Boot and the Barking Dog*, (Belfast, 1986), pp.7-8.

7. D/640/10/4, 9 June 1924. D/1700/5/5/45, 15 January 1932.

8. Letter to Craig from Cloreen, 19 July 1923 in D/1700/8.

9. D/1700/6/1/18, 8 July 1923.

10. D/640/11/2, p.107.

11. D/1700/5/3/13, –/19, –/36.

12. D/1700/5/4/80, –/93. D/640/30/2-3, –/17B. At this time, Charles Craig was coincidentally finalising the closure of the family interest in Dunville & Co: D/640/30/4.

13. D/640/7/2, 5 May 1919.

14. D/640/11/2, p.106.

15. These included the Belfast Branch of the British Legion (Chairman), the Committee of the United Services' Fund, the Building Committee of the Royal Victoria Hospital, and "two Committees of the Ministry of Labour dealing with ex-servicemen and disabled men, and three Committees under the Ministry of Pensions, dealing with ex-servicemen".

16. D/640/14/4-5, 19-23 July 1923. D/1700/8.

17. D/1700/5/18/3, 16 November 1932.

18. John A Oliver, *Working at Stormont*, (Dublin, 1978), p.58. Oliver expressed an ambivalent opinion of Spender, then Head of the Civil Service: "remote, kindly, lisping, out of touch, hospitable, croquet-playing, correct", p.17.

19. The various sources for Fred's Civil service career come from D/1700/5/4/77-82, –/92-93. D/1700/5/5/1. D/1700/5/16/33 and D/1700/10.

20. Timothy Bowman, *Carson's Army: the Ulster Volunteer Force 1910-1922*, (Manchester University Press, 2007), pp.150-151.

21. There is a reference to gun-triggers at the Sprucefield depot near Lisburn in 1939: D/1700/5/6/59.

22. D/1700/5/6/66, 21 May 1960. D/1700/5/8/11, 24 April 1944.

23. D/17005/5/23, –/29, November and December 1923.

24. David N Livingstone, 'Science and religion and the geography of reading: Sir William Whitla and the editorial staging of Isaac Newton's writing on biblical prophecy', *British Journal of the History of Science*, Vol.36 no.1 (March 2003), p.40.

25. See D/1700/5/18/3, extract from *Belfast News Letter*, c.27 March 1934.

26. D/1700/5/11/27, 8 February 1944.

27. D/1700/5/11/30A+30B, 4 June 1945. Bowman, pp.152-153.

28. D/1700/5/16/34, 16 October 1923. D/1700/10.

29. D/1700/5/11/20, 23 March 1935.

30. In fairness, the term 'rock garden' does not do justice to the transformation of perhaps the only site over which Fred had any direct control. It was visited by the Belfast Naturalists' Field Club (which he had joined in 1921) on 12 June 1928: D/1700/5/4/86, –/88. D/1700/10.

31. D/1700/5/5/49, –/52, June and July 1932.

32. D/1700/5/5/45, 15 January 1932. D/1700/5/6/19C, 16 November 1933.

33. D/1700/5/5/26, 16 January 1935. D/1700/6/1/30, 22 May 1935.

34. D/1700/5/6//24, –/30, –/37, May and June 1935.

35. D/1700/5/6/42A, –/42C, –/43, –/48A.

36. D/1415/B/33.

37. D/1700/5/6/27, 30 March 1935. D/1700/10, letters of June 1936. D/1700/7/1, September 1940.

38. D/1700/5/6/5, 13 December 1921. D/1700/5/17/1/162-163, September and October 1938.

39. D/1700/5/6/66, 21 May 1960. In the light of the events of 1914, it was also an ironic tribute. D/1700/5/5/103, 13 May 1937.

40. *The Northern Whig*, 19-21 February 1948. The press articles state that the home-made ammunition was for UVF rifles, but it probably originated from his Young Ulster days in the 1890s.

41. *Belfast News Letter*, 6 November 1952.

42. D/1700/6/1/18, 8 July 1923.

Index

A

Adgey, Robert   144, 148-149, 156, 161
Agnew, Captain Andrew   112, 180-182, 188-196, 200-201, 225-231, 234-237
Alexander Crawford & Son   9, 13, 17, 21-22, 25-26, 31-37, 45, 55, 57, 64-65, 81, 103, 114-116, 120, 127, 131, 143, 146-150, 157, 160, 169, 228, 248, 252, 257, 277-278, 281, 293, 301-302, 312
Andrews family   38-39, 52, 105, 134-135, 142, 236, 247, 306

B

Balmerino   195-196, 199-200, 203, 226, 296
Bates, Sir Richard Dawson   130, 153, 170, 194, 202, 231, 240, 255, 302, 304, 306, 308, 310
Belfast Nursery   25, 28, 46, 249, 290, 312
Boer (or South African) War   8, 17, 30, 40, 46, 56, 65, 72-73, 85-101, 107, 121, 162, 245, 255

C

Campbell College, Belfast   33, 47, 49, 65, 70-74, 85, 90-92, 96, 98, 102, 105, 132, 139, 144, 153, 158-161, 163-164, 171, 237, 245, 250, 252, 261, 264, 273, 278, 280, 288, 291-292, 295, 304-305, 309, 311
Carson, Sir Edward   37, 112-113, 123, 130-134, 139, 145, 148-149, 153-154, 157-160, 164, 170-177, 183, 192-193, 197-198, 202, 227, 234-240, 247, 250-251, 254-255, 262, 265-268, 28-283, 289, 291, 294-295, 299-300, 310
Carson, Lady Ruby   254-255, 294-295, 310, 312
Chlorine (House and Villa)   17, 21-25, 32, 39, 63, 114, 119, 124-125, 229, 312
Clark, Sir George   54, 114, 127-128, 135, 158, 161, 170, 175, 202
Cloreen   21, 46, 48, 63, 78, 111-112, 237, 248, 253, 268-269, 273, 304, 307-308, 312
Clyde Valley (or *Mountjoy II*)   198-201, 226, 229-233, 240-241, 254
Collins, Michael   246, 253, 263, 268-273, 291
Cowzer, Richard   170, 174, 179, 194, 196-199, 202, 230, 233
Craig, Sir James (Lord Craigavon)   50, 58, 87, 90, 97, 113, 130-131, 135, 145-148, 157, 170, 172-173, 175, 177, 179, 183, 185, 190-199, 204, 236-240, 249, 254, 262, 266-268, 282-284, 288, 292-296, 301, 303-304, 306-308, 310-311
Craigavon House   131-132, 135, 141, 148, 153, 158-160, 163, 172, 179, 183, 194, 197-200, 246, 266, 296
Crawford, Alexander (Fred's grandfather)   9, 17, 21-23, 26, 45
Crawford, Alexander (Fred's brother)   10, 22-23, 26-29, 47-48, 65, 67, 76-82, 91, 95, 112, 119-120, 301, 303
Crawford, Caroline (Fred's sister)   10, 23, 45, 47, 53

Crawford, Frederick Hugh
- apprenticeship   51-54
- Boer War   85-101
- businessman   26, 28, 32, 35, 55-58, 113, 119-120, 299-303
- character and piety   11-12, 31, 40, 58, 69, 74-75, 122, 133, 188, 197, 253-258, 279-280, 294, 304, 313-314
- charitable work   11, 35, 41, 300
- education   47, 50-51
- engineer   24, 46, 54-55
- gunrunning   140-152, 155-164, 169-205
- military ambitions   56, 101-107, 246-252
- parent and family man   45-46, 48-50, 91-92, 112, 118-119, 229, 302-304, 310-311
- politics   67, 86-87, 114, 120-135, 140-142, 153-155, 234-238, 261-294
- travels   58, 63-76, 116-117

Crawford, Helen (Fred's wife)   50, 88, 95, 115-119, 126, 179, 188, 229, 234, 255, 305-311
Crawford, James Wright (Fred's father)   9-11, 17, 21-41, 45-47, 51, 56, 63-64, 80, 91, 112, 118, 120, 122, 198
Crawford, Margery (Fred's mother)   26, 39, 47, 80, 118-119
Cunningham, James   148, 170, 174, 183, 192-193, 196, 199, 202, 228, 230, 262

D

Davidson, James Samuel (Sirocco Works)   64, 67, 101, 158, 161, 206, 240
Donegal Artillery   56, 87-88, 90, 93, 95-96, 99-103, 106, 129

F

Falck, Captain Ole Marthin Jensen   181-183, 189-193, 195-196, 201, 230-232
Fanny   55, 71, 107, 112, 169, 179-185, 188, 190-201, 229-233, 237, 240

G

Gelston, John FitzHugh (Commissioner)   280, 284-286, 290, 292, 294
Gleichen, Brig-Gen Count   133, 162-163, 204, 237

H

Harland & Wolff (Queen's Island)   10, 49, 51-54, 57, 74, 114, 278, 287, 300, 312

K

Kaiser Wilhelm II   235-236, 251, 268, 305
Kanzki, Elsa   175, 183, 192, 229, 240-241, 251
Kelly, Sir Samuel   171, 196-199, 203, 226, 231, 295
Knowles, Ernest   33, 57, 116, 252, 280-281

L

Londonderry, Marquis of, (family)   105, 114, 120, 134, 159, 234, 240, 254, 308, 310
Luke, Captain William   195-196, 199-200, 230-231

M

McNeill, Ronald (Lord Cushendun)   122, 128, 133, 135, 140-141, 154, 237, 265
Moore, Arthur   65-66, 72, 139-140, 144, 203, 245-247, 256

O

Old Town Hall, Belfast   132, 153, 159, 162, 169-171, 175, 179, 194, 239, 247, 284, 289, 310

R

Ranfurly, Earl of   51, 53, 88, 94, 105, 115, 123-126, 251, 254, 306, 309-310
Richardson, General Sir George   160, 170, 172, 179, 183, 192, 198, 202, 204, 226, 228, 238-239, 281
Royal Irish Constabulary (RIC)   97, 149, 151, 163, 227, 264, 269-270, 277, 284-290
Royal Ulster Constabulary (RUC)   267, 288, 290, 292

S

Schneider, Friedrich (Fritz)   174, 176, 178, 180-185, 189-190, 193-194, 229, 233
Smith, Thomas James (Inspector General)   97, 151, 157, 162, 270, 277, 281, 284
Spender, Lady Lilian   37, 112, 148, 179, 193, 202, 239, 241, 250, 254, 282, 290, 295
Spender, Sir Wilfrid Bliss   95, 120, 162, 170, 175, 179, 183, 185, 190-194, 202-204, 241, 250, 265, 267, 272, 289, 295, 302, 306-307, 310-311
Spiro, Bruno   147-151, 155-156, 161, 171, 174-180, 183-184, 187-190, 194, 229, 231, 233-241, 245

U

Ulster Special Constabulary (USC)   100, 268-269, 283-284, 289-292, 295
Ulster Volunteer Force (UVF)   37, 63, 124-125, 142, 144, 154, 157-164, 169-170, 173, 179, 183, 202-205, 225-229, 234, 237-241, 247, 250-252, 255, 262, 272-273, 281-284, 289, 295, 306, 308, 312-313

W

Wallace, Colonel R H   33, 112, 132, 135, 143, 146, 237, 250, 255, 289
Whitla, Sir William   41, 47, 116, 118, 307
Wilson, Field Marshal Sir Henry   81, 98, 253, 291, 294
Wilson Street Works   see Alexander Crawford & Son

Dear Reader

I hope you have enjoyed this publication from Ballyhay Books, an imprint of Laurel Cottage Ltd. We publish an eclectic mix of books, ranging from memoirs to authoritative books on local history, culture and institutions.

To see details of these books as well as the beautifully illustrated books of our sister imprint, Cottage Publications, why not visit our website at www.cottage-publications.com or contact us at:–

Laurel Cottage
15 Ballyhay Rd
Donaghadee
Co. Down
N. Ireland
BT21 0NG
Tel: +44 (0)28 9188 8033

Timothy & Johnson

BALLYHAY BOOKS